The British Nuclear Weapons Programme

1952–2002

Editors

DOUGLAS HOLDSTOCK
FRANK BARNABY

With a Foreword by
JOSEPH ROTBLAT

FRANK CASS
LONDON • PORTLAND, OR

First published in 2003 in Great Britain by
FRANK CASS AND COMPANY LIMITED
Crown House, 47 Chase Side, Southgate
London N14 5BP, England

and in the United States of America by
FRANK CASS
c/o International Specialized Book Services, Inc.
920 NE 58th Avenue, Suite 300, Portland, OR 97213-3786

Website: www.frankcass.com

British Library Cataloguing in Publication Data

The British nuclear weapons programme, 1952–2002
1. Nuclear weapons – Great Britain 2. Nuclear weapons –
Government policy – Great Britain 3. Nuclear weapons –
Environmental aspects 4. Nuclear weapons – Moral and ethical
aspects
I. Holdstock, Douglas II. Barnaby, Frank
355. 8′25119′0941

ISBN 0-7146-5382-9 (cloth)
ISBN 0-7146-8317-5 (paper)

Library of Congress Cataloging-in-Publication Data

The British nuclear weapons programme, 1952–2002 / editors Douglas
Holdstock, Frank Barnaby; with a foreword by Joseph Rotblat.
 p. cm.
Includes bibliographical references and index.
 ISBN 0-7146-5382-9 (cloth) – ISBN 0-71476-8317-5 (pbk.)
 1. Nuclear weapons–Great Britain. 2. Great Britain–Military
policy. I. Holdstock, Douglas, 1933– II. Barnaby, Frank. III. Title.
UA647.B8527 2003
355.8′25119′0941–dc21

                                      2003007110

Typeset in 10.25/12pt ClassGaramond by Frank Cass Publishers
Printed in Great Britain by MPG Books Ltd, Bodmin, Cornwall

THE BRITISH NUCLEAR WEAPONS PROGRAMME

This book is dedicated to the Maralinga Tjarutja
people, who were displaced from their homeland
and whose lives were disrupted by the
UK nuclear-weapons programme

Contents

Notes on Contributors

Frank Barnaby is consultant to Oxford Research Group on technical and scientific issues and has been on the Group's Council of Advisers since its inception. He is a nuclear physicist by training and a prolific author. He worked at the AWRE, Aldermaston (1951–57) and was on the senior scientific staff of the Medical Research Council. He was Director of the Stockholm International Peace Research Institute (1971–81) and Guest Professor at the Free University, Amsterdam (1981–85).

General Sir Hugh Beach is a retired Royal Engineer officer who served in north-west Europe in the Second World War and on three separate tours of duty thereafter. He subsequently commanded the Army Staff College at Camberley and was Deputy Commander-in-Chief United Kingdom Land Forces. His last army appointment was as Master General of the Ordnance, responsible for the procurement of all land service equipment for the British armed forces. More recently he was Director of the Council for Arms Control for three years. His other activities have included Wardenship of St. George's House, Windsor Castle, membership of the Security Commission and chairmanship of the boards of Bedales School, the Church Army and the Society for Promoting Christian Knowledge.

Janet Bloomfield is the British Co-ordinator of the Atomic Mirror, which works to reflect and transform our nuclear world through the arts. She was Chair of CND from 1993 to 1996 and is now a Vice-President. She is currently a member of the Global Council of the Abolition 2000 Global Network to Eliminate Nuclear Weapons. She is also a member of the Religious Society of Friends, serves as Co-Clerk of the Peace Campaigning and Networking Group of Quaker Peace and Social Witness in Britain and acts as a consultant to the Oxford Research Group.

Roger Cross recently retired as a Senior Lecturer of the Faculty of Education, University of Melbourne. He is well known internationally in the field of science education for his research into the social responsibility of science, having written eight books and over 100 articles on the subject. His recent book *Fallout: Hedley Marston and the British Bomb Tests in Australia* (2001) created considerable media interest. He is pursuing a collaborative book project with Australian veterans of the British atomic bomb tests.

Robert Green served in the British Royal Navy from 1962 to 1982, retiring with the rank of Commander. He became Chair of the UK affiliate of the World Court Project in 1991. He now works with his wife, Dr Kate Dewes, co-ordinating the New Zealand Peace Foundation's Disarmament and Security Centre, where he is promoting more ethical and lawful approaches to security and defence issues.

Douglas Holdstock is a retired consultant physician and a founder member of Medact, the UK affiliate of IPPNW. He has edited *Medicine, Conflict and Survival* since 1990, written widely on health effects of war and weapons of mass destruction and co-edited, with Frank Barnaby, *Hiroshima and Nagasaki: Retrospect and Prospect* (1995).

Ric Johnstone was a motor mechanic in the RAAF when he was present at the four Buffalo tests at Maralinga, South Australia in 1956. He co-founded the Australian Nuclear Veterans Association (which campaigns for adequate medical benefits for Australian test veterans) in 1972 and is now its honorary national president.

Bruce Kent was president of the International Peace Bureau from 1985 to 1992 and general secretary and chair of the CND between 1980 and 1990. He is vice-president of the International Peace Bureau and chair of the Movement for the Abolition of War.

Ronald McCoy is President of IPPNW and a retired obstetrician and gynaecologist. He is a member of Medact and founder and chair of Malaysian Physicians for Prevention of Nuclear War. He was a member of the Malaysian delegation making an oral submission on the legality of nuclear weapons to the ICJ in 1995 and of the Canberra Commission on the Elimination of Nuclear Weapons in 1996.

Tom Milne is a researcher at the London Office of the Pugwash Conferences on Science and World Affairs. He has published extensively on nuclear arms control and disarmament, was lead author of the British Pugwash Group report *An End to UK Nuclear Weapons* (2002) and co-editor of *Ending War: The Force of Reason* (1999) and *A Nuclear-Weapon-Free World: Steps Along the Way* (2002).

Ronald King Murray (Rt. Hon. Lord Murray) was called to the Scottish Bar in 1953 and became Queen's Counsel (Scotland) in 1967. He was Member of Parliament for Leith from 1970 to 1979, became a Privy Counsellor in 1974, was Lord Advocate from 1974 to 1979 and subsequently a High Court judge in Scotland. In August 1945 he was serving with a combined force in South East Asia Command which was preparing for a sea invasion of Japanese-occupied Malaya when the first atomic bombs were dropped. His interest in the legality of nuclear weapons dates from that time.

Alan Parkinson is a mechanical and nuclear engineer. In 1989 he developed some 30 options for rehabilitation of the Maralinga atomic bomb test site. In August 1994 he was appointed the Government's Representative to oversee the whole of the cleanup project and was also a member of the government's advisory committee (MARTAC). In December 1997 he was removed from both appointments for questioning the management of the project.

Sebastian Pease FRS is a physicist who worked in Bomber Command operational research unit during the Second World War and then for the United Kingdom Atomic Energy Authority. He was Director of Culham Laboratory and Authority Director of Fusion Research. He was chairman of the British Pugwash Group from 1981 to 2002 and co-authored their study reports *Does Britain Need Nuclear Weapons?* (1995) and *An End to British Nuclear Weapons* (2002).

Duncan Rees first became involved with CND on the 1968 Aldermaston march. He was General Secretary from 1975 to 1980 and National Organizer from 1981 to 1985. He was General Secretary of the World Disarmament Campaign from 1987 to 1988 and has worked for the *Morning Star*, the Nicaragua Solidarity Campaign and Oxfam. He is now Co-operative Affairs Officer in North Wales for the Co-operative Group.

Sue Rabbitt Roff represented human rights organizations at the United Nations in New York throughout the 1980s, with particular reference to peace and security issues in small states and territories. Since 1991 she has been teaching social sciences and medical sociology at Dundee University Medical School, including courses on the health hazards of ionizing radiation and organophosphate-based pesticides. She is also a Lay Member of the General Medical Council's Fitness to Practice Committee.

Sir Josepth Rotblat FRS was co-recipient of the 1995 Nobel Peace Prize and is Emeritus Professor of Physics at the University of London. He worked on the Manhattan Project at Los Alamos during the Second World War, but resigned in December 1944 when it became clear that Germany would not develop an atomic weapon. He is a co-founder and President Emeritus of Pugwash.

Plates, Maps and Tables

PLATES

MAPS

TABLES

Abbreviations

ABM	Anti-ballistic missile (system or Treaty)
ACS	Australian Construction Services
ADM	Atomic Demolition Munitions
ARL	Australian Radiation Laboratory
ARPANSA	Australian Radiation Protection and Nuclear Safety Agency
AWE	Atomic Weapons Establishment
AWRE	Atomic Weapons Research Establishment
AWTSC	Atomic Weapons Test Safety Committee (Australia)
BAOR	British Army of the Rhine
BASIC	British-American Security Information Council
BNTVA	British Nuclear Test Veterans Association
CAAT	Campaign Against Arms Trade
CND	Campaign for Nuclear Disarmament
CSIRO	Commonwealth Scientific and Industrial Research Organisation
CTBT	Comprehensive Test Ban Treaty
DNA	Deoxyribonucleic acid (see Glossary)
DPIE	Department of Primary Industries and Energy (Australia)
GHG	Gutteridge, Haskins and Daley Pty Ltd (Australia)
HEU	Highly-enriched uranium (see Glossary)
IAEA	International Atomic Energy Agency
ICBM	Inter-continental ballistic missile
ICJ	International Court of Justice
INF	Intermediate-range nuclear forces
IPPNW	International Physicians for Prevention of Nuclear War
ISV	In-situ vitrification
MAD	Mutual assured destruction
MARTAC	Maralinga Rehabilitation Technical Advisory Committee (Australia)
MCANW	Medical Campaign Against Nuclear Weapons (now part of Medact)
MoD	Ministry of Defence (UK)
MOX	Mixed oxide (see Glossary)
NATO	North Atlantic Treaty Organization
NGO	Non-Governmental Organization
NHSCR	National Health Service Central Register
NPT	Non-Proliferation Treaty (Appendix 3)

NRPB	National Radiological Protection Board
NWS	Nuclear-weapon state
ORG	Oxford Research Group
PAT	Pension Appeals Tribunal (UK)
PTBT	Partial Test Ban Treaty
RAF	Royal Air Force (UK)
RAAF	Royal Australian Air Force
SAC	Strategic Air Command (US)
SAM	Surface-to-air missile
SANA	Scientists Against Nuclear Arms
SGR	Scientists for Global Responsibility
SIOP	Single Integrated Operations Plan
SLBM	Submarine-launched ballistic missile
START	Strategic Arms Reduction Treaty
TAG	Technical Assessment Group (Australia)
UN	United Nations
VERTIC	Verification, Research, Training and Information Centre
WCP	World Court Project
WHO	World Health Organization
WMD	Weapon of mass destruction
WPA	War Pensions Agency (UK)

Glossary

Italicized terms are referred to elsewhere in the Glossary

Alpha particle – a nucleus of a helium atom, containing two *neutrons* and two *protons*; has a high relative biological effect as its energy is rapidly deposited over a short distance

Americium – artificial *radioactive* element with atomic number 95 (symbol Am), produced in nuclear explosions and reactors; emits *alpha particles*

Atomic bomb – see *fusion bomb*

Becquerel – modern unit of radioactivity replacing the *curie*; the activity of an amount of a radioactive material in which one nucleus decays each second

Beta particle – small electrically charged particle emitted in one form of *radioactive* decay of an *isotope*

Critical mass – the minimum mass of *fissile* material above which *fission* takes place

Curie – older unit of radioactivity; the activity of an amount of a radioactive material in which 3.7×10^{10} nuclei decay each second (see *becquerel*)

Deoxyribonucleic acid (DNA) – the hereditary material in the cell nucleus. It is abnormal in leukaemic and other cancer cells and can be damaged by *ionizing radiation*

Fissile – capable of undergoing *fission*

Fission – the process in which the nucleus of a heavy element (*uranium* or *plutonium*) splits apart to *radioactive isotopes* of lighter elements and generates *ionizing radiation* including *neutrons*, *gamma rays* and other forms of energy

Fusion – the process in which the nuclei of very light elements join together, generating large amounts of energy, principally as *neutrons* and *gamma rays*

Fusion bomb – nuclear weapon that relies on nuclear *fusion* for most of its energy

Gamma ray – form of electromagnetic radiation; *ionizing radiation* of relatively high energy

Highly-enriched uranium (HEU) – see *uranium*

Hydrogen bomb – see *fusion bomb*

Ionizing radiation – energy given off by a *radioactive* source; includes *alpha particles*, *beta particles*, *neutrons*, *protons*, *gamma rays* and so on, which are capable of damaging living tissue, especially *DNA*

Iodine – naturally-occurring element required in small amounts for the normal working of the *thyroid*. A radioactive *isotope* is created in nuclear-weapons explosions and in nuclear reactors

Isotope – form of an element containing its typical number of *protons* but a different number of *neutrons*; if unstable, is *radioactive* (emitting *ionizing radiation*)

Kiloton(ne) – 1,000 ton(ne)s

Leukaemia – form of cancer affecting the white cells of the blood. Can occur in severe (acute) or less severe (chronic) forms; the former are rapidly fatal untreated and still often fatal even after chemotherapy. Can be due to several factors including *ionizing radiation*, but usually cause unknown

Megaton(ne) – 1 million ton(ne)s

Mixed-oxide fuel (MOX) – a nuclear fuel, made from a mixture of plutonium dioxide and uranium dioxide, used in nuclear-power reactors as an alternative to uranium dioxide fuel

Multiple myeloma – a cancerous disease affecting the bone marrow in older people, frequently fatal despite chemotherapy and/or radiotherapy. Can be caused by *ionizing radiation*

Nuclear reactor – a large facility in which *uranium*, usually enriched in uranium-235, undergoes controlled *fission*, originally designed to produce *plutonium* by irradiating uranium-238 with *neutrons*, later used to generate electricity

Neutron – particle with no electric charge, comprising, with *protons*, the nuclei of all atoms; released, for example, in nuclear *fission*

Neutron bomb – a nuclear weapon designed to maximize *neutron* emission when it explodes to incapacitate and kill a large number of people by irradiation while minimizing damage to buildings, armoured vehicles and other structures

Paternal preconceptual irradiation – exposure of a prospective parent, often but not exclusively male, to *ionizing radiation* before the child is conceived. Thought by some to pass damaged *DNA* to offspring, who may become more liable to *leukaemia*

Person-sievert – unit of collective dose; the total radiation dose received by a group divided by the number of people in the group

Pile – older term for *nuclear reactor*

Plutonium – artificial *radioactive* and *fissile* element (symbol Pu) of atomic number 94; is generated in *nuclear reactors*; the *fissile* material is a key component of most modern nuclear weapons and can be used as part of MOX *fuel* in some reactors

Proton – particle with single unit of positive eletric charge, found in nuclei of all atoms; the nucleus of a hydrogen atom

Radioactive – emitting *ionizing radiation*

Radioactivity – spontaneous emission of *ionizing radiation* by the nuclei of certain *isotopes* accompanied by the emission of alpha particles, beta particles, neutrons, gamma rays and energy

Radioactive fallout – the radioactive products produced by nuclear fission when a nuclear weapon explodes

Radiation-induced genomic instability – damage to *DNA*, due to exposure to *ionizing radiation*, which is not manifest until several cell divisions after exposure and can affect cells not directly traversed by the radiation; may indicate a risk of cancerous change, including *leukaemia* in bone marrow cells, and can be transmitted to later generations

Sievert – the modern unit of radiation dose, incorporating quality factors for the biological effectiveness of different types of *ionizing radiation* (implying that *alpha particles* are 20 times more dangerous than X-rays depositing the same amount of energy in tissues)

Thyroid – gland in the neck controlling metabolism, which takes up *iodine*. Enlargement ('goitre') can occasionally be cancerous, sometimes due to exposure to *radioactive* iodine; thyroids of children are especially sensitive

Uranium – naturally occurring radioactive element with atomic number 92; (symbol U) with two principal *isotopes*, uranium-238 (99.3 per cent) and uranium-235 (0.7 per cent). Both emit alpha-particles; uranium-235 when at *critical mass*, low-enriched in a *nuclear reactor* or high enriched in a warhead, is *fissile*

Wigner energy – energy stored within a substance, particularly in graphite when bombarded by *neutrons* in the core of a nuclear reactor

Foreword

JOSEPH ROTBLAT

Fifty years of British nuclear weapons. For most of that period the British public was made to believe that our possession of a nuclear arsenal – tiny though it was in comparison to those held by the superpowers – was essential to avoid another world war, a war in which the whole civilization would have been destroyed by nuclear weapons. The obvious alternative, that there would be no nuclear holocaust if there were no nuclear weapons in the world, was not accepted by the nuclear powers. Even after the major threat ceased, with the collapse of one of the superpowers, the need to maintain nuclear arsenals was claimed as necessary for world security. But by endorsing the nuclear deterrent as an essential element for safeguarding peace in the world, we have forsaken the ethical and moral values that are the basis of our civilization.

Morality is at the core of the nuclear issue: are we going to base our world on a culture of peace or on a culture of violence? Nuclear weapons are fundamentally immoral: their action is indiscriminate, affecting civilians as well as military, innocents and aggressors alike, killing those alive now and generations as yet unborn. The consequence of their use might be to bring the human race to an end. All this makes nuclear weapons an unacceptable instrument for maintaining peace in the world. But this was exactly our policy during, and after, the cold war. Nuclear weapons were kept as a deterrent, to prevent war by the threat of retaliation.

For the deterrent to be effective the threat of retaliation must be real; we must convince the would-be aggressors that nuclear weapons *would* be used against them, otherwise the bluff would soon be called. George W. Bush, Vladimir Putin, or Tony Blair must show convincingly that they have the personality that would enable them to push the button and unleash an instrument of wholesale destruction. It is terrifying to think that among the necessary qualifications for leadership is the readiness to commit an act of genocide and this is what it amounts to in the final analysis. Furthermore, by acquiescing in this policy, not only the leaders but each of us figuratively keeps our finger on the button; each of us is taking part in a gamble in which the survival of human civilization is at stake. We rest the security of the world on a balance of terror.

In the long term this is bound to erode the ethical basis of civilization. I would not be surprised if evidence were found that the increase of violence seen in the world – from individual mugging to organized crime, to terrorist groups such as al Qaida – has some link with the culture of violence which we lived under during the cold war years, and still do. Al Qaida seems to be the consequence of American policies, particularly in the Middle East, rather than the popularly presented other way round.

I am particularly concerned about the effect on younger generations. We all crave a world of peace, a world of equity. We all want to nurture the much-heralded 'culture of peace' in the young, but how can we talk about a culture of peace if that peace is predicated on the existence of WMDs? How can we persuade the young to cast aside the culture of violence, when they know that it is on the threat of extreme violence that we rely for security?

It makes a mockery of George W. Bush's claim that his anti-terrorist campaign is based on moral principles. What sort of morality is it that justifies military action against some states, such as Iraq, because of their alleged possession of nuclear weapons, while at the same time insisting on keeping these weapons for oneself, to be used as any other military implement, even in pre-emptive strikes?

I do not believe that the people of the world would accept a policy that is inherently immoral and likely to end in catastrophe. This was evident in 1945 in the reaction to the destruction of the two Japanese cities, a reaction of revulsion, shared by the vast majority of people in the world, including in the United States. From the beginning, nuclear weapons were viewed with abhorrence; their use evoked an almost universal opposition to *any* further use of nuclear weapons. I believe this is still true today; it is reflected in the world-wide opposition to the attack on Iraq. I believe that, if properly explained, the moral argument would win general support and lead to a renewed campaign for the elimination of nuclear weapons. I hope that this book, with its factual presentation of the many facets of nuclear warfare, will contribute towards this objective.

Introduction

DOUGLAS HOLDSTOCK and FRANK BARNABY

The first nuclear explosion entirely the responsibility of the United Kingdom government took place on 3 October 1952, on the Monte Bello Islands off Western Australia. The fiftieth anniversary of this event passed with very little media attention; as remarked in a report from the British Pugwash Group,[1] over the last 15 years UK nuclear weapons have ceased to be an issue of public concern.

As Tom Milne describes in Chapter 1, 3 October 1952 was not, of course, the start of the UK nuclear-weapons programme and British-based scientists were involved from early on in work on nuclear weapons. Fission of uranium was first observed in 1938 and understood in 1939, but though a potential source of heat and power, it was not at first thought to have bomb-making potential. However, a memorandum from Otto Frisch and Rudolf Peierls,[2] refugee scientists working at Birmingham University, showed that a devastating weapon – recognized from the first as likely to irradiate many civilians – was feasible if the fissile isotope U-235 could be separated from natural uranium on an industrial scale. Work on the atomic bomb in the UK proved impracticable under wartime conditions,[3] but eventually British scientists made significant contributions to the Manhattan Project at Los Alamos, which led to the atomic bombs dropped on Hiroshima and Nagasaki. Among them was Joseph Rotblat, who left the project when it became clear that Germany would not acquire nuclear weapons. He has devoted the rest of a long life to working for their world-wide elimination and we are immensely grateful that, as part of this, he has contributed the Foreword to this book.

Not long after the end of the Second World War, the United States Congress passed the Atomic Energy Act (the McMahon Act), which ended American/British co-operation. The 1945–51 Labour government remained convinced that the UK should have nuclear weapons, in part because of the onset of the cold war but also for reasons of national prestige.[4] In January 1947 it initiated a crash programme, continued by subsequent governments of both parties, leading to the tests beginning in 1952 and eventually to the first of a series of usable nuclear weapons (Appendix 1).

If the October 1952 test was only one step in an ongoing process in which there is little public interest, why mark its anniversary? On 1 July 1968, the UK, along with the US and the USSR, signed the NPT, the full text of which is given in Appendix 3. France, China and over 180 other states have subsequently signed the Treaty and only India, Israel and Pakistan (all known or believed to have nuclear weapons) remain non-signatories. Under Article VI of the Treaty, States Parties undertake to pursue negotiations in good faith on effective measures relating to cessation of the nuclear arms race and to nuclear disarmament. As Lord Murray discusses in Chapter 2, the ICJ, in its 6 July 1996 Advisory Opinion,[5] interpreted this as an *obligation* to bring such negotiations to a conclusion at an early date.

All three depository states of the NPT, the US, USSR and UK, and the later nuclear-capable signatories, China and France, effectively ignored their undertakings under the NPT for many years. In 1968, world stockpiles of nuclear weapons were just over 38,000 (28,800 in the US, 280 in the UK). Total stockpiles reached just over 65,000 in 1986, with the UK peaking at 350 in 1975–81.[6] The UK total is now down to about 200, but the missiles and their warheads are potentially far more destructive than in the past (Appendix 1). As Sebastian Pease points out in Chapter 12, a decision on whether to replace Trident cannot be long deferred and the UK has a golden opportunity to go beyond negotiations and make a real contribution to bringing about a nuclear-weapon-free world.

RATIONALE?

What has the British nuclear-weapons programme achieved in the intervening 50 years? The standard justification is that they have helped to keep the peace in Europe during this time. Of its nature, this statement is neither verifiable nor refutable – it is impossible to re-run history. Many, including former US Defense Secretary Robert McNamara – who should know – believe that the world survived deterrence as much by good luck as good judgement, not least at the time of the Cuban missile crisis. British nuclear weapons would have been involved in a later, but much less well known crisis at the time of the NATO 'Able Archer' exercise in November 1983 – the time when Cruise and Pershing 2 missiles were being deployed here and in western Europe.[7]

In any case, the UK contribution is small in percentage terms. We have produced about 1,200 warheads since 1953, the US 70,000 since 1945.[8] No doubt the UK alone could have inflicted major, perhaps overwhelming, destruction on an enemy (presumably only the Soviet Union was ever in mind). But two leading military men, Lords Carver and Mountbatten, are among those who have expressed doubt that a British Prime Minister would ever give the order to fire – and military commanders might or might not have obeyed. Hugh Beach's chapter 'The Nuclear Battlefield' leaves one wondering whether less senior commanders really understood what they were preparing for and suspecting that the use of tactical nuclear weapons would, as an American admiral warned, only be a stepping-stone to 'blowing up the world'. The use of British nuclear weapons alone could have resulted in the obliteration of this country.

DISSENT

The motives of the protesters against both the British and other nuclear-weapons programmes were varied both between individuals and over time. As the contributors to Chapter 6 describe from their own personal experience, in the CND and elsewhere, protestors at different times included communists, pacifists, feminists, doctors and scientists among others. Within such a broad church, some differences in approach and emphasis are inevitable and pro-nuclearists took full advantage of them; communists, for example, were accused of opposing western nuclear weapons but not Russia's. In the UK, dissent was slow to develop – Australia and the Pacific were a long way away before the advent of · instant television news by satellite. There was eventually increased public concern over the possible effects, particularly of cancer and genetic damage, from fallout due to the more frequent and larger American and Russian tests. The 1963 Partial Test Ban Treaty drove testing underground – out of sight, out of mind – and the reassurance provided by détente allowed proliferation in numbers of nuclear weapons to continue largely unchecked. The issue resurfaced in the early 1980s when the combination of the Soviet invasion of Afghanistan, the hard-line leadership in the west of Ronald Reagan and Margaret Thatcher and the coming of the Euro-missiles (Cruise, Pershing 2 and SS-20, with Trident to follow) led to huge public demonstrations all over western Europe (Chapter 6). Until the relevant government documents enter into the public domain and the memoirs are written (perhaps not even then) we will not know what the majority of military men thought – though it is hard to imagine that Rob Green (Chapter 5) is alone. The 1986 Chernobyl disaster was a stark reminder of the perils of a nuclear explosion.

With the fall of the Iron Curtain and the collapse of the Soviet Union, public concern has again fallen to a low level (Sebastian Pease, Chapter 12), although the threat has far from disappeared. The massive protests of the 1980s seemed to be ignored by governments of the time, but may well have led to the INF Treaty, which eliminates a whole group of nuclear weapons. They may also have inspired the largely peaceful protests in eastern Europe before the fall of the Iron Curtain – so reducing the fear of nuclear catastrophe and, paradoxically, diminishing the call for total elimination. But there can be no doubt, for example, that the story of the Greenham women inspired others throughout the world. Mikhail Gorbachev states that the views of IPPNW (in which the UK's MCANW was prominent) strongly influenced his work for nuclear disarmament.[9]

RADIOACTIVE CONTAMINATION OF THE ENVIRONMENT

A global nuclear war could be the ultimate man-made human and environmental disaster. But even in prevention, we should recall Hippocrates' aphorism still quoted to all medical students: 'first, do no harm' – the global nuclear arms race clearly fails this criterion. Given the huge extent of the US and Soviet programmes, the pollution around their facilities is far worse there than elsewhere.[10] The area around the Mayak facility on the Techa River in central Russia may be the most radioactively polluted site in the world.[11]

Each of the main stages of nuclear-weapon production contaminates the environment with radioactive material; some contaminate it with non-nuclear toxins. Radioactive contamination arises from such activities as uranium mining and milling, uranium enrichment (to increase the amount of uranium-235 in uranium), the production of plutonium in plutonium-production reactors, the reprocessing of spent nuclear reactor fuel (to separate the plutonium from the spent fuel), the production of the fissile components (highly enriched uranium and plutonium) for nuclear and thermonuclear weapons), the assembly of nuclear weapons and the disposal of radioactive wastes.

But of all the activities involved in nuclear-weapon programmes, the human environment has been most contaminated by nuclear-weapons tests – in the atmosphere and underground until 1996 and underground only until 1998. The USA, the Soviet Union/Russia, France, China, the UK, India and Pakistan have conducted a total of 2,052 nuclear tests, 530 of them in the atmosphere. Israel has nuclear weapons but is not officially known to have made a nuclear test.

The atmospheric nuclear tests had a total explosive yield of 545 megatonnes, of which 217 megatonnes were produced by nuclear fission. Atmospheric nuclear testing resulted in global environmental effects – contaminating the global environment with radioisotopes, mainly carbon-14, caesium-137, strontium-90 and zirconium-95, as well as plutonium. These tests have exposed, and will expose, the world's people to a collective effective dose of 30 million person-sieverts.

The UK nuclear tests (Appendix 2) have contributed their share of *global* contamination. Alan Parkinson (Chapter 8) describes the environmental effects of the tests at Maralinga in Australia (Map 1) and the effort needed to clear up their aftermath. A similar clear-up was needed in other test sites, in particular Christmas Island, for them to become habitable again.

The British nuclear-weapon programme has also contaminated the *local* environment in the UK, particularly around the main nuclear-weapon establishments – Windscale/Sellafield, Aldermaston and Burghfield. A dramatic example of local contamination is the accident at a military plutonium-production reactor at Windscale. The collective effective dose caused by this nuclear accident is estimated to be about 2,000 person-sieverts.

SIAMESE TWINS: BRITISH NUCLEAR WEAPONS AND CIVIL NUCLEAR POWER

Swedish physics Nobel Prize winner Hannes Alfven described the military and peaceful atoms as Siamese twins. The link between the development of British nuclear weapons and the civil nuclear power programme is a prime example. The focus of the relationship is the nuclear establishment at Windscale/Sellafield where military nuclear reactors produced plutonium for British nuclear weapons.

The first of two plutonium-production reactors began operation in October 1950; the second started up in June 1951. The plutonium from these reactors was used in the first British nuclear test in October 1952. The short time between these events indicates the speed at which the nuclear-weapon programme proceeded.

At 1.13am on 7 October 1957 one of the two nuclear reactors at Windscale was shut down for a perfectly routine operation. Within a short time, this had become a disaster and remains by far the worst nuclear accident that has ever happened in the West. Details of what went wrong in the reactor and the scale of the disaster were kept secret for decades. The documents that have now been released tell a tragic story of incompetence by senior staff at Windscale.

Perhaps the Windscale tragedy was built into the plant. The two reactors were put up in a great hurry to make plutonium for Britain's nuclear weapons. Corners were cut because of the haste: the reactors had no containment, no operating manual was prepared, temperature gauges were put in the wrong positions and so on. In the circumstances, the Windscale accident was hardly surprising. Before 1957, Hiroshima and Nagasaki were the places associated with nuclear catastrophe. Since 1957, Windscale has been joined by Three Mile Island and Chernobyl as places made notorious by nuclear disasters.

Because disaster was associated with the name 'Windscale', the nuclear industry had its name changed to 'Sellafield'. A variety of nuclear activities continue under this now familiar name. These include the commercial reprocessing of spent fuel from civil reactors, in two reprocessing plants, and the production of MOX nuclear fuel from the plutonium produced by reprocessing. It is bad for business to remind people what happened when Sellafield was called Windscale.

The Windscale reactors used natural uranium as fuel. The fuel was surrounded with graphite. When the reactors were running the graphite became very hot and was bombarded with a large number of neutrons. Under these conditions, the carbon atoms in the graphite stored energy known as Wigner energy, after the American physicist who discovered the process.

The physicists who operated the Windscale reactors knew that unwanted Wigner energy would build up in the graphite and that they would have to get rid of it. The standard way of doing this is to rapidly increase the reactor power and then decrease it. The point of this is to increase the temperature of the graphite above its normal operating temperature so that the energy is released in a controlled manner.

When the Windscale physicists decided to get rid of the Wigner energy in one of the Windscale reactors, they seriously underestimated the amount of energy stored in the graphite. Consequently, the operation of increasing and decreasing the power of the reactor was carried out far too quickly and the graphite released its energy in a sudden extra surge of uncontrolled heat. The temperature of the reactor fuel soared to 1,300 degrees centigrade, the fuel cans ruptured, the uranium fuel caught fire and the graphite started to burn. The events at Windscale were a forerunner of the 1986 accident at Chernobyl. This may be hardly surprising as Windscale and Chernobyl had the same type of reactor.

By 6.45pm on 10 October 1957 there was an obvious glow from the core of the Windscale reactor. By 8pm yellow flames appeared. At 8.30pm blue flames appeared. As the fire at Windscale raged, highly radioactive fission products poured out of the reactor's 22-metre high chimney and spread across the English countryside. Firemen first tried to put out the fire by pumping in carbon dioxide gas, but this made the flames even worse. In desperation, vast amounts of water were pumped into the reactor. What happened then is predictable: a huge cloud of highly radioactive steam and smoke was produced and released into the atmosphere.

It was at first assumed that all the radioactivity would either fall on ground around the reactor owned by the British Atomic Energy Authority or be blown out to sea, so most of the staff were not worried about risk to people living near the reactor. This optimism was short-lived. The direction of the wind suddenly changed and the radioactive cloud was blown south-east, across most of England.

The authorities were still in no hurry to respond to the emergency; 12 hours were to pass after radioactivity began to escape from the reactor before emergency action was taken. It was not until 1.30am on 11 October that people were warned of the emergency and told to stay indoors and wear face masks, and not until 4pm on 12 October that local milk samples were analyzed. The laboratory at which the milk samples were tested was not working at the crucial time! The analysis showed that the milk was so radioactive that it was unfit for human consumption. The milk contained radioactive iodine that is concentrated in the thyroid gland. Radiation emitted by the radioactive iodine can cause thyroid cancer. Children are particularly at risk.

The scientists should not have waited for the results of the milk samples. When the fire started, on the afternoon of 10 October, large amounts of radioactivity were going up the chimney. A monitor reading showed that the radioactivity being released to the atmosphere was 50 times more than normal. Of the radioactivity released during the Windscale nuclear accident, well over half was radioactive iodine. Eventually, milk distribution was stopped over an area of more than 500 square kilometres, though far too late to prevent many people from drinking radioactive milk. Since then, Sellafield, as it is now called, has become notorious because of the relatively high number of children in the population living around the nuclear plant that suffer from leukaemia (Chapter 10). Exactly how many children contracted leukaemia because of radiation from the Windscale accident will never be known.

The radioactive isotopes released during the Windscale fire included polonium, a highly radioactive substance used in early nuclear weapons. The presence of this very toxic material was ignored at the time. In fact, the full facts about the Windscale accident were deliberately suppressed at the time. We now know that this was at the direct order of the Prime Minister, Harold Macmillan. He gave this order, in spite of the health hazards of the radiation from the accident, for fear of what the Americans may have thought.

If the full facts had been published the Americans might have ended collaboration with British scientists on nuclear weapons. Macmillan believed that the Windscale fire might have led important American politicians to conclude that Britain could not be trusted with information about nuclear weapons. At that time, the British government did not want the Americans to know too much about the plutonium being produced at Windscale for British nuclear weapons.

The two military reactors at Windscale were shut down after the accident and are still being dismantled. Robots will do much of the dismantling; there is still too much radiation in the reactors to risk exposing human workers to radiation. There may even be too much radioactivity to allow complete dismantling. If so, the Windscale reactors may be sealed in a concrete tomb, just like the one at Chernobyl. It is intriguing to speculate what archaeologists of the twenty-second century will make of these structures. Some sort of odd religious temples, perhaps?

HEALTH EFFECTS

Radiation can cause cancer and the fallout from atmospheric tests will, over time, cause around 1.5 million fatal cancers. For comparison, the Chernobyl nuclear accident (resulting in a global collective effective dose of 600,000 person-sieverts) will cause, in the long term, about 30,000 cancer deaths. Nuclear testing has caused, and will cause, 50 times more deaths world-wide than Chernobyl.[12]

The 1957 Windscale fire could have caused about 100 cancer deaths. The UK National Radiological Protection Board estimates that 260 people developed thyroid cancer because of radiation from the Windscale accident. According to the Board, 13 of these cancers were fatal. Other scientists disagree with the Board's calculations and believe that many more people died prematurely because of the Windscale accident.

The attitude to indigenous Australians described by Roger Cross in Chapter 7, though another consequence of the haste with which the whole programme was conducted, seems to go beyond carelessness and verges on negligence. Given the inadequate level of healthcare they received at any time, the extent of adverse health effects on the Aborigines will probably never be agreed but must have been significant.

The UK government has still not accepted that service personnel present at the tests have suffered ill effects as a result (Chapter 9). It is debated whether the clusters of childhood leukaemia around UK nuclear facilities are a direct effect of radiation or an indirect effect of population mixing (Chapter 10). Acceptance that the nuclear programme is a cause of these effects would lead to large compensation payments. It would also fully justify protests against the entire weapons programme. No wonder attempts were made to discredit whistle-blowers.[13]

ECONOMICS

The costs of the UK nuclear-weapons programme are very difficult to estimate. Different aspects of the programme include research and development, obtaining fissile material, procuring weapons and delivery systems, maintenance, decommissioning of obsolete weapons and support systems, such as hunter-killer submarines, spread across all three armed services. The expense of these has been divided between different parts of the defence budget, wherever possible without being clearly ascribed to the nuclear-weapons programme. Repeated questions by Lord Carver in the House of Lords eventually led to the admission that the cost of the Trident programme is over £1 billion annually, several per cent of the £25 billion defence budget at this time. The more varied programme in the past was presumably at least as expensive. Work on developing Devonport dockyard to refit nuclear submarines will cost over £900 million – suggesting that the government intend to maintain nuclear capability for a long time to come.

Even more imponderable is the cost of the overall military strategy of which nuclear weapons were an integral part. All that can be said is that a purely defensive, neutral stance would have cost much less. Throughout the post-war period, the UK defence budget has been among the highest, at several per cent of gross domestic product, of European and NATO member states. Today, for instance, Germany spends 1.4 per cent of gross domestic product on defence and will reduce this further, the UK's 2.5 per cent is rising. At the very least, the UK's part, as a nuclear power, in post-1945 geopolitics must have cost many billions of pounds which could otherwise have gone towards education, healthcare and social services.

THE FUTURE

So much for the past: what of the future? As interpreted by the ICJ, the NPT commits the NWSs to achieve nuclear disarmament and at the Review Conference in 2000 the NWSs committed themselves to elimination.[14] The British Pugwash Group reviewed the options and, as summarized by Sebastian Pease in Chapter 12, concluded that the most feasible possibility is to undertake now not to replace Trident.[15] Unless military nuclear facilities are opened to IAEA inspection, this is not verifiable and implies that the UK, although now the smallest of the five NPT NWSs, will remain a nuclear power until perhaps 2030 – scarcely an encouragement to the others. Indeed, press reports suggest that plans for the immediate future of the AWE at Aldermaston at least leaves open its capacity to prepare for a successor to Trident.

As Tom Milne comments (Chapter 1), majority public opinion has always opposed this country becoming a non-nuclear-weapons state until all others do likewise. However, the Pugwash report (quoted by Pease) notes that the nuclear threat has not been a matter of public concern for several years and we wonder if their conclusion may be too pessimistic. Scrapping Trident would certainly be a nine-day wonder, but in today's political climate it surely need no longer make a political party unelectable. Rob Green has suggested elsewhere that the UK should announce the decommissioning of the Trident nuclear programme at the 2005 NPT review conference. He believes that doing so would transform the debate on nuclear disarmament – and perhaps earn the Prime Minister of the day a Nobel Peace Prize.[16]

Of course, the nuclear powers also have individual reasons for wanting to maintain nuclear capability and there can be no certainty that others would follow our lead. Additionally, as many nuclear apologists have pointed out, knowledge of how to make nuclear weapons will always be with us. This implies an even more radical need – an end to war.[17] The contents of this book, we believe, show that in the 50 years since the first test explosion, the UK nuclear programme has caused significant harm while achieving little or nothing. The start of the second 50 years surely provides an opportunity to do better.

NOTES

1. T. Milne, H. Beach, L.J. Finney, R.S. Pease and J. Rotblat, *An End to UK Nuclear Weapons* (London: British Pugwash Group, 2002), pp.41–3.
2. O. Frisch and R. Peierls, *On the Construction of a Super Bomb* (1940), Public Records Office Doc. AB1/210.
3. M. Gowing, *Britain and Atomic Energy 1939–1945* (London: Macmillan, 1964).
4. M. Gowing, *Independence and Deterrence: Britain and Atomic Energy 1945–1952*, 2 Vols. (London: Macmillan, 1974).
5. International Court of Justice, *Legality of the Threat or Use of Nuclear Weapons*, UN Doc. A/51/218 (New York: United Nations, 1996), para.10F.
6. R.S. Norris and H.M. Kristensen, 'Global Nuclear Stockpiles, 1945–2002', *Bulletin of the Atomic Scientists*, Vol.58, No.6 (2002), pp.103–4.
7. G. Prins, *The Heart of War: On Power, Conflict and Obligation in the Twenty-first Century* (London: Routledge, 2002), pp.4, 32–3.
8. Norris and Kristensen, 'Global Nuclear Stockpiles'.
9. M. Gorbachev, *Perestroika: New Thinking for our Country and the World* (London: Routledge, 1987), p.154.
10. M. Renner, 'Environmental and Health Effects of Weapons Production, Testing and Maintenance', in B.S. Levy and V.W. Sidel (eds.), *War and Public Health* (New York and Oxford: Oxford University Press, 1997), pp.117–36; M. Goldman, 'The Russian Radiation Legacy: Its Integrated Impact and Lessons', *Environmental Health Perspectives*, Vol.105, Suppl.6 (1997), pp.1385–91.
11. Joint Norwegian-Russian Expert Group, *Sources Contributing to Radioactive Contamination of the Techa River and Areas Surrounding the 'Mayak' Production Association, Urals, Russia* (Østerås: Norwegian Protection Authority, 1997).
12. IPPNW International Commission, *Radioactive Heaven and Earth: The Health and Environmental Effects of Nuclear Weapons Testing In, On, and Above the Earth* (New York: Apex Press / London: Zed Books, 1991); R.F. Mould, *Chernobyl Record: The Definitive History of the Chernobyl Catastrophe* (Bristol and Philadelphia: Institute of Physics, 2000).
13. G. Greene, *The Woman Who Knew Too Much: Alice Stewart and the Secrets of Radiation* (Ann Arbor, MI: University of Michigan, 1999).
14. R. Johnson, 'The 2000 NPT Review Conference: A Delicate, Hard-won Compromise', *Disarmament Diplomacy*, No.46 (2000), pp.2–21.

15. Milne, *et al.*, *An End to UK Nuclear Weapons*.
16. R. Green, 'Conventionally-Armed UK Trident?', *RUSI Journal*, Vol.147 (2002), pp.31–4.
17. J. Rotblat, 'Remember your Humanity' (Nobel Prize Acceptance Speech), in M. Bruce and T. Milne (eds.), *Ending War: The Force of Reason* (Basingstoke: Macmillan, 1999), pp.165–71.

British Nuclear Weapons Policy

TOM MILNE

Since 1970 the United Kingdom has been legally committed to nuclear disarmament under the terms of the NPT (Appendix 3), a position reaffirmed in unequivocal language at the 2000 NPT Review Conference. The UK has not met this commitment and successive governments, including the current Labour one, have made clear their intention to retain nuclear weapons for as long as other nations possess them and thus for the foreseeable future.

BEGINNINGS

The history of British nuclear-weapons policy-making begins in early 1940 when Otto Robert Frisch and Rudolf Peierls sent a memorandum to the government *On the Construction of a 'Super-bomb'; Based on a Nuclear Chain Reaction in Uranium.*[1] In setting up a scientific committee to investigate the scientific feasibility of the Frisch-Peierls conclusions, the British government became the first to recognize and pursue the possibility of the atomic bomb. The committee, which came to be known as the MAUD committee, reported in mid-1941 the view that the proposed scheme for a uranium bomb was 'practicable and likely to lead to decisive results in the war' and that work should be continued 'on the highest priority and on the increasing scale necessary to obtain the weapon in the shortest possible time'.[2]

Developing a nuclear weapon in wartime came to be regarded as beyond the United Kingdom's national means and from late 1943 British work was subsumed into the United States bomb project. After its pioneering research in the field and substantial contribution to the US wartime effort, there was however a natural presumption when the war ended, at least among many of those with knowledge of the UK's activities in the field, that Britain would re-establish a national nuclear-weapons programme. Indeed, Britain had sought to send as many scientists as possible to the United States, partly with a view to acquiring knowledge and experience for possible future use.[3]

AFTER THE WAR: TOWARDS INDEPENDENCE

Quite apart from its involvement in the early history of nuclear-weapons development, the UK still had extensive world-wide interests and wanted to remain in the first rank of military powers, which meant acquiring the latest and most powerful weapon no matter what. The decision to develop the bomb also came when the future security of Europe was unclear, predating the establishment of NATO and the Marshall Plan and following the 1946 McMahon Act in the US banning the sharing of atomic information. It could not be discounted that the US might withdraw into isolationism; Attlee recalled: 'We had to hold up our position *vis-à-vis* the Americans. We had to look to our defence – and to our industrial future. We could not agree that only America should have atomic energy.'[4]

After the war, an industrial programme to produce fissile materials was thus quickly set in motion, the military services were asked to assess UK requirements for atomic bombs and in early 1947 the Attlee government took the formal decision to manufacture a British nuclear weapon. An often-quoted passage from Margaret Gowing's official history of the early years of the UK nuclear-weapons programme encapsulates the near inevitability of the decision:

> The British decision to make an atomic bomb had 'emerged' from a body of general assumptions. It had not been a response to an immediate military threat but rather something fundamentalist and almost instinctive – a feeling that Britain must possess so climacteric a weapon in order to deter an atomically armed enemy, a feeling that Britain as a great power must acquire all major new weapons, a feeling that atomic weapons were a manifestation of the scientific and technological superiority on which Britain's strength, so deficient if measured in sheer numbers of men, must depend.

The decision was also, Gowing continues, a 'symbol of independence' and an anticipated source of future influence in Washington.[5]

'OVERWHELMING RETALIATION' AND DETERRENCE

As well as deciding to develop nuclear weapons, the immediate post-war years saw the UK embark on a major programme of conventional rearmament, given added urgency by the Korean War and increasing fears that a general world conflict was imminent. The acquisition of nuclear weapons by the Soviet Union was also seen to increase the importance of conventional rearmament, since the West's nuclear weapons, it was reasoned, could henceforth serve only as a last resort.

However, British thinking on nuclear weapons changed significantly when Churchill was re-elected Prime Minister in 1951. Churchill decided that the level of military spending was unsustainable in view of wider social and economic needs. He had also long made clear his belief in the primary importance of nuclear weapons to Western defence. He therefore invited the Chiefs of Staff of the three British military services to take stock of the world situation and the impact of nuclear weapons in particular. The Chiefs' conclusion, incorporated into a so-called *Global Strategy Document*, was that the advent of atomic weapons and air power made obsolete traditional approaches to defence based on massive conventional forces.[6] The primary deterrent, they argued, must be Russian knowledge that aggression would be met by 'immediate and crushing atomic retaliation', foreshadowing the nuclear doctrine that would soon come to the fore in the US under the Eisenhower administration.

Based on the Chiefs' advice, Churchill could announce a slowing of conventional rearmament and an increased emphasis on nuclear weapons in mid-1952.[7] He claimed that the 'remorseless march of the science of human destruction' called for a new approach to world security. Government statements argued that in the event of general war both sides would be certain to use nuclear weapons and that for this reason policy had to be based on the prevention of war breaking out. The threat of 'overwhelming nuclear retaliation' was the surest means to achieve this.[8] Britain's decision to develop the hydrogen bomb, announced in 1955, was consistent with the developing strategy.[9]

By 1957 the RAF was beginning to establish an operational nuclear capability and a megaton weapon was soon to be tested. The annual Defence White Paper contained a blunt restatement of the primacy of nuclear weapons in defence planning: a military effort on the scale planned at the time of the Korean War rearmament was unaffordable and the threat of nuclear retaliation was the only safeguard against major aggression.[10] The 1958 Defence White Paper placed still further emphasis on the nuclear deterrent. It argued in tones resonant of the US doctrine of massive retaliation that a major Soviet conventional attack would lead to a *strategic* nuclear response and stressed that 'a full-scale Soviet attack could not be repelled without resort to a massive nuclear bombardment of the sources of power in Russia'.[11]

With alarm over what came to be seen as a dangerous over-reliance on nuclear weapons, the next few years saw mounting criticism of nuclear strategy on both sides of the Atlantic. In Britain the strategy was judged especially perverse in view of the nation's extreme vulnerability to nuclear attack. P.M.S. Blackett, for example, suggested that 'five to ten hydrogen bombs would almost certainly suffice to annihilate all its main centres of industry, comprising half the population of the country'.[12] As a result, nuclear weapons began to be given less prominence in UK defence planning. Likewise in the US, the newly elected Kennedy administration sought to reduce the emphasis placed on nuclear weapons in NATO strategy and to increase the options for conventional defence.

In the early 1960s the UK formally committed its nuclear weapons to NATO, both in declaratory policy and arrangements for command and control. At a meeting with President Kennedy held in Nassau in December 1962, where the US undertook to supply the UK with submarine-launched ballistic missiles on a continuing basis, Macmillan agreed that 'except where Her Majesty's Government may decide that supreme national interests are at stake, these forces would be used for the purposes of international defence of the Western Alliance in all circumstances'.[13] Existing UK nuclear weapons were formally assigned to NATO the following year, becoming part of the US' SIOP drawn up in Omaha, Nebraska,[14] and from 1967 to the end of the cold war the UK supported a NATO policy of 'flexible response' involving plans for the forward defence of Europe 'based upon a flexible and balanced range of appropriate responses, conventional and nuclear, to all levels of aggression or threats of aggression'.[15]

When first described as a contribution to NATO, in the mid-1950s, UK nuclear weapons could be presented as a significant addition to the developing US/NATO nuclear deterrent.[16] Later, as the US arsenal expanded rapidly, they became an insurance that targets of particular importance to UK security would be prioritized in a developing conflict.[17] But by the 1960s the US arsenal had expanded to such a vast scale, incorporating thousands of nuclear and thermonuclear weapons, which could be used to attack any conceivable target, that there could no longer be any question that UK forces were numerically significant. Henceforth UK nuclear weapons could only be portrayed as an 'independent contribution' to Western/NATO defence. Although the government was always careful to maintain that the UK deterrent was by itself sufficient 'to make a potential aggressor fear that our retaliation would inflict destruction beyond any level which he would be prepared to tolerate',[18] it was natural to question whether such an independent force served any purpose in view of overarching US nuclear capabilities.

A SECOND CENTRE

An additional problem facing Britain's nuclear policy-makers in the early 1960s, in seeking to justify the UK's nuclear contribution to NATO, was a widespread perception that America would 'not regret the United Kingdom's retirement from the nuclear business'.[19] Robert McNamara, then Secretary for Defense, openly sought to discourage independent European nuclear forces, arguing instead for an increase in European conventional defence capabilities and memorably characterizing independent European nuclear forces as 'dangerous, expensive, prone to obsolescence and lacking in credibility as a deterrent'.[20]

McNamara's remarks may have been directed principally at the nascent French nuclear programme, with the British force probably too well established to hope to dislodge,[21] but British nuclear forces, then comprising ageing V-bombers (Valiant, Vulcan and Victor – Plate 1) that were increasingly vulnerable to Soviet air defence, did not measure up well to his criteria for credible deterrence. However, the US had agreed in 1958 to resume nuclear co-operation with Britain,[22] and in 1962 had undertaken to supply Britain with ballistic missiles for a submarine-based deterrent (Plate 2).[23] From this point onwards the UK could look ahead to a modern, secure second-strike deterrent and for the most part ever since the US has apparently welcomed the UK nuclear programme and continued to provide substantial practical assistance.[24] A significant consideration for many UK policy-makers, in supporting UK nuclear forces, has been to endeavour to strengthen the US commitment to the defence of Europe by demonstrating a willingness on the part of the UK to shoulder an equal burden of risk and responsibility.

In terms of military strategy, the UK finally settled, in the mid-1960s, on the concept of a 'second centre of decision' as a justification for the continuing presence of UK forces alongside the more powerful US deterrent. The notion may have been a response to the prompting of French military strategists who had begun openly to question the credibility of the US extended deterrent guarantee to Europe. They argued that developing Soviet nuclear capabilities meant that the US could not be expected to risk nuclear attack in defence of Europe:

> different methods must simultaneously be used to keep the enemy's mind in that *state of uncertainty* which alone can render deterrence effective; thus to enable several methods of deterrence to be used simultaneously, *there must be several centres of decision*. This basic conclusion is contrary to American policies; in fact these have for too long been focused upon the stabilization of the nuclear threshold although it is today so stable that it needs to be, so to speak, 'destabilized' to restore its deterrent effect.[25]

British officials made the case that British (and French) nuclear weapons were significant by providing an additional, independent centre of decision-making that would give the Soviet Union pause should it (mistakenly) doubt American willingness to use nuclear weapons in Europe's defence:[26]

> The nuclear decision, whether as a matter of retaliatory response or in another circumstance, would, of course, be no less agonising for the United Kingdom than for the United States. But it would be a decision of a separate and independent Power, and a Power whose survival in freedom might be more directly and closely threatened by aggression in Europe than that of the United States. This is where the fact of having to face two decision-makers instead of one is of such significance. The risk to the Soviet Union would be inescapably higher and less calculable.[27]

Without ever attracting widespread interest or comment, the notion of a second centre of decision has at various times been an object of derision in debate on UK nuclear strategy. Should the Soviet Union have doubted American willingness to use nuclear weapons in Europe's defence, would it not, for example, similarly have doubted that Britain would invite obliteration by using nuclear weapons on its own? Senior military figures have been particularly scathing about the policy.[28] If the UK were to be so reckless as to use weapons independently, in an attempt to draw the Americans into the conflict, who is to say that the UK would not simply suffer massive Soviet reprisal while the United States stood by 'horrified but passive'?[29] But an abiding attraction of the position, at least from the standpoint of UK officials, was that without casting doubt on the US commitment to Europe (the stated concern was only that the Soviet Union might mistakenly reach such a conclusion), the policy drew attention to the British capability for independent action. In this respect it could be seen more as a diplomatic formula than strategic concept.[30]

POST-COLD WAR ROLE

Whatever its merits, the second centre rationale remained central to UK policy until the end of the cold war. It then lost all meaning – at least as far as serving as a deterrent to the erstwhile Soviet Union was concerned – and British governments have since sought to argue in more general terms that nuclear weapons remain necessary to deter (unspecified) threats to the UK's vital interests.[31] What this means in practice is unclear, but for the most part talk of deterring specific threats has given way to a generalized concept of insurance against an uncertain future.

In many ways the concept of a 'general insurance' is sufficiently vague to preclude analysis. If discussed in terms of hypothetical threats – that is, whom the UK might want to deter from doing what – few examples can be found in the literature of scenarios in which UK weapons could conceivably be used, above all independently of NATO. Speaking of Western nuclear forces in general, Michael Quinlan makes the case for 'marginalized' nuclear capabilities that would serve as a 'low key element of insurance, not directed against specific adversaries, in support of world order'.[32] Thus the UK nuclear deterrent survives, largely unchallenged, without any apparent need to say who or what is being deterred.

We are left with a visceral feeling, present from the onset of the nuclear age, that an unspecified adversary would think longer and harder about attacking Britain because of the possibility of a nuclear response; an instinct that *when the chips are down* a nuclear-armed Britain must be (porcupine-like) a painful enemy to tangle with, a customer to handle delicately'.[33] General considerations of political prestige may still play

17

some part in British thinking about nuclear weapons,[34] but most would say that this is a diminishing consideration.[35] It is also sometimes said that retaining nuclear weapons helps the UK to keep its position as a permanent member of the Security Council; historically there may be some truth in this, but today there are surely 'more likely reasons for losing that role than a change in nuclear status'.[36]

Since the end of the cold war, there has also been some change in the notion of 'sub-strategic' nuclear deterrence. During the cold war the distinction between strategic and sub-strategic weapons was simply drawn. Nuclear use was only envisaged in the context of East–West confrontation. Strategic weapons were those that were to be used against the homeland of the enemy, against their cities and industrial facilities. In the case of the nuclear superpowers, they also comprised those weapons to be used against the enemy's strategic weapons in order to prevent a similar blow to one's own homeland. Sub-strategic weapons were all other types of weapon – those for use on the battlefield to halt an enemy advance or break up tank formations, for example. Now that the invasion of Western Europe, the scenario upon which all nuclear planning was based, can be discounted, and indeed the circumstances in which nuclear use would be feasible are seen as less clear and involving other threats, this distinction has become blurred.

Speaking as Secretary of State for Defence in 1993, Malcolm Rifkind argued that a sub-strategic capability was necessary because an aggressor might, in certain circumstances, gamble on a lack of resolve on the part of the UK to make a strategic nuclear strike. For this reason any hypothetical use of nuclear weapons should be 'credibly proportionate to the importance to us of the interests which aggression would damage'.[37] In other words an enemy might doubt that the UK would be ready to carry out a strategic strike but believe that it could contemplate a lower level of nuclear use.

This idea of a 'lower level' of nuclear threat, rather than a step in an escalatory chain (as in 'flexible response'), is the thinking behind sub-strategic use of the UK nuclear deterrent. Presumably a sub-strategic strike might involve a single low-yield warhead (Appendix 1). UK governments have not, in general, given examples of scenarios in which sub-strategic strikes would be contemplated, although Secretary of Defence Geoffrey Hoon was apparently testing the water when he suggested in March 2002 that the UK would in certain circumstances be willing to respond with nuclear weapons to the use of WMDs by, for example, Iraq.[38] Although this statement goes significantly further in undermining security assurances provided to non-nuclear-weapon states than previous positions taken by government ministers, it evoked little and only passing reaction outside the peace movement.

The UK has been involved in four major conflicts, outside the cold war context, since possessing operational nuclear forces, in Suez, the Falkland

Islands, the Persian Gulf and Kosovo. It has not seriously contemplated using a nuclear weapon in any of these, never having been placed in such dire circumstances that the use or threat of use of nuclear weapons could be considered.

OPPOSITION

There have been two major periods of public protest on nuclear issues in Britain. The first, in the late 1950s and early 1960s, was based mainly around concern about the potential health and environmental effects of atmospheric nuclear testing. The second, in the late 1970s and early 1980s, was triggered by the proposal to introduce new American nuclear missiles into Europe (Chapter 6). Although anti-nuclear sentiment was stronger in the UK than in any other of the nuclear-weapon states, with the CND an important mass movement helping to ensure that the atomic bomb has never come to be thought of as 'just another weapon', the notion of unilateral nuclear disarmament has at no time come close to having a majority of public support. Accordingly, for the most part the major political parties have seen few or no electoral advantages, only potential risks, in raising the question of the UK's nuclear status.

In opposition the Labour Party has at different times espoused policies of unilateral nuclear disarmament, but it is doubtful whether such a policy was ever likely to have been implemented. Least enamoured of the nuclear deterrent were the Wilson governments. In 1965 it was decided and announced that no further warhead designs were needed; the UK alone of the five nuclear-weapon states conducted no nuclear tests between 1965 and 1974. The nuclear-weapons programme was scaled down and some civil work initiated at the UK AWE. Wilson also sought to lower the profile of the UK deterrent, emphasizing the extent of dependence on the United States.[39] Internal government discussions were held on the future of the UK nuclear force, including the option of unilateral disarmament when, or before, it was assumed that the then strategic deterrent, Polaris, would no longer remain a credible delivery system. The option of announcing such a decision to relinquish nuclear weapons in conjunction with signing the NPT was raised but apparently not seriously considered.[40] More recently, Labour's advocacy of unilateral disarmament in the 1980s, though strongly supported by the party's rank and file, proved politically untenable. Subsequent assessment of the policy found that:

> people had a simple, common-sense view of the issue – if you have a dog, no one will attack you; if someone else has a knife you should have a knife also. There was some support for multilateral disarmament, but none for unilateralism.[41]

19

As in all areas, the UK's enthusiasm for pursuit of multilateral nuclear disarmament has varied from one government to the next. The elimination of nuclear weapons has long been the UK's officially recognized objective, as noted at the start of this chapter. While making generally constructive contributions to international disarmament work, however, including playing an important role in the prohibition of nuclear testing, the UK has in the main only been able to operate at the margins of the nuclear issue, with the arms race dictated by the United States and the Soviet Union.

Today the UK places a strong emphasis on multilateral verified arms control. A serious and independent commitment to nuclear disarmament on the part of the UK, a longstanding nuclear-weapons power, which is a member of NATO, the European Union, the G-8 and one of the five permanent members of the Security Council, would place it as a leader among the growing band of 'middle powers' campaigning for a nuclear-weapon-free world.

SUMMARY

It has not been my purpose in this chapter to argue for or against UK possession of nuclear weapons, but only to suggest that, for historical reasons, it was almost inevitable that the UK would develop nuclear weapons after the end of Second World War and that, once in place, there has been little prospect of the UK giving these weapons up. Views will continue to differ on the purported contribution of UK nuclear weapons to NATO cold war nuclear deterrence. Otherwise, UK weapons have apparently had little if any significant impact on the course of events, except perhaps serving to encourage France to develop nuclear weapons and, more generally, contributing to a world climate in which nuclear weapons are considered legitimate.

NOTES

1. The Frisch-Peierls Memorandum, reproduced in M. Gowing, *Britain and Atomic Energy 1939–1945* (Basingstoke: Macmillan, 1964).
2. *Report by MAUD Committee on the Use of Uranium for a Bomb*, reproduced in Gowing, *Britain and Atomic Energy*.
3. Gowing, *Britain and Atomic Energy*, pp.241–2, 321.
4. F. Williams, *A Prime Minister Remembers: The War and Post-War Memoirs of the Rt. Hon. Earl Attlee* (London: Heinemann, 1961), p.119.
5. M. Gowing, *Independence and Deterrence: Britain and Atomic Energy, 1945–52* (London: Macmillan, 1974), Vol.1, pp.184–5.
6. Ibid., p.441.
7. Winston Churchill, *Hansard*, House of Commons, Fifth Series, v.504 (30 July 1952), Cols.1492–509.

8. *Statement on Defence 1955*, Cmd.9391 (London: HMSO, 1955).
9. L. Arnold, *Britain and the H-Bomb* (Basingstoke: Palgrave, 2001).
10. *Defence: Outline of Future Policy*, Cmnd.124 (London: HMSO, 1957).
11. *Report on Defence: Britain's Contribution to Peace and Security*, Cmnd.363 (London: HMSO, 1958).
12. P.M.S. Blackett, *Atomic Weapons and East-West Relations* (Cambridge: Cambridge University Press, 1956).
13. *Bahamas Meetings December 1962: Texts of Joint Communiques*, Cmnd.1915 (London: HMSO, 1962).
14. L. Freedman, *Britain and Nuclear Weapons* (London: Royal Institute of International Affairs, 1980), p.25.
15. Communiqué issued after the North Atlantic Council Ministerial Session, Brussels, 13–14 Dec. 1967.
16. L. Freedman, 'British Nuclear Targeting', in D. Ball and J. Richelson (eds.), *Strategic Nuclear Targeting* (Ithaca, NY: Cornell University Press, 1986).
17. Winston Churchill, *Hansard*, House of Commons, Fifth Series, v.537 (1 March 1955), Col.1897.
18. *Statement on Defence 1962: The Next Five Years*, Cmnd.1639 (London: HMSO, 1962).
19. A.J. Pierre, *The British Experience with an Independent Strategic Force 1939–70* (London: Oxford University Press, 1972), p.209.
20. L. Freedman, *The Evolution of Nuclear Strategy* (Basingstoke: Macmillan, 2nd Edn. 1989), p.307.
21. Ibid., p.307.
22. *Agreement for Cooperation on the Uses of Atomic Energy for Mutual Defense Purposes*, Cmnd.357 (London: HMSO, 1958); *Amendment to Agreement between the Government of the United Kingdom of Great Britain and Northern Ireland and the Government of the United States of America for Cooperation on the Uses of Atomic Energy for Mutual Defense Purposes of July 3, 1958*, Cmnd.859 (London: HMSO, 1959).
23. *Bahamas Meetings December 1962*.
24. J. Simpson, *The Independent Nuclear State: The United States, Britain and the Military Atom* (Basingstoke: Macmillan, 2nd Edn. 1986).
25. A. Beaufre, 'The Sharing of Nuclear Responsibilities: A Problem in Need of Solution', *International Affairs*, Vol.41, No.3 (1965), pp.411–19. Original emphasis.
26. *Statement on Defence 1964*, Cmnd.2270 (London: HMSO, 1964); *Defence in the 1980s: Statement on the Defence Estimates 1980: Volume I*, Cmnd.7826-I (London: HMSO, 1980).
27. F. Pym, *Hansard*, House of Commons, v.977 (24 Jan. 1980), Cols.678–9.
28. Lord Bramall, *Hansard*, House of Lords, v.584 (17 Dec. 1997), Cols.679–81; Lord Carver, *Hansard*, House of Lords, v.403 (18 Dec. 1979), Cols.1628–30.
29. Freedman, *Britain and Nuclear Weapons*, p.131.
30. Ibid., p.129.
31. *Strategic Defence Review*, Cm.3999 (London: HMSO, 1998), para.61.
32. M. Quinlan, 'The Future of Nuclear Weapons: Policy for Western Possessors', *International Affairs*, Vol.69, No.3 (1993), p.496.
33. H. Beach, 'A Nuclear Weapons Convention and the British Deterrent', in *Brassey's Defence Yearbook 1996* (London: Brassey's, 1996), p.240. Original emphasis.
34. R. O'Neill, 'Britain and the Future of Nuclear Weapons', *International Affairs*, Vol.7, No.4 (1995), pp.747–61.

35. N.K.J. Witney, 'British Nuclear Policy After the Cold War', *Survival*, Vol.36, No.4 (Winter 1994–95), pp.96–112.
36. M. MccGwire, 'Shifting the Paradigm', *International Affairs*, Vol.78, No.1 (2002), pp.1–28.
37. M. Rifkind, 'The Role of Nuclear Weapons in UK Defence Strategy', *Brassey's Defence Yearbook* (London: Brassey's, 1994), p.28.
38. Geoffrey Hoon, Statement to the House of Commons Defence Committee, Missile Defence, Minutes of Evidence 20 March 2002, HC644-ii (London: HMSO, 2002).
39. Harold Wilson, *Hansard*, House of Commons, v.707 (4 March 1965), Cols.1553–76.
40. *British Nuclear Policy*, paper requested by the Prime Minister in minute No.94/67 of 24 July [1967] to the Foreign Secretary, Public Records Office, Kew.
41. P. Gould, *The Unfinished Revolution* (London: Little, Brown, 1998), p.70.

The Legality of British Nuclear Weapons

RONALD KING MURRAY

The war in the Pacific in the 1940s began with an act of infamy, the unprovoked attack by the Japanese on Pearl Harbor. It ended in an act of infamy – in the eyes of many at least as great – with the dropping of the atomic bombs by the United States on Hiroshima and Nagasaki. The United Kingdom was not without complicity in this, having formally consented to the bombings on 4 July 1945 in terms of the 1943 bilateral Quebec agreement with the US.[1] Happily for humanity the bombings proved to be the only actual use of nuclear weapons since they were invented. Unhappily, they spawned many subsequent exploratory and proving tests by a number of states in the following two decades. These atmospheric tests were so damaging in themselves that world opinion demanded their cessation as more urgent than measures to outlaw nuclear weapons or restrict their spread. This set the scene for the 1963 PTBT which has been largely honoured, with beneficial effect.[2] It is to the UK's credit that its atmospheric testing programme was by far the most limited and least polluting of all.

TREATIES

The close atomic wartime collaboration between the US and the UK was soured by the unmasking of the atomic spies and US institutional isola-tionism. By 1949 it had virtually ceased. Thrown back on its own resources, the UK began its own series of bomb tests at Monte Bello, off the coast of Australia, on 3 October 1952 and others followed at various locations in Australia and the south Pacific. The series, comprising 21 tests altogether, ended on 23 September 1958 (Map 1, Appendix 2). By the early 1960s the ban on atmospheric tests and improved nuclear relations with the US led to joint US–UK underground tests, which continued until a moratorium in 1991.

The PTBT forbade nuclear-weapon tests in the atmosphere, in outer space and underwater. Its preamble sets out its principal aims as 'the speediest possible achievement of an agreement on general and complete disarmament under strict international control in accordance with the objectives of the United Nations' and 'to achieve the discontinuance of all test explosions of nuclear weapons for all time'. The first part of this ambitious declaration was repeated and reinforced in the shape of Article VI of the 1968 Nuclear NPT,[3] becoming an integral part of that international agreement, a point taken forcefully in the judges' unanimous view in the ICJ Advisory Opinion of 8 July 1996 (see below).

The 1968 Treaty (Appendix 3) drew a distinction between parties that are nuclear-weapon powers on the one hand and non-nuclear powers on the other. The former were required not to transfer nuclear weapons nor ancillary material to the latter. The latter were reciprocally required not to receive or seek them. Non-nuclear powers had to agree to international safeguards and verification of compliance. Nuclear powers had to promote the peaceful use of nuclear energy, including peaceful use of nuclear explosion. The Treaty was to extend initially for 25 years when a review conference was to be held to decide whether to continue it indefinitely or for a fixed time. Initially extensions were for five years at a time but in 2000 it was extended indefinitely subject to regular reviews. A majority of the world's states, numbering 188 in November 2002, are party to the Treaty; a key minority comprises India, Israel and Pakistan. The latest signatory is Cuba, which became a state party at the 2002 UN General Assembly. However, North Korea withdrew from the Treaty at the end of 2002. The failure of the Treaty to make progress can also be seen in Article VI, which required states to pursue negotiations to end the nuclear arms race at an early date in a treaty providing for disarmament under strict and effective international control. Review conferences are preceded by preparatory committee (Prep-Com) meetings, the latest of which took place in New York from 8 to 19 April 2002. At the latest review conference (held from 24 April to 20 May 2000), all of the major nuclear-weapon states undertook unequivocally to accomplish the total elimination of their nuclear arsenals. Prep-Coms usually conclude with an official report reached by consensus, but the April 2002 meeting did not because of sharp divergences of view. Failure to produce anything but the chairman's factual summary was due at least in part to the non-nuclear states' dissatisfaction with the major nuclear-weapon states' inability to demonstrate serious progress on their unequivocal undertaking in 2000 to eliminate their nuclear arsenals.

The Prep-Com chairman's summary did record that there was strong support for the early entry into force of the third of the main nuclear limitation treaties, the 1996 CTBT.[4] This is currently stalled by the present failure of more than one-quarter of the designated states (those with a civil nuclear programme) to ratify it, including two of the major nuclear-weapon states, the US and China, which are permanent members of the Security Council. With its annexes and protocol, the Treaty is unfortunately not the most transparent of documents, although its essential thrust is simple and clear. What complicates it is the elaborate organization it sets up and its detailed verification regime. Article 1 begins: 'Each State Party undertakes not to carry out any nuclear-weapon test explosion or any other nuclear explosion, and to prohibit and prevent any such nuclear explosion at any place under its jurisdiction or control.' Taken out of context and read literally the generality of this provision would appear to outlaw the explosion of any nuclear weapon in any circumstances on the one hand and any peaceful civil engineering explosion on the other. But taken in context the provision is no doubt intended to forbid only nuclear-weapon testing and nuclear explosions directed to similar ends, namely the testing of other destructive devices. The wider interpretation would appear to have outlawed nuclear weapons at a stroke.

The UK has signed and ratified the CTBT and thereby has accepted its provisions. It may have access to information from the US 'sub-critical' tests and, if sufficient computing power is now available at AWE Aldermaston, will be able to simulate nuclear tests with computers. These activities will not be banned under the CTBT even if or when it enters into force.

THE ADVISORY OPINION OF THE
INTERNATIONAL COURT OF JUSTICE

Coincidentally, the 1996 Treaty was adopted some two months after the ICJ issued its advisory opinion on the legality of the threat or use of nuclear arms (at the behest of the UN General Assembly).[5] This was the first judicial determination upon the issue in a court or tribunal of international jurisdiction. It was not, however, the first judicial decision; that was made in Japan by three judges of the superior district court of Tokyo in 1963.[6] The case was brought by Japanese citizens who had suffered grievous loss and injury through the atomic bombing of Hiroshima and Nagasaki. The court held that under international law as it stood in 1945 the bombings were acts of illegal hostilities as indiscriminate aerial bombardment of undefended cities and that, even if directed only at military objectives there, the acts involved greatly disproportionate damage comparable to that of indiscriminate bombardment. Having succeeded in the point of principle the court nonetheless held that the claimants failed as they had no title to sue the Japanese state. In reaching its decision the court deliberately put aside considerations special to atomic or nuclear weapons since their full horrendous effects had not been established before their first use. If the court had taken those effects into account the case against legality would surely have been overwhelming. It is true that this decision was that of a Japanese court, but its reasoning was carefully and fairly set out without evidence of bias. No serious doubt about its soundness seems to have arisen since.

In 1995 the issue of legality was put directly to the ICJ when the UN General Assembly posed the question whether there were any circumstances in which the threat or use of nuclear arms were permitted under international law. A bench of 14 judges, including the presiding judge, considered the question, which one supposes the General Assembly took to mean 'Is it ever legal under international law to threaten to use or use nuclear weapons – yes or no?' However, it is expecting too much of any assemblage of lawyers to give a clear-cut answer to a complex question, especially where there is reference to circumstances, and they did not give one. Instead, the judges unanimously asserted two basic principles on which an answer should proceed:

- 'A threat or use of force by means of nuclear weapons that is contrary to Article 2 para. 4 of the UN Charter and that fails to meet all the requirements of Article 51, is unlawful';[7] and
- 'A threat or use of nuclear weapons ... should be compatible with the requirements of the international law applicable to armed conflict, particularly those of the principles and rules of international humanitarian law, as well as the with specific obligations under treaties and other undertakings which expressly deal with nuclear weapons'.[8]

Article 2 paragraph 4 of the Charter bars states from 'the threat or use of force against the territorial integrity or political independence of any state, or in any other manner inconsistent with the purposes of the United Nations'. Article 51 reserves the right of self-defence under certain limitations. Both principles would have to be complied with before an intended nuclear strike could be considered lawful.

The really difficult issue faced by the ICJ judges was whether compliance would ever be possible with nuclear arms. The court attempted to deal with this in a two-part answer. The first part was that it followed from the two principles which they had identified 'that the threat or use of nuclear weapons would generally be contrary to the rules of international law applicable in armed conflict, and in particular the principles and rules of humanitarian law'.[9] Apart from reservations about the use of the word 'generally', this was uncontroversial. The second part occasioned a strong divergence of opinion. It stated that in view of the current state of international law and the factual material before the court it could not 'conclude definitively whether the threat or use of nuclear weapons would be lawful or unlawful in an extreme circumstance of self-defence in which the very survival of a state would be at stake'. The judges were evenly divided, seven to seven, on the merits of this second part and so the two-part answer was approved only on the casting vote of the presiding judge. However, scrutiny of the judges' separate opinions shows that three of the dissenting judges did so not because they regarded threat or use of nuclear weapons as sometimes lawful, but because they judged their use to be always unlawful. It follows that an absolute majority of the judges were not prepared to affirm that there is any definitely lawful use at all for these weapons. History does not relate whether a vote on a direct yes/no answer was attempted, but in its absence we are left with the judges' somewhat Delphic pronouncement. Standing that, pro-nuclear apologists can contend that, in the absence of a direct prohibition, use of the weapons is permitted; while anti-nuclear protagonists can say that, if they have no definitely legal use at all, then they are illegal. In this regard attention should be given to the important caveat registered by the court's president, whose casting vote determined the final outcome. In paragraph 11 of his declaration (opinion) he stated that he could not emphasize enough that the court's inability to go further than its formal conclusion could not be taken as in any way leaving a door half-open to recognition of the lawfulness of the threat or use of nuclear arms.[10]

It is suggested that a firm conclusion can indeed be reached on the court's formal pronouncement along with the presiding judge's caveat, namely that the threat or use of nuclear weapons is of highly dubious legality and that because of this suspect and precarious legality, it would be unwise and unsafe for a state to rely on nuclear weapons for its defence or nuclear deterrence for the maintenance of world peace. In any event nuclear weapons could have no more than a possibly legal role as a last resort, *in extremis*, to avoid annihilation (as the ICJ determined).

SCOTTISH COURT HEARINGS

The Scottish legal jurisdiction was given the opportunity to consider the ICJ Advisory Opinion of 8 July 1996 through the dedication of three intrepid, if imprudent, anti-nuclear campaigners whose activities led them to face three charges of malicious damage to a naval craft and its equipment moored at the Trident nuclear submarine base at Coulport on the Clyde. The craft had an auxiliary role in support of the Trident submarines that carry out regular patrols on the high seas armed with nuclear missiles. The three accused (respondents in the later proceedings) were tried on indictment before a sheriff and jury. Despite objection by the prosecution, expert evidence was led for the respondents that the foregoing deployment of nuclear missiles was contrary to customary international law and so illegal, amounting in the circumstances to criminal conduct which the respondents were justified in resisting as best they could. This they said they did and in so doing committed no offence. The trial judge upheld the respondents' international law contention *inter alia* and directed the jury to acquit. Accordingly the jury unanimously found the respondents not guilty. It being incompetent for the prosecution to appeal against the jury's acquittal, the Lord Advocate petitioned the Scottish appeal court (the High Court of Justiciary), under a statutory provision not affecting the jury's acquittal, for the court's opinion on several legal points. These included whether it was competent to lead evidence of the content of customary international law at a jury trial and whether there was any rule of customary international law which justified a private individual in damaging property in opposition to nuclear weapons. In dealing with those issues the court declared:

- That a rule of customary international law was a rule of Scots law and, as such, was a matter of law for the judge not evidence for the jury, so that it was not competent to lead a witness before the jury as to the content of customary international law;
- That the rules of international humanitarian law referred to in the ICJ advisory opinion related to wartime and times of armed conflict and did not regulate states in time of peace;
- That the continuing deployment of nuclear weapons as a deterrent in time of peace did not constitute a threat in international law; and
- That customary international law did not justify a private individual in seeking to stop or inhibit criminal wrong-doing by others by an act that would otherwise be criminal itself.

The case is reported in the official Scottish law reports and fully discussed in an article by Charles Moxley Jr. in *Juridical Review*, the law journal of the Scottish Universities.[11]

The first of the High Court's pronouncements on the application of customary international law deserves, I think, a positive welcome. While there have been some indications in court decisions and academic commentary that customary international law may apply directly in UK domestic law, the High Court unambiguously affirmed this. As law is a matter for the judge and fact for the jury the trial judge should not have allowed expert evidence on the content of international humanitarian law to be led before the jury. Treated as foreign law, it would have been fact in issue for proof. While the court's view marks progress in the rule of international law, it poses practical problems for the presentation of the content of international law, on which the court makes some later observations.

The High Court's second pronouncement is that international humanitarian law in the advisory opinion relates 'to warfare and times of armed conflict' and so does 'not regulate states in times of peace'. While its first pronouncement is unexceptionable, its second is not. A number of doubts can be canvassed about the accuracy of the latter statement. First, there is the logical point that the assertion that something applies to A does not imply no application beyond A. Second, from a common sense point of view it is obvious that the law applicable to road traffic, for example, does not cover only situations where there are moving vehicles on roads, which are indeed its primary application, but also extends to a number of related matters. By the same token one would expect the laws of war and armed conflict to have some application to what states may do before hostilities break out and after they have ended and to neutral states which are not at war at all. Third, it is clear from Article 2 paragraph 4 of the UN Charter, and from the Advisory Opinion itself,[12] that all threats to do acts which contravene international law are themselves unlawful. Fourth, the High Court's assertion is hardly reconcilable with the conviction of some of the accused at the Nuremberg war crimes trial for planning and preparation for a war of aggression before war broke out. Fifth, it suggests the bizarre possibility that Trident missiles directed on hair-trigger alert at rivals' target cities could cruise the high seas under legal immunity in peacetime but not in wartime.

The High Court considered that it had identified two fundamental flaws in the respondents' case. I have sought to show that the first is a misconception and not a valid ground for rejection. The second is more substantial. The case for the respondents failed to establish that current peacetime deployment of Trident nuclear missiles constituted a hostile threat within the meaning of the Advisory Opinion. In the absence of hard facts about peacetime deployment of these missiles, in particular as to their readiness to fire, one can hardly get beyond official assurances that they are now de-targeted, that is, not targeted at any specific objective in any particular state's territory. Taking these assurances at face value, the respondents could hardly expect to establish the existence of a real threat against an adversary short of war or imminent armed conflict. However, it is understood that the concept of de-targeting depends on rather fine distinctions, making it less potent than it sounds. Potential Trident targets are stored in software retained in the submarine's computer so that, if de-targeting takes place, the missiles can be re-targeted by the crew in 30 minutes or so. If this is indeed the case, the second flaw may not be quite so fundamental (according to Moxley there is no second flaw[13]).

Proceeding on the flaws in the respondents' case that they discerned, the High Court was not strictly required to rule upon the legality or illegality of the UK's Trident nuclear defence policy. The observations they did make on it are therefore *obiter*, that is, not a binding fiat but rather a courteous outline of their thinking on what has been seriously argued before them. What they said was to the effect that continuing deployment of Trident as a deterrent in peacetime was in no sense illegal because it involved no threat within the meaning of international law.[14] More important in following their interpretation of the Advisory Opinion is their observation that 'head E of the *dispositif* identifies no rule, expressly or by implication'.[15] Having carefully recorded that the Advisory Opinion is not binding upon them, they proceed to apply it, concluding that with Trident in particular as with nuclear arms as a class there can be no general assertion of illegality (or of legality for that matter). It all depends on circumstances. The circumstances to which the respondents looked were not enough. Doubt about the legality of actual threat or use remains unresolved by the court's opinion.

CONCLUSION

The patently dubious legality of the threat or use of nuclear arms together with their horrendous quality have so far failed to make any obvious impact on the attitudes of the five major nuclear-weapon states. It is astonishing that they continue to cling to a weapons regime that is militarily bankrupt, morally indefensible and legally suspect.

Taking an overall look at the international community's efforts since 1952 to contain nuclear weapons, let alone achieve nuclear disarmament, the resonant tone of the 1963 Treaty's preamble rings somewhat hollow. While the START process has produced real reductions in a gross excess of superpower nuclear capacity and the UK has curtailed its nuclear defence somewhat, there are more nuclear-weapon states than there were in 1963. Underground testing will not be banned until the CTBT enters into force and sub-threshold testing continues. Chernobyl shows that even a nuclear explosion rated at less than a kiloton can cause continent-wide harm. There is no sign that nuclear-weapons states will accept a time limit to their own possession. If not, on what basis of principle can they demand nuclear self-denial of the non-proliferation non-nuclear states (including Iraq, by force if need be) while retaining their own nuclear arsenals indefinitely? The time has surely come for a bold initiative in the UN Security Council (or failing this, in the General Assembly) to get not just agreed declarations but results.

NOTES

1. Dennis D. Wainstock, *The Decision to Drop the Atomic Bomb* (Westport, CT and London: Praeger, 1996), p.57.
2. *Treaty Banning Nuclear Weapon Tests in the Atmosphere, Outer Space and Under Water*, Cmnd.2245 (London: HMSO, 1963).
3. *Treaty on the Non-Proliferation of Nuclear Weapons*, Cmnd.4474 (London: HMSO, 1968).
4. *Comprehensive Nuclear-Test-Ban Treaty*, Cm.3665 (London: HMSO, 1996).
5. ICJ, *The Legality of the Threat or Use of Nuclear Weapons, Advisory Opinion* (Den Haag: ICJ Reports, 1996), p.226. Also available as UN Doc. A/51/218 (New York: United Nations, 1996).
6. *Shimoda vs. the State*, 32 ILR (1963), p.626.
7. ICJ, *The Legality of the Threat or Use of Nuclear Weapons, Dispositif* (2) para.C, p.266.
8. ICJ, *The Legality of the Threat or Use of Nuclear Weapons, Dispositif* (2) para.D, p.266.
9. ICJ, *The Legality of the Threat or Use of Nuclear Weapons, Dispositif* (2) para.E, p.266.
10. Presiding judge's declaration: ICJ, *The Legality of the Threat or Use of Nuclear Weapons*, para.11. Author's translation from the original French.
11. *The Lord Advocate's Reference No.1 of 2000*, at 2001 J.C. 143; Charles J. Moxley Jr., 'The Unlawfulness of the United Kingdom's Policy of Nuclear Deterrence – The Invalidity of the Scots High Court's Decision in *Zelter*', *Juridical Review* (2001), Part 6, pp.319–43.
12. ICJ, *The Legality of the Threat or Use of Nuclear Weapons*, para.38, p.244.
13. Moxley, 'The Unlawfulness of the United Kingdom's Policy of Nuclear Deterrence', p.337.
14. *The Lord Advocate's Reference*, 2001 J.C. 143 at 177B–178D.
15. *The Lord Advocate's Reference*, 2001 J.C. 143 at 174H.

The Nuclear Battlefield

HUGH BEACH

Fortunately there has never been such a thing as a nuclear battlefield. Nevertheless the British Army of the Rhine spent much time and effort in trying to imagine what such a battlefield might look like and in preparing to cope with it. During the 1950s and 1960s these efforts were taken very seriously. It would give an incomplete account of Britain and nuclear weapons if we did not pay some attention to it. I start with two vignettes that give the views of military men, both American as it happens, on nuclear war as it could have affected them.

The first comes from William F. Burns, a retired American gunnery general, who ended up as a United States representative to the Intermediate Nuclear Force negotiations and then head of the US Arms Control and Disarmament Agency – a 'big gun' therefore. He writes of the mid-1950s when the US Army was first coming to terms with tactical nuclear weapons, in this case the eight-inch howitzer shell:

> The first nuclear weapon I saw was a training round. It contained only Uranium 238, not Uranium 235 and was not capable of nuclear detonation. It was in the back of an M 109 [howitzer] van tied down with a frayed piece of hemp, and a corporal in the van was going to tell us how to put five components together and make a 8-inch projectile. After about three hours and after many false starts on his part, with the manual we were able more or less to put the projectile together. After this we were certified as being able to put together 'a nuclear round', and two weeks later we deployed to the United States Army Europe.
>
> In Europe we suddenly found ourselves proud owners of not only a training round but several of those olive green nuclear rounds. It was an interesting situation because there was very little guidance compared to the guidance in later years. This was before the days of Permissive Action Links or very elaborate release systems. Release was basically tied to the command chain. *I had no doubt in my military mind that if my battalion commander said 'Shoot', we would shoot, and if my battalion commander said 'don't shoot', we would not shoot. It was as simple as that.*[1]

We move forward 20 years to hear from another important American, Admiral Stansfield Turner, who rose eventually to become head of the Central Intelligence Agency. In 1975 he had been appointed NATO's Commander of the Allied Forces in southern Europe, with his headquarters at Naples. Being a naval man he sought expert advice on how best to stop a Warsaw Pact advance through the Brenner Pass:

> I decided to start by talking with Colonel John B. Keely of the U.S. Army, a good friend whom I knew to have an imaginative approach to such problems. Just before coming to the staff of the southern flank, John had commanded the 2nd brigade of the US Army's 3rd Armoured Division. This division was positioned astride Fulda Gap, the principal invasion route from Eastern Europe into West Germany. Although the terrain at the gap was different from that at Brenner Pass, I wanted to talk to John about defense of passes and gaps.
>
> John described the tactics he and his superiors had envisioned for plugging the Fulda. He mentioned that they included atomic demolition munitions (ADMs) to blow up a hillside and send debris cascading on to a key highway. With a wry smile, John said that he had an interesting story about these demolition munitions. During his tour in command, the brigade had been relocated from one position to another just a few miles away. That made it necessary for John to adapt his plans to the differences in terrain. He discovered there was no sensible way to employ ADMs in the new location. He sent his plan for defending his portion of the gap without the use of ADMs up the chain of command. It quickly came back disapproved. His superiors said that the ADMs simply had to be included. Argue as he might, John found there was no way he could turn them in or just hold them in reserve. He had to find the least worst way to incorporate them into his plan. That left him the dilemma of what he would actually do in the event of war. *It was clear that the purpose of these weapons was more for deterrence than for fighting.*[2]

This conversation led Admiral Turner to ask about plans for using ADMs on the Brenner. He discovered that the plan was to use them to blow up the slender concrete piers supporting the highway. When he asked whether conventional munitions would not do the job just as well he was greeted by stunned silence.

> The fact that we had nuclear weapons that would do the job more assuredly than any other option was enough. There were no calculations to compare not only the effectiveness of the two kinds of explosives but also their ancillary effects, like radioactive fallout, fires, and electromagnetic interference. Getting the road closed and making use of these weapons, not the total consequences, were what mattered. I did not take these ADMs out of the war plans. It was not worth the probable arguments. *I just assumed I would not use them if war came.*[3]

In those three extracts the italicized sentences sum up fairly accurately where the tactical nuclear project stood in military thinking: the first in the mid-1950s, the second two in the mid-1970s. The change over that period is very striking. The questions arising include how the technology of tactical nuclear weapons developed, what policies emerged to justify their use, how they became incorporated into orders of battle and war plans, the doctrine that sought to make sense of these plans and the exercises and training that followed from the doctrine.

TECHNOLOGY

The total nuclear stockpile of the United States, at its highest point, had an estimated explosive yield of some 9 billion tons of high explosive and the Soviet stockpile must have been much the same. In the 20 years from 1945 to 1965 nuclear warheads evolved to fill every possible ecological niche on the battlefield and in numbers far greater than any rational person could possibly have considered useful. Why this occurred is an interesting topic for historians; I believe that a large part of the explanation must lie in 'technology push' rather than 'demand pull'.

The effects of a nuclear explosion are not pleasant to write about, but necessary. First comes the heat flash carrying about one-third of the total energy. X-rays from the explosion are absorbed by the surrounding air and progressively re-radiated on longer wavelengths. This leads to the formation of a luminous mass of air called the fireball that grows and rises. The resulting heat can sear the flesh of people in the open and dry-roast or asphyxiate those in shelters. If it touches the ground the fireball gouges a crater and vaporizes everything in it. Over a town the effect of heat flash can cause a firestorm. Against troops dispersed, protected and under the cover of armour or dug in, it is much less of a hazard.

Blast comes next, carrying about half the weapon's total energy. Its effects depend on the height of burst. In an airburst at medium height the blast front extends out in two spheres, from the point of detonation and in an echo from the ground, merging into a single so-called mach front with roughly double the intensity of each. Behind this come winds of up to several hundred miles an hour. The human body stands up well to blast and can take up to twice the normal atmospheric pressure. Much more dangerous are the shards of masonry, glass and the like, propelled with all the deadly effects of a cluster bomb.

The rest of the energy emerges in the form of radiation: neutrons, X-rays, gamma rays, alpha and beta particles. Dose for dose neutrons are more dangerous to the human body but do not travel as far as gamma rays. The effects of radiation fall off faster than blast or heat and of course work more slowly, but it is possible to engineer a weapon so as to increase the amount of neutron flux relative to the other effects. This is the principle of the so-called neutron bomb. Adroit propaganda characterized this as a 'capitalist' weapon because it killed people without destroying property – which is absurd. The point was that within a radius of, say, one kilometre, it could kill troops even in tanks or slit trenches with overhead cover (relatively immune to blast or heat) while causing the least possible 'collateral damage' to the whole area because the total yield could be much smaller.

In addition to prompt radiation a nuclear explosion releases some 300 different radioactive products, with half-lives ranging from a fraction of a second to millions of years. These condense on the pulverized fragments of the bomb itself and later on any dust and ash thrown up if the fireball touches the ground. As the mushroom cloud cools these materials fall back to earth in a plume, the footprint of which is shaped by local climatic conditions. When in contact with the human body these materials irradiate the tissues and affect the cell nuclei, chromosomes and genes. The tissues most sensitive are lymphoid tissue, bone marrow, spleen, testicles and the gastrointestinal tract. Victims get sick, perhaps quite quickly, and sooner or later they will die.

Finally, in speaking of the effects of nuclear weapons on the battlefield, one must not overlook the psychological impact. Armies know from experience how soldiers stand up to the hazards of being bayoneted, hit by rifle or machine gun fire, or by shrapnel from mortars, guns, howitzers or rockets. They know how people cope with being brewed up in tanks or armoured personnel carriers, rocketed or bombed from the air, attacked with napalm or even gas; how they tackle booby traps and anti-personnel minefields. These are all horrible things in their different ways but they have some familiarity. What about nuclear weapons? The first British military publication to tackle this point offered the following thoughts:

> Wide dispersion and isolation, lack of information and fear of the unknown will in future greatly increase the tension of all ranks in battle; and these will be in addition to the awe-inspiring effects of enemy nuclear explosions which will occur throughout the battle area. Furthermore the impact of high nuclear casualties occurring in a moment of time, rather than being built up over a period, must inevitably tend to affect morale. Indeed morale will depend on a frame of mind induced by a mixture of anger, hope and confidence, and based upon strict discipline. Morale has always been a prime factor in the conventional battle; in the nuclear battle it will be the supreme factor.[4]

Others, no less wise perhaps, have suggested that after one nuclear weapon had gone off on the battlefield that would be the end of it; armies would simply refuse to fight. It is impossible to know which view is right, though my own view is closer to the official one than to the radical doubters. Let us hope that humankind never finds out.

BATTLEFIELD WEAPONS

On 17 August 1945 there were no more nuclear weapons left, all three having been expended. The Americans promptly set about making more and in the next ten years were to amass an inventory of 20,000. In 1946 the US SAC was formed and nuclear tests carried out at Bikini Atoll. By 1948 the first large Boeing bombers, B-50 and B-36, became operational. In the summer of 1949, 32 B-29 SAC bombers arrived in Britain. Surprisingly soon the huge and cumbersome weapons of 1945 had been miniaturized and streamlined to tactical proportions. First came free-fall bombs, shortly followed in the 1950s by artillery shells, both eight-inch and 155-millimetre. By 1958 these had been followed by the 'Honest John' free-flight rocket with a range of some 15–20 miles (not much more than a gun); the 'Corporal' missile with a range of 70 miles (to be replaced in the 1960s by 'Sergeant' with solid fuel propellant and an inertial guidance system); and the 'Redstone' missile, derived from the German V-2 of the Second World War (to be replaced by 'Pershing', a two-stage solid-fuelled version with a range of 300 miles). At much the same time (early 1960s) it was decided to equip 'Nike Hercules' SAMs with nuclear warheads and to produce nuclear landmines (the ADMs already referred to) as well as nuclear depth charges for anti-submarine warfare. Finally, and most absurdly among tactical nuclear weapons, came 'Davy Crockett', described as a two-man weapon carried by hand or mounted on a small truck, usable by any infantry battalion (or even company) in place of an ordinary mortar.[5] Davy Crockett went into service in the early 1960s. It had a range of 2,000 metres and a sub-kiloton yield. It was soon realized that in most tactical settings one's own forward troops would be within the danger radius for blast and after about five years Davy Crockett was quietly withdrawn. Yet it took a further 20 years, until the mid-1980s, before NATO recognized just how dangerous, and for very similar reasons, the nuclear air-defence missile and the nuclear landmine were and made plans for their removal.

An unofficial inventory of NATO's tactical nuclear stockpile in Europe in the 1970s lists:

- 2,250 artillery shells;
- 1,850 free-fall bombs;
- 700 Nike Hercules SAMs;
- 300 ADMs;
- 400 anti-submarine warfare weapons;
- 180 Pershing 1as;
- 90 Honest Johns; and
- 97 Lance (SAMs).[6]

There are two important points to note. First, all the warheads for these weapons were in American ownership and custody. One-third were for use by American forces, the rest were for use by other nations under 'dual key' control. This meant that bilateral agreements had been reached with the governments of Britain, the Netherlands, Germany, Italy and Greece whereby the aircraft, missile or gun belonged to the 'host nation' while the warhead, shell or bomb remained the property of the US, even after launching. When the moment came to fire, this needed the concurrence both of the American and the 'host nation' officers at the firing point, each having been properly authorized *via* his own national chain of command by his respective national release authority. This could all take a long time, even days. A second very important point is that, with a few years time lag perhaps, the Soviet Union matched the Americans in nearly all this weaponry. But they did not make their weapons available to Allies under a 'dual key' system, no doubt because they did not trust them. Nor, as far as is known, did they have anything to match the Davy Crockett. For many years their inventory of tactical nuclear weapons was assessed as being about half that of NATO, but this imbalance had little operational significance. For all practical purposes, where tactical nuclear weapons were concerned, the situation between NATO and the Warsaw Pact was symmetrical.

STRATEGIC CONCEPTS

For 15 years from 1945 the United States enjoyed a period of unchallenged nuclear superiority, in spite of the explosion of a Soviet atomic bomb in 1949 and the development of thermonuclear weapons in the 1950s. Without intercontinental missiles and with their long-range bomber programme proving a fiasco, the Soviet Union could not get anywhere near the continental United States. In the Eisenhower era there was no doubt who would 'win' a nuclear war. The strategic policy of 'punishing aggression' by what was called 'massive retaliation at times and places of our own choosing' against Soviet centres of power – often described as the 'Dulles doctrine' – was typically arrogant but believable. A complementary strategy was evolved for NATO. The conventional forces being mustered on the continent would need to be sufficient only to identify aggression and delay advancing forces until the forces of SAC could be brought to bear. It was not a policy that anyone much liked but was unavoidable until such time as NATO's forces could be built up to constitute a deterrent in their own right. Until then their task was to act as a 'tripwire' or, even more disparagingly, as a 'plate glass window'.

Nor did the process of force development go at all smoothly. At Lisbon in 1952 NATO ministers had adopted the goal of building up defensive forces to a level of 96 divisions ready within 30 days. Twenty-five of these divisions were to be stationed in peacetime on the central front. Two years later this goal was abandoned as unrealistic and a new target adopted of 30 divisions on the central sector, including the 12 divisions to be supplied by Germany under the Paris agreement of 1954. These divisions were all to be armed with 'modern' (that is, atomic) weapons and NATO planning was officially based for the next ten years on the principle that nuclear weapons would be used tactically from the outset in response to almost any aggression. Where the major powers were concerned limited war was inconceivable.

Despite the enthusiasm that greeted this decision and the American undertaking in 1957 to accelerate delivery of suitable weapons, their arrival was in fact very slow, only really getting under way at the end of the decade. The make-up of the 'shield' force of 30 divisions was set out in the supposedly confidential but much publicized NATO document MC 70 of 1957 but the reality never quite caught up. The tally in 1962, for example, came to 23-and-one-third divisions made up as follows: Germany eight (with four more to follow), US five, UK three, France, Belgium, Netherlands two each and Canada one brigade. In principle all these were to be equipped and trained with nuclear weapons. As Fred Mulley commented in 1962:

> Twenty eight full strength divisions would be enough to discharge the tasks allotted to the Shield forces, but unhappily it is unlikely that the additional forces will be forthcoming in the near future. The present paper force of twenty-three-and-one-third divisions represents a fighting equivalent of no more than sixteen to nineteen divisions.[7]

No wonder that, as the *Times* said:

> The nuclear artillery has been enthroned in the training manuals as the queen of the battlefield and the infantry and the armour are now regarded as its support-ing arms. Through no fault of its own Rhine Army is not organised to react promptly with conventional weapons.[8]

Exercise 'Spearpoint' in 1961, the largest manoeuvres of the nuclear epoch up until then, revealed that BAOR would be incapable of defend-ing itself even for a short time without nuclear support, even if its strate-gic posture was to be changed to conform to the developing NATO policy of seeking to 'enforce a pause' by conventional means.[9]

America has always been prone to scares and the arrival in orbit of the Russian artificial earth satellite *Sputnik I* in 1957 was a turning point. The huge rocket that had lifted it was relatively crude but could have delivered a warhead to the United States. The development of true ICBMs began at the same time. It was clear that the period of assured US ascendancy was soon to end. With the US itself vulnerable, massive retaliation in response to a conventional challenge in Europe was no longer believable. The arrival of the Kennedy administration, and the new Secretary of Defense Robert McNamara, brought a new formulation:

> We believe in a policy of controlled, flexible response where the military force of the United States would become a finely tuned instrument of national policy, versatile enough to meet with appropriate force the full spectrum of possible threats to our national security.[10]

At the strategic level the first response was to emphasize 'counterforce'. Soviet weapons were the strategic targets and senior commanders still talked as though a nuclear war could be 'won'. Then the danger of this approach dawned. As the Soviet Union slowly developed the means of delivering a massive blow against the United States, so the notion of 'riding out' a first strike and then delivering a counter-blow on what could only be empty silos and deserted bomber bases became highly unattractive. The result was a shift back to 'city-busting', holding the people rather than the weapons as hostages; 400 one-megaton weapons able to hit area targets would suffice. This totally amoral doctrine was dressed up under the term Mutual Assured Destruction and its appropriate acronym (MAD).

The tactical counterpart to this change of heart took a further five years to mature. It came to be realized that large-scale assault on NATO, while still a deadly danger, was by no means the only or even the most likely contingency. Attacks with relatively limited objectives must also be anticipated. McNamara's 'flexible response', which became the short title for the whole new concept, clearly required a better-balanced mixture of conventional, tactical-nuclear and strategic-nuclear forces. The new policy emerged finally in the NATO Document MC 14/3,[11] which underlay the 'Athens guidelines' of 1967. These were later amended by the Nuclear Planning Group guidelines of 1969, the 'first strike' guidelines of 1972 and various biannual ministerial guidelines thereafter. The essence of this policy was to defend at three possible levels:

1. Direct defence (that is, conventional defence) against a non-nuclear attack for as long as possible;
2. Controlled escalation through the use of tactical nuclear weapons; and
3. General nuclear response if all else failed.

While obviously much more sensible than the preceding 'tripwire' strategy, this had the unwelcome consequence of requiring NATO to provide larger conventional forces in Germany backed up by immediately available reinforcements. At that time all the Allies were feeling a financial pinch and, apart from the resuscitated Germany, were seeking to reduce spending on defence. The idea of producing expensive additional conventional forces to 'raise the nuclear threshold' was to nobody's liking. Indeed the size of RAF Germany was sharply reduced in the early 1960s and the French hardly helped by withdrawing from the military structure altogether in 1966. This dilemma was never resolved, though certainly valiant efforts were made to upgrade the quality and firepower of tanks, tactical aircraft and so forth as well as their logistic backing. In the mid-1980s General Hackett's best-selling book on the Third World War was expressly designed to point the moral that stronger conventional forces were still needed on the North German Plain.[12] Whether or not the book was understood that way is a different question.

ORDERS OF BATTLE AND PLANS

The British were unique in having a treaty commitment to maintain a minimum number of troops on the continent. Under Article VI of Protocol No.II to the modified Brussels Treaty of 1954, the British undertook to keep four divisions on mainland Europe as a confidence-building measure related to the re-armament of Germany. Within four years, despite the extreme reluctance of their partners, the British had whittled the force down to three divisions. In the financial squeeze of the mid-1960s one of the remaining six brigades was re-located to the UK but to Britain's credit this was sent back again in 1970. The commitment was a large one – some 55,000 men all told (including the brigade in Berlin) or about one-third of the British Army's strength. The troops were accompanied by an equal number of wives and children and were supported by some 30,000 civilians. On mobilization the strength was planned to more than double, with additional regular troops and a host of reserve units and individuals to be sent from the UK. It is hard to see how Britain could have done much more.

In 1950, before the build-up of forces under NATO had begun, the only Allied formations available to defend the sector between Hamburg and the Harz mountains had been the British occupation forces consisting of the 2nd Infantry and 7th Armoured Divisions, a weak Dutch Corps in Holland, a Belgian armoured division and a Canadian brigade group. The intelligence experts appreciated that the Russians, if they got around to invading West Germany, would be able to use the greater part of some 50 tank divisions and 30 mechanized divisions. All of these were equipped with the impressive tanks that had recently defeated the Wehrmacht so conclusively. The best that the Headquarters BAOR could devise was a plan based on trying to defend the Rhine while trusting that the American bombers would come to the rescue in time.

By 1952 there were three British armoured divisions on the scene, a British nuclear bomb had been successfully exploded and the first tests of an American eight-inch nuclear cannon shell were imminent. Information from these and earlier test explosions appeared to show that armoured vehicles moving at speed through irradiated areas provided their crews with far more effective screening than any other means, quite apart from shielding against blast and heat. With growing confidence it was decided to move the main defensive line up to the River Weser. A decade later the adoption of 'flexible response' required more fresh thinking. It meant that against a massed, heavily reinforced thrust from the east NATO forces would have to win the politicians a few days grace by the use of conventional weapons alone. It meant that the idea of hundreds of square miles of ground in the heart of Europe devastated by nuclear explosions had been recognized to be a military as well as a political nonsense. It meant that tactical nuclear weapons, instead of being the means to redress NATO's conventional inferiority and produce a stalemate on the battlefield, had become in effect political weapons whose purpose would be to stop the fighting and produce negotiations to end it. It meant that the Allies had to be prepared to engage in a pell-mell armoured battle from the outset and in planning terms it meant that the first principal engagements would have to take place further forward still. This clearly had great political advantage so far as the Germans were concerned, but it meant that the BAOR would have to fight with a major water obstacle behind it. Forward dumps were needed and there were other logistical implications. All these were a direct consequence of MC 14/3 and were in train by the late 1960s.

TACTICAL DOCTRINE

Although the first exercise in BAOR to practise the tactical employment of atomic weapons was held as early as 1954, there was no established doctrine and commanders improvised from their own resources. In 1958 there arrived a short booklet entitled *The Corps Tactical Battle in Nuclear War* whose garish cover led to its being nicknamed 'The Purple Pamphlet'. But after the emergence of the 'Athens Guidelines' in 1967, as we have seen, the doctrine of 'direct defence' required the tactical battle to be fought without nuclear weapons and only when defeat was imminent could nuclear 'release' be countenanced. It follows that only for the ten years from 1958 to 1968 did the British Army genuinely have a nuclear battle-fighting doctrine.

The Purple Pamphlet made obvious assumptions about the British order of battle. It was strong in armour, with most of the infantry carried in armoured personnel carriers (all able to swim) and by way of nuclear firepower was equipped with the eight-inch gun, Honest John and Corporal. The role of the tactical air force was to destroy the enemy's

41

airfields and nuclear delivery means and to impede his forward movement and supplies. Direct close air support would be quite exceptional. The life and work of the fighting soldier would not be much affected except for frantic digging. There would be a huge premium on concealment and the need to fight and move at night. Up the chain of command there was a need to countenance much greater dispersion and a new type of battle plan. Some interesting general points were made. First, the possibility of sudden and violent changes in the battle situation called for greater flexibility on the part of commanders and the need to work from broad directives rather than detailed orders and battle procedures as in the past. Second, the effect of ground was redefined. Instead of the long-standing notion of holding ground 'vital to the defence' it seemed that the future value of ground was to provide observation and affect movement. Control of an area would have to be retained by 'offensive mobile' operations. Third, nuclear artillery would become the predominant arm. Planning would centre on the positioning of the nuclear missile launchers. Nuclear target acquisition and analysis became key staff functions, as did the calculation of safety distances and the warning of our own troops when our own strikes were imminent. Time had to be allowed for this and warning procedures devised. There was much discussion of how to deal with the 'crust' of enemy forces left between our front lines and the nearest enemy positions that could safely be struck with nuclear weapons.

The Corps tactical plan was still to be based on a major obstacle, preferably a river line but possibly consisting of demolitions and minefields. This was seen as even more important than before. There were four phases to the battle. First, the delaying action beyond the obstacle, carried out by screen forces including engineers. The aim was to identify the enemy axes of advance, cause delay and possibly force the enemy to concertina, thus creating a nuclear target. This was expected to last only a day or so. The second phase, called 'On the obstacle', aimed to cripple the enemy forces, so that they could not develop their offensive, by using nuclear missiles against unprotected troops (that is, those doing the assault crossing) and taking toll of his engineers and bridging. If he succeeded in crossing in force there followed a confused phase called 'stabilizing' or 'containing' in which the aim was to hold him within five or ten miles of the obstacle by means of rapid anti-tank screens and pre-planned demolitions, maintaining contact if at all possible. The guidelines at this point contained a warning against improper or ill-conceived movement that it regarded as hazardous in the extreme. This sat oddly with a doctrine for highly mobile operations. Finally, and most exciting, came the much-debated 'Corps counter stroke'. This was in essence a nuclear strike upon an enemy formation preparing to continue the advance, followed on our part by an armoured thrust from some unexpected direction and mopping up. A divisional HQ was normally left out of battle to plan for this.

Clearly the selection of the objective, preliminary movement and timing were matters of delicacy. The question of the 'crust' was of great concern. This was to be the British Army's last great effort; after that it was assumed that strategic nuclear activity would have forced the enemy to cease, desist and sue for peace.

The Purple Pamphlet reads surprisingly well today. It was a brilliant attempt to make sense of an impossible situation. Its life span coincided with the currency of the Weser Strategy. There really was some depth in the position and a major obstacle to be defended. The Army began to receive the lavish scale of armoured personnel carriers, rapid digging equipment and mechanically laid mines that the plan required. A few nuclear strikes on the Weser crossings would have posed major problems for the Warsaw Pact. The Allies might have held them off for five days or so, which was roughly what the plan required. Once the main defensive position had been moved well to the east things got much more difficult and this phase of planning coincided with MC 14/3 and the need to forgo nuclear strikes for tactical purposes. But in one sense planning for this was much more realistic because the great nuclear unknown had been removed from the battle-fighting phase.

The main component of battle management that the Purple Pamphlet had failed to foresee, at least in so many words, was the concept of the 'killing ground'. This was an ancient idea given a new colour. Before you can cope with an enemy advance satisfactorily you have to lure him into some kind of dead end and then strike him, whether it be by nuclear or conventional means. The mental picture is of a cul-de-sac. The killing ground could be located on the near side of an obstacle, as was envisaged in the Purple Pamphlet for the containing phase and corps counter-stroke. In operations east of the Weser one could use the wooded valleys in that part of Germany, thickened up with well-hidden minefields covered by observation and fire. The model could be applied almost anywhere and within a few years it became one of the most crucial elements in all planning and discussion; a key concept in the short nuclear-battle-fighting age.

TRAINING

It was very difficult to carry out realistic exercises with troops to practise the nuclear phase of a battle. Simulating a nuclear strike meant detailing a party of sappers from the control staffs to light some oily rags in an empty 40-gallon oil drum, let off a loud bang and then, because neither of these had been noticed by anybody, sending the umpires round to tell the troops in the notionally affected area that they were either fried, shot-blasted or radioactive and probably all three. Realistically this meant the end of the exercise for the victims. If there were any woods around, these would have been flattened by blow-down. That meant stopping all movement – an obvious difficulty in an exercise that was supposed to involve manoeuvre. It followed that, so far as exercises with troops was concerned, nuclear release tended to coincide with the end of exercise.

One notable exception to this rule had occurred as far back as 1954, when the British Corps attacked a Belgian Corps in Exercise 'Battle Royal'.[13] The Belgians, who were in defence, notionally made use of seven nuclear shells (although of course such things hardly then existed) and the list of what they hit provides one of the most instructive visions of the nuclear battlefield. The first, based on good information from a Belgian SAS patrol, hit HQ 7th Armoured Brigade, 6th Field Regiment (self-propelled) and a squadron of the Royals, knocking them out completely, plus 100 other miscellaneous vehicles. The second was accounted a failure, causing only 100 casualties to a motor battalion of 7th Armoured Division; there was no obstacle and the target was largely guesswork. The third, based on the capture of a marked map, hit 61 Brigade at H-hour for an assault across the Ems in their concentration area and the brigade was virtually destroyed. The fourth fell on HQ 1st British Corps, accurately located by an agent. Though the HQ was well dispersed it would actually have become non-functional, but for exercise reasons it was allowed to carry on. The fifth was aimed at an assault on the Teutoberger Ridge but only 'hit' a gunner regiment causing 100 casualties. The sixth was aimed at an atomic cannon in the Netherlands sector but ground zero was changed at the last moment and it 'hit' an engineer regiment and some bridging. The seventh was 'dropped' on the British Maintenance Area, causing 40 casualties and destroying 25,000 rations and 1,000 tons of fuel. At this stage the exercise was stopped and declared a draw.

It is easy to see why this sort of thing was never popular where exercises with troops were concerned. Instead reliance was placed on tactical exercises without troops, model exercises and command post exercises of various kinds. During the 1960s major exercises were held each year in the great Exhibition Hall in Luxembourg. The various Corps, Division and Brigade Headquarters were all placed in cubicles, connected by telephone in a realistic way, and the exercise was run to a timetable by an elaborate control staff. One distressing feature was that it ran at double time. The whole day was played between 6am and 6pm after which the players returned exhausted to their hotels and came back in time for 6am next morning. There was plenty of nuclear play. On one such exercise the Commander Royal Engineers of 2nd Division lost a lot of bridging equipment to a Russian nuclear strike but actually succeeded in letting off an ADM. An exercise like that can be very realistic. For many participants it provided by far the most vivid vision they had of the nuclear battlefield.

When it came to exercises with troops, an entirely different form of war was played. The big divisional exercises often took the form of long advances to contact and assaults across real water obstacles using real bridging. These were very demanding. Any nuclear episodes would have slowed things to a standstill. It is an open question why exercises tended to take this form. Was it because an offensive exercise was a better test of commanders and troops? Or was there a deeper reason? Did everyone, deep down, look on the very idea of a massive Warsaw Pact assault, let alone a nuclear response, as unreal? The real action, what the British Army always *did* as opposed to planning and training for, was offensive action – usually undertaken to throw dictators out of lands they had improperly seized. This was what they had done in the Second World War from El Alamein onwards and in Korea and Suez. It was what they were to do in the Falklands and the Gulf. It was necessary to be trained for it, not least on the North German Plain.

During the second half of the cold war from 1969 onwards, NATO had only a feeble concept of fighting a nuclear battle. The great project of the 1980s was the stationing of Pershing and Cruise missiles in Europe and the harnessing of surveillance and target acquisition to precision guidance and other smart technologies. Once the Russian Empire had collapsed the British were quick to announce that they no longer planned to conduct operations with theatre nuclear weapons. Perhaps the whole notion will come to seem a historical aberration. Certainly there was always room for doubt that nuclear weapons would truly favour the defence rather than the assault, just as one can never know for sure how much the nuclear balance of terror contributed to keeping the peace in Europe anyway. But at the time the nuclear battlefield seemed all too real – at least in the Luxembourg Exhibition Hall.

NOTES

A version of this chapter first appeared in *Flattering the Passions: Or, the Bomb and Britain's Bid for a World Role* by the author and Nadine Gurr (London and New York: I.B. Tauris, 1999). We are grateful for permission to reprint it here.

1. W.F. Burns, 'The Future of US Nuclear Weapons Policy', *Arms Control Today*, Vol.27, No.7 (Oct. 1997), p.3. Emphasis added.
2. S. Turner, *Caging the Nuclear Genie: An American Challenge for Global Security* (Oxford: Westview Press, 1996), pp.74–5. Emphasis added.
3. Ibid., p.75. Emphasis added.
4. *The Corps Tactical Battle in Nuclear War 1958* (London: War Office, 1958), p.17.
5. F. Mulley, *The Politics of Western Defence* (London: Thames and Hudson, 1962), p.76.
6. C. Campbell, *Nuclear Facts: A Guide to Nuclear Weapons Systems and Strategy* (London: Hamlyn, 1984), p.131.

7. Mulley, *The Politics of Western Defence*, p.128.
8. *Times*, 25 Jan. 1961, quoted in Mulley, *The Politics of Western Defence*, p.145.
9. Mulley, *The Politics of Western Defence*, p.146.
10. Campbell, *Nuclear Facts*, p.33.
11. Ibid., p.132.
12. J. Hackett, *The Third World War August 1985: A Future History* (London: Sidgwick and Jackson, 1978), *passim*.
13. I.R. Graeme, 'Northern Army Group Exercise Battle Royal', *British Army Annual*, No.2 (1955), pp.9–22.

My First Trip to Ground Zero

RIC JOHNSTONE

After many years some details like time and date are difficult to remember, but I still have very vivid memories of my first trip into the blast area of the first nuclear weapon detonated at Maralinga (Map 1). After being a kind of roving mechanic in the early days of preparation for the first explosion (like an RAC road service person) and helping with the positioning of target response vehicles, about a month before the first detonation I was assigned to work at the main decontamination centre which was a few kilometres from the Maralinga village toward the airstrip, with its own entrance into the forward area, called the dirty track.

Corporal Bill Hughes (known as Paddy – he was Irish) and I, both members of the RAAF and both motor transport mechanics, were shown how to dress in protective clothing and how to enter and leave the contaminated areas by members of the Canadian Army's No.1 Radiation Detection Unit, Corporals Dennis Newbury and James Ripley, who were also stationed at the decontamination centre. My job was to salvage and decontaminate any yellow vehicles that might break down in the contaminated area and rescue their occupants. I was also involved in the assessment of mechanical damage to target response vehicles.

Paddy and I both had yellow Land Rovers and had radio contact with each other in the 'hot' areas. His call sign was Yellow One; mine was Yellow Two. We also had our own vehicles that we used for the clean areas and were on call 24-hours a day. Yellow vehicles were normal Land Rovers and trucks that had their mudguards painted yellow to indicate that they were for use only in the contaminated areas and were never to be driven into the clean areas.

The Canadians had their own special vehicles that they looked after themselves as some of their equipment was still top secret. I recall one very large van, a Dodge, I think, that had lots of strange rods, probe-like structures, pointing out from it. A rear spring U-bolt broke on this vehicle during trials before the first detonation. We repaired it for them but were not allowed to look inside the van, where there appeared to be many instruments in boxes with dials and switches. These vehicles were kept separate from ours and closely guarded; they were also kept spotlessly clean.

For us, the decontamination of motor vehicles was much the same work as we might do everyday; we used the same equipment to steam clean and degrease motor vehicles and their engines as part of our normal duties. The difference was that we now had to do this dressed in protective clothing and wearing huge boots and gloves. This proved impossible in most cases; we could not undo the wing nuts retaining the carburettor oil-filled air cleaners and we had to remove the gloves and the breathing gear because of the heat. We were used as guinea-pigs for different types of protective clothing and breathing gear.

While we were doing this job others dressed in full protective clothing (two or three scientists of some sort we assumed) took readings with Geiger counters and pointed to the worst contamination. This was usually around the sump gasket or the gearbox – anywhere that oil showed, in particular the oil-bath air cleaners on the carburettors.

THE FIRST TEST

We watched the detonation of the first bomb from the compound near the village, wearing our everyday clothes. We were told to turn our backs to the blast area. There was a countdown over loud speakers from ten seconds after which we could turn to face the blast. While our backs were to the blast there was a white flash that seemed to come through the back of one's head and a warm feeling on the back of the neck. When we turned we were amazed by the fireball, which was slowly turning into the now familiar mushroom cloud. As it grew it seemed to be right over us. Then came the hot air and a sound that shook up some people. It sounded like a huge clap of thunder, trailing off to a sound like 100 locomotives crossing the desert. We stood amazed for some time and then returned to our respective huts.

NEXT DAY

After breakfast at about 7am, Paddy and I reported to the decontamination centre. We were told that the Canadians would go towards ground zero and take readings, but before they did we would have to take them in for a preliminary run in our vehicles – they wanted to keep their vehicles clean until they knew exactly where they could go.

We went through the entry procedure and suited up. I had Dennis Newbury and another person whom I think was a Canadian officer or scientist with me. I drove up the dirty track toward ground zero to wherever they indicated they wanted to go. They were taking readings all the time. It was an amazing sight, the vegetation was blasted away, shrubs were burning, vehicles were on their sides or on their backs and some were burning. Buildings that I remembered in certain areas were no longer there.

After a couple of hours looking around and taking readings we returned to the decontamination centre via the dirty track. I parked the vehicle in the designated yellow ('hot') area and we all went through the decontamination procedures together and then re-entered the clean area. The others went off to do their paperwork and I went to the village for lunch.

After lunch I returned to the decontamination centre, suited up and re-entered the hot area. I retrieved the vehicle we had used in the morning from where it was parked and placed it on the concrete slab where, under the direction of a scientist, I proceeded to decontaminate it. Others had also entered the hot area and on return had parked their vehicles in the yellow area, so now there were more vehicles to decontaminate. Paddy arrived shortly after to give me a hand. Under the supervision of the boffins we cleaned two or three vehicles and then ourselves. After using the exit procedures we left the area and went for dinner in the village.

LATER

Some of the things that happened to Paddy and me in and out of the forward areas after may one day fill a book. Paddy and I both did the same kind of work from then on and throughout the four detonations of Operation 'Buffalo'. Toward the end of this work I began to suffer bouts of vomiting and diarrhoea and reported to our flight sergeant medical orderly. He said it was just the food we were eating, I accepted that as the problem and did not worry about it. As my tour of duty was at an end and I had accumulated three months leave on full pay, I was going home to be married to a girl I had been writing to throughout my time at Maralinga.

But when I arrived in Adelaide from Maralinga the bouts of illness continued. We were married in Adelaide and then returned to my home base in New South Wales, where I had rented a house close to my depot, which was HQHC Lapstone near Penrith. Although I was still on leave, I reported ill to the local doctor in Penrith and then to the RAAF doctor at Lapstone. Blood tests were taken and on the strength of the results of those I was admitted to No.3 RAAF Hospital, Richmond NSW.

The doctor said he thought I had radiation poisoning and he would devise some form of treatment for me. He had to stop the red cells eating the white cells or visa versa – I'm not sure now which way round it was! Anyhow, I was in the hospital for a couple of weeks, during which time I had blood transfusions and many pills. Then I was told that I had been lucky, my bone marrow had recovered and was now producing good red cells. I was discharged from hospital and told that I might now have some kind of nervous condition. I was put on light duties – the cover-up had begun.

Eventually, after a few more trips into hospital, I was discharged from the RAAF in late 1957 as medically unfit for further service due to a nervous condition. I guess the rest of the story might make another book or a film. Some of the official cover-up is beginning to unravel for them now due to the release of some documents and other events. Both my sons were born with hair, skin and teeth defects, which may be due to radiation.

TODAY

Bill Hughes is now dead and I am told that Dennis Ripley and James Newbury both died from cancer. The person who took over my job, a RAAF mechanic named Yet Foy, also died from cancer. I took the government to court in 1989 and won, but it was a Pyrrhic victory – they won on the amount of damages and the cost to me and the cover-up continues. Other cases have been settled out of court for large sums of money, but with secrecy clauses so that evidence that could be put before the court would not become public knowledge.

Why I Rejected Nuclear Weapons

ROBERT GREEN

In 1969 I was a 25-year-old Royal Navy Lieutenant serving in the British aircraft-carrier HMS *Eagle* as back-seat aircrew in its Buccaneer nuclear strike jet squadron. 'Observer' is the Fleet Air Arm's traditional term for bombardier-navigator, whose job is to navigate the aircraft and help the pilot operate its weapons system. During the next three years, I accepted without question an elite role with my pilot as a 'nuclear crew', with an assigned target from NATO's SIOP. Our task was to be ready to deliver a free-fall thermonuclear bomb of over 100 kilotons explosive power to detonate above a military airfield on the outskirts of Leningrad – which is now St Petersburg's airport.

Thirty years later, I landed there to speak at a conference reviewing nuclear policy and security on the eve of the twenty-first century. In a television interview, I apologized to the citizens of St Petersburg since, had my nuclear mission been completed, it would inevitably have caused horrific indiscriminate casualties and long-term poisonous effects from radioactive fallout, quite apart from extensive collateral damage to their beautiful ancient capital. I now concluded that nuclear weapons would not save me – and they will not save the Russians either.

Following a decision by the British government that it could no longer afford strike carriers, in 1972 I switched to anti-submarine helicopters. A year later, I was appointed Senior Observer of a squadron of Sea King anti-submarine helicopters aboard the aircraft-carrier HMS *Ark Royal*. Our task was to use radar, variable-depth sonar and other electronic sensors plus a variety of weapons to detect and destroy submarines threatening the force.

All was well until we were ordered to be ready to use a thermonuclear depth-bomb because our lightweight anti-submarine homing torpedoes could not go fast enough or deep enough to catch the latest Soviet nuclear-powered submarines. The explosive power of that depth-bomb was more than that of the atomic bomb that devastated Hiroshima. If I had pressed the button to release it, it would have vaporized a large volume of ocean – and myself because (unlike the strike jet) the helicopter was too slow to escape before detonation; this would have been a suicide mission. There would have been heavy radioactive fallout from the depth-bomb plus the nuclear submarine's reactor and any nuclear-tipped torpedoes it carried; this could have escalated the Third World War to nuclear holocaust. All this, just to protect our aircraft-carrier.

Yet all these concerns were brushed aside. Soothing responses included the claim that 'going nuclear' would only arise in deep water far from land (where nuclear submarines would use their speed advantage), so no civilians would be involved and 'the Soviets wouldn't even detect it'. Because I was ambitious and was assured that there would almost certainly be no need to use it, I decided to obey. From then on, however, my absolute trust in my leaders was shaken and I realized that nuclear weapons were militarily useless.

NUCLEAR CUCKOO IN THE NAVAL NEST

In December 1979 in the House of Lords, former UK Chief of Defence Staff Field Marshal Lord Carver declared:

> I have never heard or read of a scenario in which I would consider it right or reasonable for the Prime Minister or Government of this country to order the firing of our independent strategic force at a time when the Americans were not prepared to fire theirs – certainly not before Russian nuclear weapons had landed on this country. And, again, if they had already landed, would it be right and reasonable? All it would do would be to invite further retaliation.[1]

Just over a year before, on promotion to Commander I went to the MoD in Whitehall, London as Personal Staff Officer to an Admiral who had the responsibility of recommending the replacement for the Polaris nuclear-armed ballistic missile submarine force. I witnessed the debate in the Naval Staff and watched the nuclear submariners – known as the 'Black Mafia' – go ruthlessly for a scaled-down version of the huge US Trident submarine system, even though it grossly exceeded UK requirements, introduced a destabilizing first-strike capability with its greater firepower and accuracy and its massive cost threatened the future of the Royal Navy as a balanced, useful force.

When Margaret Thatcher became Prime Minister in May 1979, she quickly demonstrated that she was determined to have Trident – and the Chiefs of Staff were whipped into line. The Navy is increasingly embarrassed by the ridiculously over-capable, and hence unusable, Trident force. Meanwhile, the British surface fleet is now smaller than the Japanese Navy's, and shrinking, and a brand new class of conventionally powered submarines has been leased to the Canadian Navy.

THE FALKLANDS WAR

In my last appointment as Staff Officer (Intelligence) to Commander-in-Chief Fleet, I ran the team providing round-the-clock intelligence support to Polaris as well as the rest of the Fleet from the command bunker in Northwood, near London. In 1982, Britain suddenly found itself at war with an erstwhile friend, Argentina, over the Falkland Islands. During the war, which was directed from Northwood, my intelligence team expanded four-fold. Having just been granted redundancy in a defence review, I was allowed to leave the Navy once it was over.

I know what a close-run thing that war was. If Argentine aircraft had sunk one of the troopships before the landing force had got ashore, the British might have had to withdraw or risk defeat. What would Thatcher have done? Polaris had clearly not deterred Argentina's President Galtieri from invading. With victory in his grasp, it is doubtful that he would have believed Thatcher would have seriously threatened a nuclear strike on Argentina. Yet rumours emerged after the war that a Polaris submarine had been moved south within range of Buenos Aires. If she had so threatened, Galtieri would have very publicly called her bluff and relished watching US President Reagan try to rein her in. In the last resort, would the Polaris submarine's Commanding Officer – briefed by me on the Soviet threat before he went on so-called deterrent patrol, but faced with a bizarre shift of target and new rules of engagement – have either refused the firing order or faked a malfunction and returned to face a court martial with a clear conscience? In the event, this nightmare did not arise but I suddenly saw the huge danger of placing any leader in such a crisis with the nuclear option at their disposal. The failure of nuclear deterrence could have led the Royal Navy to multiply the ignominy of defeat by being the first to break the nuclear taboo since Nagasaki.

THE GULF WAR

My doubts over nuclear weapons grew when the Berlin Wall came down in 1989, but it took the 1991 Gulf War to make me break out of my pro-nuclear brainwashing. It was very traumatic. My military intelligence training warned me that the US-led coalition's blitzkrieg strategy would give Iraq's President Saddam Hussein the pretext he needed to attack Israel, in order to split the coalition and become the Arabs' champion. If sufficiently provoked, he could use Scud ballistic missiles with chemical or biological warheads. Israel's Prime Minister Shamir would come under heavy domestic pressure to retaliate with a nuclear strike on Baghdad. Even if Saddam Hussein did not survive (and he had the best anti-nuclear bunkers that Western technology could provide), the entire Arab world would erupt in fury against Israel and its Allies, its security would be destroyed forever and Russia would be sucked in.

The first Scud attack hit Tel Aviv on the night of 17 January 1991. A week before, I had become the first ex-British Navy Commander with nuclear-weapon experience to speak out against them when I addressed a crowd of 20,000 anti-Gulf War demonstrators from the foot of Nelson's column in Trafalgar Square, of all places. For the first time, the second city of a *de facto* nuclear state had been attacked and its capital threatened. Worse for nuclear deterrence dogma, the aggressor did not have nuclear weapons. The Israeli people, cowering in gas masks in basements, learned that night that their so-called 'deterrent' had failed in its primary purpose. Some 38 more Scud attacks followed. Seymour Hersh recounts how Israel reacted:

> The [US] satellite saw that Shamir had responded to the Scud barrage by ordering mobile missile launchers armed with nuclear weapons moved into the open and deployed facing Iraq, ready to launch on command. American intelligence picked up other signs indicating that Israel had gone on a full-scale nuclear alert that would remain in effect for weeks. No one in the Bush administration knew what Israel would do if a Scud armed with nerve gas struck a crowded apartment building, killing thousands. All Bush could offer Shamir, besides money and more batteries of Patriot missiles, was American assurance that the Iraqi Scud launcher sites would be made a priority target of the air war.
>
> Such guarantees meant little; no Jews had been killed by poison gas since Treblinka and Auschwitz, and Israel, after all, had built its bomb so it would never have to depend on the goodwill of others when the lives of Jews were being threatened.
>
> The escalation didn't happen, however; the conventionally armed Scud warheads caused – amazingly – minimal casualties, and military and financial commitments from the Bush administration rolled in. The government of Prime Minister Yitzhak Shamir received international plaudits for its restraint.
>
> American officials were full of private assurances for months after the crisis that things had been under control; newsmen were told that Israel, recognizing the enormous consequence of a nuclear strike, would not have launched its missiles at Baghdad. The fact is, of course, that no one in America – not even its President – could have dissuaded Shamir and his advisers from ordering any military actions they deemed essential to the protection of their nation.[2]

Meanwhile, in Britain the Irish Republican Army just missed wiping out the entire Gulf War Cabinet with a mortar bomb attack from a van in Whitehall. A more direct threat to the government could barely be imagined. What if instead they had threatened to use even a crude nuclear device? A counter-threat of nuclear retaliation would be utterly incredible.

BRITANNIA WAIVES THE RULES

Belatedly forced to research the history of 'the Bomb', I discovered that the British scientific-politico-military establishment bore considerable responsibility for initiating and spreading the nuclear arms race. Having alerted the US to the feasibility of making a nuclear weapon, the UK participated in the Manhattan Project. On being frozen out of further collaboration by the 1946 McMahon Act, in 1947 the UK began to develop its own nuclear arsenal. The UK became Saddam Hussein's role model: the first medium-sized power with delusions of grandeur to threaten nuclear terrorism. I began to realize that the doctrine of nuclear deterrence had always been flawed in terms of its practicality, was immoral and unlawful and there were more credible and acceptable alternative security strategies.

In 1991 I became Chair of the World Court Project's UK affiliate. This world-wide network of citizen groups helped to persuade the UN General Assembly, despite desperate countermoves led by the three NATO nuclear-weapon states, to ask the ICJ (known as the World Court) for its Advisory Opinion on the legal status of nuclear weapons. In 1996 the ICJ confirmed that the threat, let alone use, of nuclear weapons would generally be illegal. For the first time, the legality of nuclear deterrence had been challenged (Chapter 2).

One aspect of the ICJ's decision was especially important. It confirmed that, as part of international humanitarian law, the Nuremberg Principles apply to nuclear weapons. In particular, Principle IV states: 'The fact that a person acted pursuant to order of his government or of a superior does not relieve him from responsibility under international law, provided a moral choice was in fact possible for him.' This has serious implications for all those involved in operating nuclear weapons, but particularly those military professionals who, unlike the Prime Minister, really would have to 'press the button'. What is at stake here is a crucial difference between military professionals and hired killers or terrorists: military professionals need to be seen to act within the law.

NOTES

This chapter is adapted from the author's book *The Naked Nuclear Emperor: Debunking Nuclear Deterrence* (Christchurch: Disarmament and Security Centre, 2000). We are grateful for permission to reprint it here.

1. Lord Carver, *Hansard*, House of Lords, v.403 (18 Dec. 1979), Cols.1628–30.
2. S. Hersh, *The Samson Option* (New York: Random House, 1991), p.318.

Resisting the British Bomb: The Early Years

DUNCAN REES

It is commonly perceived that the post-Second World War atomic bomb programme was simply a natural progression from wartime fears that Nazi Germany would be the first to develop nuclear weapons and the need to use the atom bomb to ensure the defeat of Japan. The pro-nuclear argument was based upon nuclear weapons being just a natural evolution to a more modern (and more destructive) form of weapon. The idea that nuclear weapons can take their place as part of our state's legitimate armoury has been an article of faith for British governments ever since the 1940s (Chapter 1). Initially, however, the political and moral implications of possessing and being prepared to use such weapons were not widely debated.

However, even as early as 1948, the distinguished physicist P.M.S. Blackett, winner of the Nobel prize for physics in that year, said that 'the dropping of the atomic bombs [on Japan] was not so much the last military act of the second world war, as the first act of the cold diplomatic war with Russia'.[1] By 1953, with the United Kingdom atomic bomb operational, Prime Minister Winston Churchill was moved to say that 'We had one and let it off – it went off beautifully'[2] – no apparent moral qualms there! In 1957, Prime Minister Harold Macmillan confirmed Blackett's opinion when he said that:

> We have made a successful start. When the [nuclear] tests are completed ... we shall be in the same position as the United States or Soviet Russia. We shall have made and tested the massive weapons. It will be possible then to discuss on equal terms.[3]

Such were the illusions. The political and military consensus in favour of a UK weapons programme has always been well established – even if not particularly well thought out – from Attlee to Blair. It is hard to envisage Tony Blair trying to justify UK nuclear weapons of the twenty-first century on the grounds that they achieve some kind of parity with the superpowers. Yet since its creation, the 'British Bomb' has succeeded in sustaining delusions of past grandeur among generations of politicians who should really know better.

THE CAMPAIGN FOR NUCLEAR DISARMAMENT

Launched publicly at Central Hall Westminster on 17 February 1958, the CND has played a central role in the evolution of the movement against nuclear weapons in the UK and become one of the largest mass protest movements that the UK has ever seen. The emergence of CND resulted from the coming together of a diverse range of campaigning groups and concerned people at a time when the pace of external events connected with nuclear weapons suddenly quickened. By 1957 both the Churches and the scientific community were becoming increasingly concerned about the moral and ethical implications of nuclear weapons. Also in that year, the heat in the political debate was turned up, as Aneurin Bevan shook the Labour Party by forcefully supporting the British bomb in his notorious 'naked into the negotiating chamber' speech at the annual party conference. Opponents of nuclear weapons were stung into action – an article by J.B. Priestley in the *New Statesman* attracted the interest and support of figures such as Bertrand Russell, A.J.P. Taylor, Kingsley Martin, P.M.S. Blackett and Canon John Collins.[4] Meanwhile MPs such as Michael Foot and Tony Benn (then Anthony Wedgwood Benn) had also become involved. For a time, it may have seemed that any anti-bomb protest would be confined to high-level pressure group work. However, for all the heavyweight intellectual backing (CND's initial list of founders included 13 who featured in *Who's Who*), the campaign was also, from the outset, a popular grass-roots movement.

Among the groups instrumental in setting the scene for the emergence of CND was the National Campaign for the Abolition of Nuclear Weapons Tests, which had local groups in the Golders Green, Finchley and Hampstead areas of London. Another was the Emergency Committee for Direct Action Against Nuclear War (Direct Action Committee). It was the Direct Action Committee that organized the first Aldermaston march at Easter 1958 (with support from the newly formed CND). Making its way from London to Aldermaston, during a miserably cold Easter, the 1958 march grew from 5,000 to around 10,000 people on its final stages and crucially established a key symbolic focus for the new campaign. By 1960 and 1961, the Aldermaston nuclear-weapons plant had become the starting point for the Easter march, by then organized by CND, and the numbers filling Central London at the end had swollen to over 100,000.

CND was not only the first campaign against the nuclear bomb to have a coherent national and international strategy, it also (mostly) managed to bring together its diverse elements into an effective and powerful campaigning body. This success was achieved despite the many different persuasions involved – pacifists, communists, Labour Party members, Christians of differing denominations, anarchists and many others – but also because of the discipline that some of the groups exerted among their supporters. The pacifist/anarchist tradition, for example, was the backbone for much of the pioneering non-violent direct action which marked the early years of protest, whilst the Labour and trade union movement provided key organizational and administrative skills and personnel. Yet to say that CND was 'controlled' by the communists, Churches, trade unions, anarchists and so on, as often happened, was missing the point. CND was one of the first truly 'popular' mass public protest movements of the later twentieth century and its very success in attracting support made it very difficult for any one faction to control. The biggest internal CND battles of the 1960s were perhaps over the issues of direct or non-violent action and the question of support for 'peripheral' campaigns such as Vietnam or Greece, yet these were issues that in any case divided opinion within political parties.

The issue of using non-violent civil disobedience or direct action as a tactic took on huge significance after the Committee of 100 was formed in 1960 as a direct successor to the Direct Action Committee. With big popular support and CND President Bertrand Russell at its head, the Committee of 100 sought to become a kind of 'cutting edge' to the campaign against nuclear weapons, but was opposed by Canon John Collins and most of the CND executive. However, the Committee of 100 certainly played its part and established a key principle: that in order to overcome a great immorality, the breaking of the law could in some circumstances be justified. Most in CND agreed on the point of principle, the divisions arose mainly over the perceived effectiveness of civil disobedience. Fortunately, the lessons learned meant that during the CND revival of the 1980s such disunity was far less significant.

The political parties which supported CND to a greater or lesser extent (Labour, Communist, Liberal and Scots/Welsh Nationalist) all did so on the understanding that CND was 'a broad Church'. Groups that sought to hijack CND, such as Trotskyite groups during the 1980s, not only lacked support, but were also firmly countered by the supporters of the 'broad Church'.

EVOLUTION

Some idea of how CND evolved through the 1960s and 1970s can be gained by recalling the challenges that faced its full-time officials. I was the first CND General Secretary who was also at the time a Communist Party member, but I was preceded by a member of the Labour Party and followed by a Catholic priest – a truly broad Church one might say.

The late Peggy Duff (General Secretary from 1958 to 1967) was a brilliant organizational inspiration behind not only the campaign, but in particular, the Aldermaston march. She was equally at home supervising the logistics of the march like a military campaign, or handling the ranks of the great and good who lined up to speak in Trafalgar Square. Many who followed, including myself, made a backward nod in acknowledgement of what she did to make the marches into the powerful statement against British nuclear weapons that they became.

In 1967 John Minion from Birmingham stood in as secretary. John later went on to keep the CND flag flying in the West Midlands and was one of the stalwarts from the 1960s who kept going into the 1980s. Dick Nettleton, who died in 1988, was General Secretary from 1967 to 1973. He was a large, easy-going Mancunian, with a cheery smile and an avuncular manner, yet was a tough and efficient organizer – and had to be. To Dick fell the task of managing CND's decline in the late 1960s and 1970s. It is enormously to his credit that he succeeded in keeping the campaign together, welding it close, but not too close, to the anti-Vietnam War campaign and actually inspiring the campaign to begin the process of re-inventing itself for a new decade.

My immediate predecessor, Dan Smith, served from 1973 to 1975. He accelerated the process that Dick Nettleton had begun, appreciating that if CND was to remain relevant it had to re-focus its resources and personnel into new ways of working and campaigning.

For myself, my first proper introduction to CND came as a child of seven taking part in a march with my parents and younger brother in Cardiff. I remember vividly the terror that the Cuban missile crisis created. Belonging to a political family (we took the *Daily Worker/Morning Star* every day), I was not lacking in opportunities to become involved in campaigns. One of these of course was CND and the peace movement, which the *Morning Star* and the Communist Party enthusiastically championed. But by the time I became involved, things had moved on from the early 1960s.

In the mid- to late 1960s CND became increasingly identified with the anti-Vietnam War movements, indeed many of its principal officers were shared with the British Campaign for Peace in Vietnam. However, despite the broad base of the British Campaign, it was inevitable that the message about nuclear weapons, especially British ones, would be diluted. By that time, perceptions about the nuclear threat had changed. Nuclear conflict, if it featured at all as a concern, was more likely to be seen as a terrible by-product of the United States war in south-east Asia or the conflict in the Middle East. The US–Soviet arms race and the British bomb had ceased to be of prime concern. As the Vietnam War grew ever more brutal and ugly, it became the main focus of protest for many young people.

On my first CND Aldermaston march in 1968, I felt I was marching more for the suffering people of Vietnam than to rid the world of nuclear weapons, but it was a big march and I supported the anti-Vietnam War movement so I was happy, if footsore. In 1970, travelling back from the Easter CND march in London, poorly attended and with little support from my hometown of Cardiff, I had begun to wonder what I was doing there. By then the anti-Vietnam War movement was attracting less support and CND's national and regional organization had dwindled to a tiny fraction of its size even five years earlier. My reaction was to study the arguments over nuclear weapons more carefully and the result was an increasing conviction that we needed to do something to re-invigorate CND.

In 1972 I participated in another CND Aldermaston march, again poorly attended, except at the end when the device of a pop concert featuring the band Hawkwind drove the numbers up to around 10,000. At this time new CND groups, like those that I had helped to set up in both my hometown of Cardiff and at Liverpool University, were a rarity. Nationally however, the statistics presented to CND's National Council (to which I was elected in 1972) made depressing reading: 2,120 members and just 50 local groups were all that remained. (CND's national membership scheme only started in the late 1960s when decline in support was already well advanced.)

By 1974 CND marches had reached a nadir. From hundreds of thousands in the 1950s and early 1960s, the Aldermaston march had dried up to just a trickle. In that year just 200 set off from Aldermaston and there was plenty of room for the pigeons in Trafalgar Square beside our tiny crowd of about 2,000. Nuclear weapons seemed to be on virtually no one's political agenda.

RECONSTRUCTION AND REVIVAL

There was much talk of where CND should go next. I took over as General Secretary from Dan Smith in 1975. We began a programme of monitoring our membership statistics. This revealed that in 1975 there were about 60 groups nation-wide (perhaps half of them viable), 2,500 members, three full-time staff and 158 affiliated organizations. In the absence of sufficient active public support, and given that the formal backing for CND from the late 1970s came from groups like the Churches, trade unions and the Labour Party, it is perhaps not surprising that we looked particularly to strengthen our links with affiliated organizations. We combined this with moves to develop an authoritative voice on nuclear and other defence matters, aimed at key opinion formers.

With the support of MPs such as Robin Cook, Stan Newens and the late Jo Richardson, we began to build up a reputation for authoritative and consistent pressure on nuclear issues within parliament. Within our 'broad Church' remit we did not forget other parties and so it was that in 1977 the then Chair of CND, John Cox, and myself (Communist Party members both), encouraged, though obviously did not become involved in, the setting up of a Liberal Party CND group.

In the trade unions, the work of Labour CND and the Lucas Aerospace Shop Stewards Committee broadened debate on alternatives to arms manufacture. This work aimed to show that the moral dimension of disarmament had a practical side, creating or saving jobs at the same time as reducing work on armaments. In the Churches, the work of Quakers (Friends Peace Committee) such as Frank Williams and Rowland Dale and our other colleagues in the Anglican and Catholic Churches helped both the theological and public debate on nuclear-weapons issues. One of the critical developments at this time, which was to have big implications after 1980 when protests against UK nuclear weapons reached new heights, was the revival of Christian CND and the role that this played in bringing together an organized multi-denominational movement against nuclear weapons. This expressed itself both in the broadening of the debate publicly and also in specific policy discussions, for example, within the General Synod of the Church of England. It was interesting that by 1977 CND had Bruce Kent, a Catholic priest, as Chairman and myself (a Communist) as General Secretary. We have both moved on in many ways since, but it worked well at the time. Another key figure from that time was Barbara Eggleston who was a driving force behind Christian CND (and its full-time organizer during the 1980s). Eggleston, who sadly died in 2002 at the early age of 47, was one of several of the idealistic 20-somethings who worked or volunteered for CND in the 1970s and were able to experience the sheer excitement and joy when the campaign really took off again in the 1980s.

By 1979 our annual report noted that membership had increased to over 4,000, with 150 CND groups and 274 affiliated organizations. As part of our programme of taking the message out to the country, I had spoken to audiences totalling more than 20,000 at showings of the film *The War Game* across the country. *The War Game*, commissioned by the BBC, had been directed by Peter Watkins in the 1960s and was a dramatized account of a nuclear attack on the UK. Fearful of the effect its powerful images might have, the film was withheld from general viewing on television until the 1980s. CND obtained copies of the film from the British Film Institute in 1975 and used it extensively in public meetings around the UK.

APPRAISAL

The anti-nuclear-weapons movement in the UK has always been something of a rollercoaster, influenced not only by its own initiatives and expertise, but also driven one way or another by the tides of political fortune in this country and the rapidly changing world picture. I would like to think that we have been a successful campaign. Although we have not, obviously, attained our general objectives in full, we have still achieved much. We have put the issue on to the political agenda, raised arguments that would otherwise have remained absent from public debate and forced successive governments to detail and justify their military programmes in a way never seen before, but above all we have set a moral benchmark. Norman Moss summarizes this neatly in the title of his book, *Men Who Play God*.[5] CND resolved the dilemma by saying simply 'we will not live with the nuclear threat'. CND has succeeded in a sense by telling people the facts – simply stated by the headline in one of its earliest campaigning leaflets in the 1950s and 1960s: 'if it [nuclear war] ever happens – don't say we did not tell you.'

The early years of CND from 1958 to 1978 were marked by formation, then rapid expansion, lack of consolidation, diversification and then rapid decline followed by slow re-building. The re-emergence of the campaign in the 1980s, with protests even bigger than those of the 1960s, were partly a result of the decision to site US cruise missiles in the UK. I say partly, because CND was, and is, always keen to stress that one of our prime concerns is with UK nuclear weapons and the example that getting rid of them would pose to the rest of the world. So in the late 1970s, while CND started addressing the issue of cruise missiles, we also concentrated heavily on what was, for Britain, an even more fundamental and yet very poorly understood and discussed issue – the replacement of the Polaris missile system by Trident.

Even among supporters, this was sometimes difficult. Arousing fear of US missile bases (planned or existing) was almost always easier than arguing against UK nuclear military facilities, the reason being the usual syndrome 'Not In My Back Yard'!

There is perhaps a gut feeling among some people that although we do not want to be made a target by the presence of US bases, somehow it is alright for the UK to have its own 'little deterrent'. This of course gets right to the core of the whole debate. CND's initial premise, and the argument that attracted me among many others, was the moral/non-pacifist argument. In other words, we do not expect unilateral disarmament, but we do expect unilateral nuclear disarmament irrespective of whatever other countries may or may not do. My own father, who fought in the Second World War, was a member of Ex-Services CND and I think this attitude was an example for many of us who, though not necessarily opposed to all wars in all circumstances, can see that nuclear weapons cross a crucial dividing line in terms of what is and what is not acceptable in warfare.

This is our responsibility. We can argue until the proverbial cows come home about American policy, but at the end of the day, it is the example provided by the UK that is the centre of the CND argument. If we are seriously arguing that the world is a safer place without Indian or Pakistani or Israeli nuclear weapons, then why are UK nuclear weapons any different? For as long as there are nuclear weapons in the world, it remains the case that the greater the number of nuclear-armed states, the greater the chances of global nuclear war.

I have argued with Tory ministers, Labour ministers and soldiers, in public school debating chambers, on radio phone-in programmes and, yes, even with the man or woman on the bus or in the pub. I have yet to hear a logical, coherent, rational, moral, economic, military, political or convincing case for the UK having its own nuclear-weapons programme.

NOTES

1. John Cox, *Overkill* (New York: Peacock Books, 1977).
2. Ibid., p.27.
3. Ibid.
4. J.B. Priestley, 'Britain and the Nuclear Bombs', *New Statesman*, 2 Nov. 1957.
5. Norman Moss, *Men Who Play God: The Story of the Hydrogen Bomb and How the World Came to Live With It* (New York: Harper and Row, 1968).

Resisting the British Bomb: The 1980s

BRUCE KENT

No one guessed that for CND's world the 1980s would turn out to be such an exciting and interesting decade. The 1978 United Nations First Special Session on Disarmament had attracted scarcely a ripple of British political interest. Even in the peace world its powerful Final Document was received in semi-silence. Yet, though we did not realize it, public opinion on nuclear matters was massively on the move. I have always wondered why it was that the government did not understand how much it did during Margaret Thatcher's reign to boost CND's flagging fortunes.

The Conservative government announced that Britain would not only host American cruise missiles, but would also build Trident submarines as a replacement for Polaris, with American missiles and British warheads. It followed up this chilling and expensive news with an entirely ludicrous pamphlet called *Protect and Survive*,[1] which told the public what to do in case of nuclear war. Not only were the recommendations in themselves ridiculous (hide under the stairs for 14 days, for example) but the message was clear. The nuclear deterrence that we were told was foolproof was not so foolproof after all. If it was, then why all the concern for civil defence?

It now began to dawn on a wider public that 'our' nuclear weapons were there even to be used first as a last resort in a war in which the enemy had not used nuclear weapons. The glossy blue cruise missile brochure produced by the MoD made this first use function quite clear. The aim of using cruise missiles 'would be to persuade the Russian leadership – even at the eleventh hour – to draw back'.[2] The idea that some rational purpose could be served by setting off a flight of cruise missiles, each carrying a warhead with about ten times the destructive power of the Hiroshima bomb, was not convincing.

New memberships poured in by the hundreds every week. The graph we had on the wall outgrew the wall and had to be taken across the ceiling. Many of those who had been activists in the 1960s returned to renew their subscriptions. Membership shot up in three years from barely 2,000 to well over 100,000. All over the country anti-cruise missile groups sprang up, most of which eventually turned themselves into CND groups.

DEMONSTRATIONS

By October 1980 CND was clearly back in business. The decision to hold an outdoor rally in Trafalgar Square on Sunday 26 October 1980 was not easily made. I thought Trafalgar Square was over-ambitious, but by the time the day came we knew that we were on to a winner. Coaches were coming from all over the country, trains had been booked and there was an astonishing feeling of expectation.

It was an amazing, magical afternoon. The square was full and went on filling. As many as 80,000 people turned out. Banners were flowing down from Piccadilly like the sails of ships. By 4.30pm it was already getting near dusk and still they came. A number of invited guests and several uninvited ones made speeches. Philip Noel-Baker, Fenner Brockway (later to found the World Disarmament Campaign together) and the Japanese monk Fujii Guruji (the inspiration behind the Milton Keynes and Battersea Peace Pagodas) were lined up in their wheelchairs. Edward Thompson thrilled the massed thousands with his great cry, 'Feel your strength!' His pamphlet, *Protest and Survive*,[3] published in answer to the official civil defence absurdities, put the match to a powder-barrel of alternative thinking.

It was Thompson who gave us international vision as well as indignation. CND was still a very British-directed organization and, though there was a new interest in the work of the United Nations, it had a limited international perspective. The European Nuclear Disarmament Appeal, launched in 1980, gave us a new framework for a united, bloc-free Europe and a new idea of people's power. It also linked disarmament and human rights in a positive way.

The biggest demonstration by far that I ever attended was not in London but in New York on 12 June 1982. People seemed to have come from all over the United States. There were bands and a trick cyclist and people walking on stilts. But there were also thousands and thousands of ordinary people, carrying signs and posters saying 'Bread Not Bombs', 'Stop the Arms Race', 'No More Nukes' and the like. It was a joy to me personally to see the Catholic religious orders go past – Dominicans, Benedictines, Jesuits, Franciscan nuns and Sisters of St Joseph of Peace, too many to count.

DEBATING

Demonstrations, local, national or even international, were only part of the endless work of the 1980s, which involved television and radio appearances, making international connections, talking to Church people, trade union leaders and politicians, and visiting local groups from Cornwall to the Shetlands.

Denis Healey, who had taken a rather snooty view of CND at its foundation in 1958, was generous enough by December 1982 to admit that CND had already achieved the most impressive recorded victory for single issue politics. Perhaps he was too generous, but clearly our numbers and success in debate, when one could find a serious Conservative with whom to debate, were looked at with interest and hostile concern by the right wing of British politics. The sharp end of Conservative attacks on CND came from a body called the Coalition for Peace through Security – two of its founders are now Tory MPs. The Coalition, with its headquarters in Whitehall, would never reveal the sources of its own finance, but nevertheless made outrageous allegations about CND's funding.

Lack of hard evidence did not bother those who wanted to throw mud. Lord Chalfont, much more establishment than the members of the Coalition, used the House of Lords in 1981 to say that 'It would be strange indeed if the CND were not substantially assisted from communist sources'.[4] He claimed that the Soviets spent £100 million a year 'financing peace movements in Western Europe'.[5]

More damaging than any direct assault was the steady drip of the mainstream media. What was said at meetings or demonstrations was not important. What mattered to the press was how many were arrested, what went wrong, how few came and what the negative police comments were. Long before I arrived on the CND scene the media had divided the world into two camps – the multilateralists against the unilateralists. The multilateralists were good; the unilateralists were bad. If the government was against a proposal, it must be unilateralist. If the government was for it, it must be multilateralist. The United Nations had said in 1984, 'There is no either/or choice between unilateral and negotiated measures of disarmament. Both are needed in view of their complementary nature.'[6] But this made not the slightest difference; no one had read this UN report. To be against cruise missiles was to be a unilateralist. To be for *Star Wars* was to be a multilateralist.

When the media were not dividing the 'unis' from the 'multis' they were concentrating on 'balance'. Theirs was a bean-counting world and of course the answers they came to about balance depended on the military beans they chose to count. That both East and West were already admirably equipped to blow up the world did not seem to count. What mattered was how many of *this* they had compared to how many of *that* we had. The implication was that the arms race proceeded in a planned way, with one deployment matching or balancing another. No wonder the media swallowed and passed on to a believing public the idea that cruise missiles somehow 'answered' SS20s. Rarely does anything answer anything else. When about to deploy a new technology, which had probably taken about ten years to develop from drawing board to production, each side regularly justified it on the grounds that it was a response to something else.

Granted the political bias of our media, I do not think that there was a genuine debate about nuclear policy in the 1980s. To criticize NATO or British assumptions and policies was simply to be soft on the Soviets, full stop.

Today, much that was official gospel in the 1980s now looks somewhat incredible. Who really believed then that the Warsaw Pact – a disparate collection of assorted tyrannies and opposing nationalisms all of which were being bankrupted by the arms race – actually intended to overrun Western Europe, and that having done so, would be able to administer what was left of the smoking ruins to its own advantage? Yet that the Soviet Union was poised for a massive westward strike was the endless assumption of journalists and politicians. Their malign intentions had, it seemed, always to be determined by their massive capabilities. Our benign intentions, on the other hand, were to be accepted by the Soviets without question, despite our equally fearsome capabilities.

Such double standards were rarely challenged. Media conformity was the order of the day. Graham Greene, speaking at Hamburg University in 1969, called for writers to maintain the one virtue of disloyalty, so much more important than chastity, unspotted from the world. But most of them did not.

NON-VIOLENT DIRECT ACTION

In its 1980s second phase CND managed to avoid the splits over 'direct action', which had damaged the campaign of the 1960s. A conference resolution was passed supporting 'considered' non-violent direct action and thus we avoided the trap which had so divided Canon Collins and his followers from Bertrand Russell and his. Nearly everyone in the second phase knew well that there were circumstances in which national law ought to be broken. Martin Luther King broke the law and became an international hero. So did the conscientious objectors of the First World War, who suffered dreadfully for their principles. So did the Pankhursts and their companions in the early days of this century.

Perhaps it was the Greenham women who most imaginatively broke the law in defence of the law with their various escapades inside and outside the American cruise missile base (Plate 3). Theirs is, of course, a tale to be told in full by someone else. It is my own conviction that one day the courage, humour and determination of those women will be recognized and honoured in our national history. The effect they had on women around the world was incalculable. In remote towns in Australia, through translators in Japan, at private meetings in the German Democratic Republic, I was often asked first of all, 'How are the women of Greenham?' That incredible day in December 1982, when women ringed the entire nine-mile perimeter fence, was one of the most remarkable of those ten years. They left the wire covered with pictures, poems, photographs of children and grandchildren and thousands of touching reminders of our common humanity.

DISAPPOINTMENTS

The two great disappointments of the 1980s were the general elections of 1983 and 1987. Though CND policy was to urge people to vote for the candidate who, in the voter's opinion, would do most for disarmament, outside Wales and Scotland that in effect meant a Labour vote. In 1983 the media had so effectively carved up the Labour Party and ridiculed its leader that the mess the party made of the defence issue hardly mattered. Opportunities were thrown away by the barrelful. I remember ringing the Labour headquarters in Walworth Road in the middle of the campaign to ask when they were going to start exposing the Tory record on arms sales, on the NPT, on a nuclear test ban, on the Trident escalation and on the recommendations of the 1978 UN General Assembly Special Session. Soon, I was promised – but soon never came.

In 1987 Labour produced a defence and nuclear policy that was doomed from the start. It challenged none of the assumptions of the cold war, or the presumption that nuclear weapons enhanced security. All it did was to promise that Britain would get rid of hers while compensating with more conventional weapons and sheltering under what was claimed to be an American nuclear umbrella. The umbrella theory itself was an odd one. It assumed what was highly unlikely – that an American president would risk Washington or New York for London or Rome. It was a dog's dinner of a policy and it suffered the fate that unconvincing stitch-ups deserve.

The sad fact is that the Labour Party and many, but not all, of its supporting unions have never set about the process of internal education about international relations and disarmament that must precede a policy change. Something very different happened in Sweden, which could also easily have become a nuclear-weapon power. In 1957, 40 per cent of the Swedish public wanted a Swedish bomb, 36 per cent did not, 24 per cent were uncertain. In 1969 only 17 per cent were still in favour, 69 per cent were against, 14 per cent were still uncertain. The shift in opinion was no accident; it was the result of pressure group and political campaigning and education.

Even in Britain today our dominant political fixation is our nationalism. It was that nationalism that gave us nuclear weapons nearly half a century ago. Ernest Bevin, then Foreign Secretary, said that 'We've got to have this thing over here, whatever the costs. We've got to have the bloody Union Jack on top of it.'[7]

CND cannot escape its own share of responsibility for failing to move public opinion further, as it might have been moved, despite the media odds against us. It was too easy to assume that popular opposition to cruise missiles, civil defence and Trident submarines meant that people had come to realize that British nuclear threats were both immoral and pointless, decreasing rather than increasing our security. This was always the key issue. Nuclear weapons were still discussed as if they were weapons. We did not persuade the majority of the public that promising to blow up your own house is not a very intelligent way of dealing with burglars, or that threatening to fire Chernobyls at one another does nothing to enhance real security.

ACHIEVEMENTS

Whatever its responsibility in the 1980s for failing to demolish British faith in nuclear deterrence, and the usefulness of British nuclear weapons, CND certainly played a major part in putting the nuclear-weapon issues back on the agenda of public discussion. Civil defence had been successfully ridiculed. Much more attention was being paid to the disarmament proposals of the United Nations. Links were made between militarism and world poverty. CND pressure had contributed to the withdrawal of cruise and Pershing 2 missiles. The fragility of nuclear deterrence was much better understood, granted the publicity CND had given to the many nuclear-weapon accidents.

In Mikhail Gorbachev appeared a world statesman who actually talked about the abolition of war itself. With the cold war apparently over, the 1980s ended on a note of hope. Everyone was talking of a new world order and a peace dividend. It was not to be. We have moved instead towards a very old world order – the dominance of one superpower in military, political, economic and even cultural terms.

NOTES

1. *Protect and Survive* (London: HMSO, 1980).
2. *Cruise Missiles* (London: MoD, no date).
3. E.P. Thompson, *Protest and* Survive (London: Campaign for Nuclear Disarmament/Nottingham: Bertrand Russell Peace Foundation, 1980).
4. Alun Chalfont, *Hansard*, House of Lords (20 July 1981), Cols.41–4.
5. Alun Chalfont, *Hansard*, House of Lords (9 Dec. 1981), Col.1336.
6. *Unilateral Disarmament Measures*. Report of the Secretary-General to the 39th United Nations General Assembly, 1984 (New York: United Nations, 1984).
7. Alan Bullock, *Ernest Bevin: Foreign Secretary, 1945–1951* (London: Heinemann, 1983), p.352.

Resisting the British Bomb: Recent Times

JANET BLOOMFIELD

In November 1995 the United Kingdom Attorney General, Sir Nicholas Lyell MP QC, stood before the judges of the ICJ at the Peace Palace at The Hague and argued the case for the legality of British nuclear weapons. Among those observing that day were Claudia Peterson, an American woman from Utah whose family had suffered greatly from the effects of nuclear testing; Joan Wingfield, an Australian Aboriginal woman from south Australia whose native lands covered the area of Maralinga (Chapter 8); a group of Hibakusha from Japan and dozens of British citizens. The ICJ, in its historic Advisory Opinion of 8 July 1996, ultimately rejected the arguments that Lyell made that day.[1] It was a pivotal moment in the long struggle against the British bomb and the high point of 1990s anti-nuclear work. The efforts made to bring the bomb to trial and the effects of the judgement framed resistance to the British bomb in the 1990s.

AFTER THE COLD WAR

At the beginning of the 1990s all the talk was of the Peace Dividend and the arms trade. The Gulf War dominated the peace movement's agenda, while the media and the public breathed a sigh of relief that the cold war was over and the nuclear nightmare had been consigned to history. Membership of CND dropped again. Many activists moved into other areas of concern, such as the environment or development, or simply took a well-deserved break and got back to their everyday lives.

Those who continued to work on nuclear-weapons issues began to focus on the possibility of using the end of the cold war as an opportunity to close the book on the nuclear age. The CTBT, a possible fissile material cut-off treaty and the nuclear NPT began to move into the front of the picture. The more research-based groups that flowered in the 1980s, such as BASIC, ORG and VERTIC, developed credibility with the media and decision-makers. Professional groups such as SANA and MCANW which had flourished in the 1980s reviewed their strategy and broadened their agendas to include more general security issues. SANA became SGR and MCANW, with the Medical Association for Prevention of War, became Medact.

THE NON-PROLIFERATION TREATY PROCESS

In 1993 a debate began within CND and other groups about how to use the 1995 review conference of the NPT as a focus for campaigning. CND decided to focus on the NPT and produced a Blueprint for a Nuclear-Free World that advocated ten steps governments should take to bring this about. It proposed that the NPT should be given a limited extension of ten years as a way of applying pressure on the nuclear-weapons states to fulfil their Article VI obligations. Of the research groups only ORG advocated the same position. BASIC and VERTIC favoured an unlimited extension (the position of the nuclear-weapon states) on the basis that the NPT was such a crucial instrument of world security that it needed to be given an unlimited life rather than take the risk of a shorter extension.

As 1995 approached two groupings formed. The Acronym Institute (BASIC, VERTIC and others) came together to monitor and interact with NPT process, with Rebecca Johnson as Director. (The work of Acronym has recently been transferred to the Simons Center for Peace and Disarmament Studies, Vancouver.) A loose grouping based around the National Peace Council brought together grass-roots organizations including CND, Quakers and CAAT to develop joint projects marking the fiftieth anniversary of the end of the Second World War. For those concerned about nuclear weapons, the fiftieth commemoration of the atomic bombings of Hiroshima and Nagasaki loomed large.

But what was happening to direct resistance to the British bomb as all this was going on? Faithful campaigners were maintaining the peace camp outside the Trident base at Faslane, women were witnessing at Aldermaston and Sellafield, nukewatchers were consistently tracking nuclear convoys and those affected by British nuclear testing were seeking redress and compensation. The government was ostensibly reducing nuclear weapons whilst planning an all-singing all-dancing system on Trident submarines that would allow it to be used for both strategic and sub-strategic purposes. Those who were paying attention to this were not about to give up.

WORKING FOR ABOLITION

A literal bombshell was dropped into the midst of all this by French President Jacques Chirac and the Chinese when they resumed nuclear testing immediately after the end of the NPT review conference. After all the lobbying US and UK governments got their way; the NPT was extended indefinitely and nuclear testing resumed. But a new initiative was born at the NPT called Abolition 2000. NGOs from around the world frustrated with the lack of radical action by governments produced an 11-point statement calling for the abolition of nuclear weapons. Within weeks several hundred groups, including Greenpeace and IPPNW, had signed up. Later in the year representatives of NGOs who were attending the oral hearings before the ICJ at The Hague formed the Abolition 2000 Global Network for the Abolition of Nuclear Weapons and soon after Abolition 2000 UK came into being. Long-time advocate of nuclear disarmament Frank Blackaby became the first President of Abolition 2000 UK.

CND became the focal point for public outrage against French and Chinese nuclear testing. On the day the French tests resumed a small meeting of the nascent Abolition 2000 UK network was taking place at the CND office. It immediately called for a boycott of French wine and other produce and went down to the French embassy in London to protest. A weekly vigil started and Youth and Student CND mobilized a noisy and colourful presence that included many of the young Australians and New Zealanders in London. I remember returning from the fiftieth anniversary of the Hiroshima and Nagasaki bombings to take part in the vigil and hearing honking horns, chanting and music as I came out of the Underground. It was clear that people were outraged by nuclear testing in the Pacific and shocked that nuclear weapons had shown their ugly face again in world politics.

In October 1995 the anti-nuclear movement received a huge boost with the award of the Nobel Peace Prize to Joseph Rotblat. He had worked on the Manhattan Project and was the only scientist to leave before the bomb was used – realizing that Germany would not acquire it. Since then he has devoted his life to working for nuclear disarmament.

Not all activity was based in London. Many of the local groups that had formed in the 1980s continued to hold public meetings and street stalls, work with local media and lobby their local MPs about the continuing nuclear danger. CND organized a number of long walks around the country aimed at raising awareness. Bruce Kent led a number of these walks in his capacity as Vice-President of CND and continued to work for nuclear disarmament throughout the 1990s with Abolition 2000 and Pax Christi. In 1996 a pilgrimage was organized by the Atomic Mirror, which spent three weeks travelling around England, Scotland and Wales visiting nuclear and sacred sites, culminating at Sellafield on 26 April – the tenth anniversary of the Chernobyl disaster. Every summer from 1997–99 CND took educational materials and a mock-up of a Trident missile around the country.

THE WORLD COURT PROJECT AND THE ICJ OPINION

From the early 1990s WCP-UK focussed on obtaining the opinion of the highest court in the world, the ICJ, on the legality of the use and threat of nuclear weapons. Local groups around the country collected Declarations of Public Conscience to take to The Hague. In the end 151,534 were collected in Britain, adding to the world-wide total of 3.8 million. Chaired by former naval Commander Robert Green and organized by George Farebrother, WCP-UK was one of the most active parts of the WCP world-wide. The WCP was an initiative of lawyers and activists, initially based in Aotearoa/New Zealand, which grew to encompass most of the world. After its launch in 1992 it worked so effectively that within a year a resolution was passed at the World Health Assembly calling on WHO to ask whether the use of nuclear weapons in war would violate international law relating to their health and environmental effects. The United Nations General Assembly then passed a resolution which extended the WHO question to whether the threat of use or use of nuclear weapons would be permitted under international law. This question then went forward to the ICJ; it was at the oral hearings into this question at the end of 1995 that Nicholas Lyell tried and failed to argue the case for the legality of nuclear weapons.

CONTINUING RESISTANCE

After the Advisory Opinion of the ICJ was given in July 1996, a new wave of resistance was unleashed using the law to peacefully disarm Trident. The core of the judgement stated that the threat or use of nuclear weapons was generally illegal and that the nuclear-weapons states had a legal obligation to move rapidly to complete nuclear disarmament (Chapter 2). Soon activists were taking up the judgement and using it in 'civil obedience' to inspect nuclear facilities for potential crimes. In August 1997, Angie Zelter circulated a letter inviting people to join an open, accountable and non-violent campaign to disarm British nuclear weapons. She was inspired by the US Ploughshares movement and realized that the World Court had given great potential to the legal arguments for non-violent direct action. People were asked to sign a Pledge to Prevent Nuclear Crime and an attempt was made to engage the British government in dialogue prior to any action. Trident Ploughshares 2000 was formally launched on 2 May 1998. Since then over 1,800 people have signed the Pledge, over 1,700 have been arrested, 277 trials have taken place (with more in the legal pipeline) and 1,615 days have been spent in prison (not counting police cells). Fines and compensation orders totalling £41,016.70 have been imposed.

The most famous case so far involved was the *Maytime* incident. Three women (Angie Zelter, Ulla Roder and Ellen Moxley) climbed aboard the *Maytime* Trident-related research station moored in Loch Goil, adjacent to the Gareloch, and threw its computers overboard. Sheriff Margaret Gimblett acquitted them in the Court in Helensburgh. The Scottish High Court subsequently made a highly contentious ruling that the acquittal was incorrect (Chapter 2). The inspiration of Trident Ploughshares has been crucial in maintaining resistance to British nuclear weapons in the late 1990s.

The struggle against the British bomb continues, but the greatest success of the anti-nuclear movement culminated on 8 April 2000. The last nuclear weapon left Greenham Common in March 1991. It was finally re-opened to the people as common land again after over 50 years as a military base; 19 years after seven women walked there from Cardiff demanding debate with the UK government on the siting of US cruise missiles in Britain. The groundbreaking decision in favour of a commemorative garden and sculpture at Greenham took place on 8 September 2001 and the sculpture was put in place just over a year later.

So where now? In the aftermath of 11 September 2001 and the resulting war on terrorism, it would seem that the window of opportunity for abolition that was on the lips of so many in the mid-1990s has firmly closed. Trident still lurks in the Gareloch; it is on patrol 24 hours a day, 365 days a year. The dangerous work of refitting Trident's reactors is now taking place at Plymouth following the closure of the naval dockyard at Rosyth. The AWE at Aldermaston is housing a huge new development for continued research and development into nuclear weapons. Within the next few years the government will decide what to do about replacing Trident (Chapter 12). Resistance to the British bomb has still a long way to go before the dream of a nuclear-free Britain in a nuclear-free world is realized, but the persistence and creativity described here will continue.

NOTE

1. International Court of Justice, *The Legality of the Threat or Use of Nuclear Weapons.* Advisory Opinion: Document A/51/218 (New York: United Nations, 1996).

British Nuclear Tests and the Indigenous People of Australia

ROGER CROSS

The concept that Australia was *terra nullius*, 'a country without a sovereign recognized by European authorities' or, secondly, a territory where – conveniently – 'nobody owns any land at all', dates back to James Cook's landing on the east coast of the continent in August 1770. The arrival of Governor Phillip and the First Fleet of convicts in January 1788 led to the eventual destruction of the majority of Aboriginal tribes with whom they came into contact. Their experience over the atomic bomb explosions at Monte Bello, Emu Field and Maralinga, and the subsequent trials at Maralinga (Map 1), is primarily tied to the European perception of Aborigines as human beings and mirrors what Australian indigenous people experienced during the first century of European settlement.

Sadly, the history of Australia since 1788 is one of the subjugation of one people by another. As Australian common law developed in the second half of the nineteenth century it became accepted practice to completely ignore pre-European ownership of the land, despite the evidence that Australia in 1788 (or indeed in 1770) was by no means 'a tract of territory practically unoccupied, without settled inhabitants or settled land'. It took until 1992 for the High Court of Australia to protect Australian common law and overturn the second interpretation of *terra nullius* that the Aborigines had no claim to freehold land.[1]

From the early nineteenth century onwards the prevailing attitude of white settlers towards the indigenous people can be summed up in the epithet 'Australian Savage', with Aboriginal society considered one of the lowest forms of civilization in the British Empire and of interest to anthropologists alone. Only in the last quarter century have Australian historians turned their attention to what current prime minister John Howard has disparagingly called the 'black arm band view of history' and the toll of those who perished during the period of white domination has still to be assessed. What is certain is that many of the Aboriginal tribes were annihilated by forces that included European diseases, battles with squatters and genocide, as well as intertribal disputes caused by the stresses of displacement.[2]

Despite the declaration of *terra nullius*, the land was actually 'owned' and occupied by a complex matrix of tribal groups, often living richly off the land. Yet in the 1950s, as the British and Australian governments prepared to contaminate the vast majority of Australia, its 'red centre', the perception prevailed that they were dealing with useless uninhabited desert. This introduces another factor into the story of the inland-dwelling Aborigines and the British bomb: by the 1950s the last remnants of indigenous people still practising totally tribal ways of living were in the most inaccessible regions, including the outback.

The right to vote, previously existing in certain of the colonies, was taken away upon Federation in 1901 and the indigenous people were not allowed to vote in Federal elections. They were not included in any National Census until finally granted the vote after a referendum in 1967.[3] In the 1950s there was no co-ordinated body caring for Aboriginal welfare. Had such a body existed during the tests, it could have found out the whereabouts of the threatened Aborigines, despite their omission from census records (which would later enable *The Report of the Royal Commission into the British Tests* to give details of Aboriginal populations and their 'country').

Thus, the Aboriginal experience during the atomic bomb tests was consistent with the belief in the supremacy of British civilization and the cultural hegemony that goes with Western thought – involving at best an ignorance of other lifestyles and at worst a systematic destruction of lifestyles alien to its own.

This chapter discusses each of the atomic bomb sites (Monte Bello, Emu Field and Maralinga), touching on the impact of the bomb tests on the Aboriginal people; the so-called minor trials at Maralinga contaminating the site with plutonium are described by Alan Parkinson in Chapter 8.

THE ATOMIC WEAPONS TESTS SAFETY COMMITTEE

Australia had no formal oversight of the conduct of the earliest tests (one in 1952, two in 1953). This changed with the introduction of the Australian watchdog AWTSC, constituted by the Menzies Government on 21 July 1955 to oversee further atomic bomb tests. However, the composition of this 'safety committee' was to cause many problems.[4] The following is part of its charter of responsibilities:

(a) To examine information and other data supplied by the United Kingdom Government relating to atomic weapons tests from time to time proposed to be carried out in Australia for the purpose of determining whether the safety

> measures proposed to be taken in relation to such tests are adequate for the *prevention of injury to persons* or damage to livestock and other property as a result of such tests.[5]

Unfortunately for public safety, with the exception of Australia's most senior meteorologist (co-opted after its first meeting), the members were all physicists without the expertise necessary to form judgements about the biochemical impact of radiation exposure! This state of affairs led to what was arguably the most acrimonious dispute in Australian science, when Hedley Marston, Chief of the Division of Biochemistry and General Nutrition at CSIRO, became incensed at AWTSC's public announcements that the bomb tests were perfectly safe.

Marston's concerns do not appear to have embraced the indigenous people as part of the Australian population at large. However, from the wording of the statement above it can be assumed that Aborigines were to be included in the concerns as to 'injury to persons' – although there was no special reference to them and the particular problems that would soon become apparent, such as culture, isolation, language, remnant nomadic tribal life, diet and association with the land. There was certainly no one on the AWTSC who had the slightest professional knowledge of Aboriginal culture and lifestyle so the committee can be dismissed as being a factor in protecting the Aboriginal population.

MONTE BELLO ISLANDS (1952):
OPERATION 'HURRICANE'

Little was known about the status of Aborigines at this time and certainly Ernest Titterton, Vice-Chairman then Chairman (from 1957) of AWTSC and the leading apologist for the British tests, put his ignorance on public record. Giving evidence before the Royal Commission on the bomb tests in 1984 Titterton, a migrant to Australia from the UK some 30 years before and the only 'Australian' nuclear scientist the British bomb group was prepared to trust, suggested that if the Aborigines had objected to the tests they could have voted the government out (although, as indicated above, they did not gain voting rights until 1967 ...).

Titterton was not alone in his ignorance. The first full-scale nuclear device, in what was termed Operation 'Hurricane', was detonated in 1952 on the Monte Bello Islands, an uninhabited group lying off the coast of Western Australia, north-west of Onslow. For information on the presence of Aborigines on the mainland in the vicinity of the Monte Bellos, the British authorities relied upon such authoritative documents as the *Pocket Book of Western Australia*. The Royal Commission was not impressed:

Scant attention was paid to the location of the Aborigines during the Hurricane test. The Royal Commission found no evidence to indicate that any consideration was taken of their distinctive lifestyles which could lead to their being placed at increased risk from given levels of radiation.[6]

The following cultural issues were not taken into account:

- Aborigines' lack of clothing and footwear.
- Diet, which at that stage was a mixture of 'western' and traditional foods of a hunter gatherer society; the biological magnification of radioactivity would have been significant.
- Unknown movement pattern.
- General health status.
- Distribution within the danger area.
- Methods of communication between white and Aborigine Australians.

EMU FIELD (1953): THE TOTEM TESTS

The Emu Field site in the desert of South Australia was recognized almost immediately to be a logistical nightmare and is recorded as being a disastrous choice.[7] The site was in an area about 200 miles north of the future Maralinga site and 300 miles from Woomera, the rocket range that had been in existence since 1946. It is desert country with no water, the sand in the surrounding sand-hills is soft and yielding and it is prone to violent dust storms. After the two Totem bombs were exploded, the total unsuitability of Emu Field ensured that it was not used again.

In choosing a claypan called Dingo as the Emu Field site, only passing thought was given to the possibility of nomadic or semi-nomadic Aborigines using the area. This was, after all, an area of Australia that was little known and very few were aware of their presence. One who did know was Len Beadell, nowadays remembered as one of the last great Australian adventurers, who found plenty of evidence of occupation of the land.[8] Beadell suggests that the British had no idea just how isolated the area was and that it was chosen so the radiation would not interfere with the rocket work at Woomera.[9]

Beadell and others came across some remarkable sacred sites, which he dubbed 'Aboriginal Stonehenge' and which were close to the Dingo claypan bomb site. By the time the tests were scheduled to take place, traditional patterns of Aboriginal movement had broken down due to the establishment of missions. The Pijantjatjara people of the north moved further south to the transcontinental railway line, where they set up camp at the Ooldea Mission, others had moved to various missions and pastoral stations, the attraction of European food being a powerful incentive. However the area was still used, as the 1984 Royal Commission reported, for:

hunting and gathering, for temporary settlements, for caretakership and spiritual renewal. ... From an unknown time – but certainly for long before the arrival of white people – Aboriginal people had used the lands where the tests took place ... people were constantly traversing the country.[10]

In contrast, William Penney asked W.A.S. Butement, Australia's chief scientist with the Department of Supply, about indigenous Australians. He was told that: 'I am given to understand that the area is no longer used for Aborigines ... there is no need whatever for Aborigines to use any part of this country around the proposed area.'[11]

As far as the (earlier) Woomera rocket range was concerned, a native patrol officer, Walter MacDougall, was appointed in 1947. After his transfer to the Federal Department of Supply in 1949, he undertook regular trips into the outback making contact with and helping scattered Aboriginal groups. This one man had increasingly large areas to patrol as he struggled to ensure the safety of the Aborigines in the areas that might be affected by the Woomera rocket tests. As his work increased, so too did the problems of keeping contact with the tribal people. By 1950 he had become concerned that there was not even a census of the people living in this vast area: the range stretched 1,200 miles across South Australia's far north to the Western Australian coast.

By 1951 MacDougall was known to the Aborigines as a respected friend, a white man they could trust and was called '*Kuta*', or 'brother'. Yet in August of that year, he came across some tribal Aborigines who did not even know of him as they had been avoiding contact with whites. He gradually extended his patrols and by March 1952 had undertaken a journey of over 2,000 miles in some of the most difficult country imaginable, finding yet more groups living in the northern boundaries of the Central Reserve, people who again rarely made any contact with the white missions.

In April 1953 MacDougall was dispatched to search an area called Granite Downs within reach of the Totem site and was able to map traditional Yankunytjatjara people's territory. Even so, many uncertainties remained, especially over the water sources, such as the rock holes that tribal people used, and it was clearly impossible for one man to deal with migrating people throughout such a vast area. The minutes of the Totem Panel's fourth meeting, held 2 April 1953, illustrate the level of concern over the Aboriginal problem: first came the thefts by Aborigines from the Totem site; second came concern over the danger of them entering the contaminated area at the actual test site.[12] It was decided to undertake aerial patrols of the test area – at most covering a 20-mile range. Warnings of the coming trials were sent to pastoral station managers in August 1953.

Once again, no special consideration was given to the Aboriginal lifestyle. In an exact replica of Operation 'Hurricane', the authorities conveniently forgot that these people were largely or wholly unclothed. They cooked and ate in unsheltered locations and had a diet liable to biological magnification of radioactive contamination, for example, lizards such as goannas and snakes. It is now known that people at Wallatinna Station, a pastoral property on Granite Downs only 108 miles from Totem 1 (a ten-kiloton bomb), were seriously contaminated and suffered radiation sickness after what has become infamous as 'the Black Mist incident'.[13] In a report that July, the secretary of the Pitjantjatjara Council, Robert Stevens, claimed that a black mist had rolled across the outback affecting a large number of people, some of whom subsequently died. About 45 Yankunytjatjara Aborigines were enveloped in a black mist one or two days after the explosion. Within 48 hours many were reported to be suffering from rashes, vomiting and diarrhoea, all typical signs of radiation sickness. It was said that many children became temporarily blind after 72 hours, that the old and the frail died within a few days and that nearly 20 people were buried on the outer fringes of the Wallatinna Station following the incident.[14]

The Adelaide *Advertiser* had earlier reported a claim from Trevor Cutter, a member of the Central Australian Aboriginal Congress working for an Alice Springs health service, that there had been between 30 and 50 Aboriginal fatalities among up to 1,000 people affected. He stated that Aboriginal people who had been in five different locations (Coffin Hill, Ernabella, Kenmore Park, Everard Park and Granite Downs) recalled the terror of the 'Black Mist'.[15] When this first came to light in 1980, Ernest Titterton responded to an Australian Broadcasting Corporation programme by denying the possibility:

> No such thing can possibly occur. I don't know of any black mists. No black mists have ever been reported until this scare campaign was started. ... If you investigate black mist sure you're going to get into an area where mystique is the central feature.[16]

Despite Titterton's remarks, an inquiry was initiated by the Federal Minister for Science and the Environment on 18 September 1980 and was carried out by the Australian Ionising Radiation Advisory Council. Its report lends credibility to the incident.

There the matter rested until in 1982 when Yami Lester, an Aboriginal man of the Yankunytjatjara people, who was in Alice Springs heard a radio interview with Titterton, who gave the categorical assurance that no Aboriginal people had been harmed by the tests. Lester, who had been working as a boy on Wallatinna Station at the time of the Totem tests, could not believe his ears. So angry was he that he rang the *Advertiser* in Adelaide and the paper then ran a series of reports on the tests.[17]

The 1984 Royal Commission visited Wallatinna Station and heard evidence from a number of the Yankunytjatjara tribe who had been camped in the area at the time. Yami Lester spoke of his own experience:

> a big bang – a noise like an explosion and later something come in the air … [it] was coming from the south, black-like smoke. I was thinking it might be a dust storm, but it was quiet, just moving … through the trees and above that again, you know. It was just rolling and moving quietly.[18]

White station owners also saw and experienced the cloud. A Mrs Lander reported seeing the cloud passing through Wallatinna – a cloud that rolled along dropping a fine sticky dust as it went. Ernest Giles at Welbourne Hill Station also heard the explosion and saw a 'mountain of smoke in the distance'.

Lester recounts how the old people were scared, fearing that it was a spirit, and how they tried to direct it away from their camp with *woomeras* (implements used to propel spears at distant objects with great force). Others told of how the cloud was low to the ground; it was, they said, like a black mist rolling over the scrub. Afterwards the water tasted sweet. They told of how they became ill, all vomiting and some developing headaches. Later, people began to suffer from sore eyes. Younger members of the group went temporarily blind and a few lost their sight permanently. (Lester claims that as a result of the 'Black Mist' he went temporarily blind in his left eye and permanently blind in his right.) Some developed diarrhoea, others irritated and peeling skin. People died, but the number was unknown. Deaths of old people began about five days after Totem 1; others lingered for 12 months.[19]

The 'Black Mist' incident was certainly real and radioactive contamination did cause illness. David Barnes, the British health physicist responsible for safety at the Totem tests, stated under cross examination by the Royal Commission that 'We might very well have taken more account of the Aboriginal population' and that Totem 1 was designed to be five kilotons but in fact was ten kilotons. The fallout over Aboriginal hunting ground had been 100 per cent above the recommended safe level.

The Report of the Royal Commission attempted to reconstruct the radiation dose received by the Aboriginal people around Wallatinna Station at the time. This included external and internal doses. The estimated total dose was 93.4 rem, but the contribution of the overall dose made by the particular Aboriginal diet and the consequent biological magnification that would have taken place was ignored. (Note that the vomiting experienced by the people at Wallatinna Station is consistent with a dose of 80–100 rem in five to ten per cent of people exposed.) In the final analysis the Royal Commission believed the Aboriginal explanation – with the one qualification that the illnesses experienced could have been psychogenic and arising from the frightening experience, or could have been a combination of causes. It also concluded that there had been a failure to consider the distinctive lifestyles of the people. On reflection this seems an extraordinarily weak statement.[20]

The Aboriginal people of the Coober Pedy area are currently fighting the prospect of a nuclear waste dump on their land. Their Irati Wanti website describes the effects the radiation experienced in the 1950s:

> The Government used the Country for the Bomb. Some of us were living at Twelve Mile, just out of Coober Pedy. The smoke was funny and everything looked hazy. Everybody got sick. Other people were at Mabel Creek and many people got sick. Some people were living at Wallatinna. Other people got moved away. Whitefellas and all got sick. When we were young, no woman got breast cancer or any other kind of cancer. Cancer was unheard of. And no asthma either, we were people without sickness.
>
> We've been fighting about it, the Government for years. We know about the radioactivity, we were here with the bomb Emu/Maralinga. We never saw our old people sick before this. They used to walk very long ways. After that, they were just dropping here and there, crippled, sick, short of breath. Died.[21]

RETURN TO THE MONTE BELLO ISLANDS (1956): MOSAIC

Two more bombs were exploded at Monte Bello in the Mosaic tests of 1956. These were the first tests in which the Atomic Weapons Tests Safety Committee was involved. Mosaic 2 was the biggest of the 12 atomic bombs exploded in Australia and that second explosion, on 19 June, remains the most shameful episode of all. 'The blast was terrifying. Buildings jolted at Onslow more than 100 kilometres away … roofs rattled at Marble Bar, an inland town 400 kilometres to the east, where radioactive rain was later reported.'[22] The radioactive fallout swept right across the top half of Australia, drifting east and exiting from the mainland over the Queensland coast. It was many years before Geoffrey Pattie, Minister of Defence Procurement in 1984, inadvertently admitted the yield to have been 60 kilotons, although it is widely rumoured to have been of the order of 90 kilotons.

When William Penney gave evidence before the Royal Commission, he was asked whether he or his staff had ever considered the Aborigines living in north-west Western Australian. He answered 'Not to my knowledge' and stated that he would have relied on advice from the Australians. The Royal Commission concluded that the extra vulnerability of the Aboriginal population on the mainland near the Monte Bello Islands was not taken into account.[23]

The Australian public found out that something was wrong with Mosaic 2 on 22 June 1956 in the strangest way imaginable. A prospector called Jack Tunny was prospecting for uranium with a Geiger counter near Mount Isa in Queensland. While he was boiling rainwater in his billycan for a cup of tea his counter went off the scale.[24] Of course, at the time, the Minister for Supply Howard Beale poured – cold – water on Tunny's story, but he later admitted that this incident nearly ruined him.[25] The whole affair illustrates the extent of the contamination of the northern half of Australia, the area with the greatest concentration of Aboriginal people.

MARALINGA: 1956 ONWARDS

Maralinga was established in 1955, a short distance from the Watson siding on the Trans-Australian Railway. William Penney described it as a first-class site and said that 20 weapons could be tested there. A great deal of the necessary supplies could be brought up by rail and then transported to Maralinga village, thus it was better in all respects than the sandy Emu Field. From the point of view of the indigenous people of the area, however, things could not have been worse.

Ooldea Soak, three miles north of another siding at Ooldea, had for centuries been an important centre for the indigenous people from a vast area around. After the intervention of Prime Minister Menzies and Thomas Playford, the premier of South Australia, the Ooldea Aboriginal Reserve was revoked on 25 November 1953 and relocated to Yalata, near Fowlers Bay. In his plans for Maralinga William Penney held discussions with W.A.S. Butement over possible inconvenience due to the presence of Aborigines; Butement reportedly said that he 'was given to understand that the area has now been abandoned'.[26]

With another civilization, this might have been an acceptable conclusion, but not for the Aboriginal people and for his part, the native patrol officer, Walter MacDougall, was far more cautious. He said, in effect, that it was not known how many sacred and hunting sites the Aborigines visited; information obtained showed that people still used the area and frequently moved around to attend ceremonies. (MacDougall had gone as far as removing sacred objects to Yalata, but this did not alter Aboriginal perception of the 'bad' country and nothing could change the significance of a birth and death location.) The Maralinga people did not like the coastal country: it was not *their* country and they tried to continue their lives as before. From 1954 onwards large- and small-scale movements by the Aboriginal population still occurred throughout the region.

No matter. The Maralinga Tjarutja people's country and culture was devastated.[27] Not only were seven atomic bombs exploded on their traditional lands in 1956 and 1957, but the tragic minor trials from 1957 to 1962 in which plutonium was scattered around the trial site – and then blown all over the area – has changed their country forever, despite repeated clean-ups (Chapter 8). Following legislation in 1984, the main Aboriginal settlement after the tests was, and is, Oak Valley, about 60 miles north of Maralinga. In 1987 it was reported that particles of radioactive plutonium and caesium were discovered close to the school (having about 70 children) and white teachers refused to work there.

A short excursion north-west of Maralinga demonstrates another disastrous contact with the indigenous population. In preparation for reliable meteorological forecasting west of Maralinga for the forthcoming 1956 tests, the Giles Meteorological Station was established in one of the most isolated areas in the country, the Rawlinson Ranges in Western Australia.

Little was known about the Western Australian Aborigines living in the area. They were considered true nomadic people who had virtually no contact with white Australians and western civilization. MacDougall was positively alarmed at the prospect of such a contact, as the weather station personnel would disrupt the lives of these people and, at the very least, subject them to those 'white-man's diseases' that had proved so disastrous.

MacDougall was recognized as a man who expressed his views on the welfare of the Woomera Aborigines forthrightly.[28] He had been appointed a protector of Aborigines in 1955 and now threatened to go to the press over this matter. He was feared by the authorities, as the only person in the country with detailed knowledge of the indigenous people of the desert regions of South Australia, but all the same this was a tactical error. Butement told MacDougall that he was not to be concerned with policy matters and that he showed a lamentable lack of balance in placing the affairs of a handful of natives above those of the British Commonwealth of Nations. He lost support and was officially silenced; the station went ahead as planned.

MacDougall continued his survey of the Rawlinson Range and, far from finding a handful of 'natives', found over 100. By May 1956 his worst fears had been realized. Aborigines were 'very sick with chesty colds' (unknown to people of the desert) and they 'were all in mourning'. As the Royal Commission put it: 'scientists and policy-makers knew little about aborigines but this was not going to stop them preparing for the tests.'[29]

There are many recorded instances of official indifference towards Australia's native peoples – in many cases based on total ignorance. Howard Beale, Minister for Supply in the Federal Government, under whose ministry the bomb tests came, declared, for example, that the Giles weather station occupied a mere 50 acres in the Central Aboriginal Reserve in Western Australia; was sited away from Aboriginal watering places and the Western Australian Aboriginal Department had carefully controlled contacts between the indigenous people and whites. These were in fact lies: Giles was sited at a known watering place; construction workers broke the cohabitation law and they photographed a native birth – a taboo act.[30]

Back in Adelaide, Hedley Marston's staff at the CSIRO Division of Biochemistry and General Nutrition were to be involved in collecting samples of sheep and cattle thyroids across outback Australia in order to determine the uptake of radioactive iodine-131. Sometime before the tests, in their briefing by one of the scientists from the British Biological experiments group (led by Oxbridge scientist Robert Scott Russell), one of the staff allegedly put a question about the Aboriginal people. The response, that they were a dying race and therefore dispensable,[31] provides another instance of callous disregard.

Only a few days before the first Buffalo test in September 1956 it was clear that Aboriginal people were moving about the area. A party of 90 Aborigines had walked all the way from Yalata on the Nullabor Plain to Coober Pedy (a distance of some 250 miles as the crow flies) for a *corroboree* (Aboriginal dance ceremony). Emu Field (north of Maralinga) was also occupied, by 31 Aborigines who were 'bareheaded and in various states of nakedness'. Prime Minister Menzies was advised that aircraft patrols were undertaken before the Buffalo trials, yet evidence of only two such flights has come to light. An officer, B.L. Smith, was supplied on the ground to help in rounding up, or alerting, the Aborigines in this vast area. Smith, however, admitted to having no knowledge whatsoever of the Aborigines, or any knowledge of the conditions of this most harsh part of the Australian outback. This was well known to those who sent him there. He was only appointed as a decoy to counter possible adverse press reports when it could be shown that action had been taken – another measure of official cynicism and indifference.

The report of the Royal Commission notes the total ignorance at high levels about Aborigines and their way of life. A certain Group Captain Menaul claimed that they sleep most of the afternoon (perhaps he was thinking of kangaroos) so that a single search each day was all that was required. Yet despite the totally inadequate search procedure, Aborigines were seen in dangerous locations. F. Smith, a member of the Australian Radiation Detection Unit, was treated with scorn and disbelief when he submitted a radio report of a sighting of Aboriginal people in the prohibited zone. He was asked if he realized 'what sort of damage [he] would be doing by finding Aboriginals where Aboriginals could not be'. It later came to light that a traditional Aboriginal 'road' ran right through the Maralinga range.[32]

An interesting commentary on both the British and Australian attitude towards the Aborigines can be gauged from the testimony of the British Government health physics advisor in the 1950s, Geoffrey Dale, who told an Australian newspaper in 1985 that a supply of boots was sent to

Kenmore Park Station 150 miles north-west of Maralinga to help protect Aborigines against contamination. Sadly the boots did not fit any of the 100 they were intended for – but it is questionable whether they would have worn them if they had. Ignorant of the cultural aspects of Aboriginal life, those in authority did not bother to find out.[33]

The story of Eddie Milpuddie is the most poignant of the whole 1956–57 Maralinga period. It had a special place in the Report of the Royal Commission and is known as the 'Pom Pom incident'. At the time of writing, Eddie is 71 years old and one of the elders of the Maralinga Tjarutja people. Her family's story graphically illustrates the incompetence of those who were in charge of security and the safety of the indigenous population. In the face of the breathtaking cynicism of the British and Australian authorities, her fortitude is amazing.

In 1955, one year before the Maralinga tests began, the Milpuddies set off from the Everard Ranges for Ooldea, not knowing that the Aboriginal people had been removed to Yalata. They made use of a new system of dusty tracks that passed for roads, as well as using local knowledge gained over thousands of years. They followed the old rock waterhole route ensuring access to water and crossing apparently waterless terrain, eventually they came to Maralinga. 'WARNING. You Are Approaching A RADIOACTIVE AREA. Read All Notices', proclaimed the signs placed around the site – signs that Eddie and her family could not read.[34]

The second 1956 bomb was a ground burst of 1.5 kilotons on 4 October at the Marcoo site. It left a large crater. On 14 May 1957, Eddie, her husband and children were camping in the crater itself. She tells how soldiers came and took her and her family to the Maralinga village. It was a shocking trip; they had never ridden in a vehicle before and they vomited everywhere.[35] At Maralinga they were given the first showers of their life, with soap that got into their eyes and blinded them. It was a frightening experience, made worse for Eddie by the fact that initially she thought there was another woman in the shower with her – until she realized it was a mirror and she was alone. The Royal Commission reported that the *lubra* cried. The family were showered four or five times before the Geiger counter showed an acceptable level of radioactivity and they were given clothes.[36] The soldiers shot their four hunting dogs. No medical follow-up occurred. Eddie was pregnant at the time of the incident and she subsequently buried a stillborn baby, which she believed was because of poison in the ground. Her next baby died, aged two, of a brain tumour in 1963 and the next was born very premature.

The Milpuddie incident was considered extremely serious for the AWTSC (it was not recorded in the minutes of the committee). After all, it exposed the flaws in the security at the Maralinga site. Colonel Durance, the range commander, also viewed the incident in the light of its possible political ramifications and Walter MacDougall helped cover it up by meeting the family and telling them that 'they had accidentally seen something of a whiteman's ceremony [and] they should not declare anything to other white men'.[37] Durance told the Royal Commission that the Pom Pom incident caused a fuss in government and military circles and could have led to the cancellation of the tests.[38] As the Royal Commission observed, hushing up the affair was one thing, doing nothing about it was another. The health of the surviving members of the Milpuddie family was not monitored until after 1980.

The Royal Commission summed up the Buffalo series of explosions as follows:

- Regard for Aboriginal safety was characterized by incompetence and cynicism;
- The Buffalo site was chosen on the false premise that it was no longer used by the traditional owners;
- The Giles Meteorological Station brought intruders into an extremely sensitive area;
- The native patrol officer, Walter MacDougall, was placed in an impossible situation of increasing conflict with the bomb authorities;
- The Pom Pom incident illustrated the flaws in security and lack of consideration for the Aboriginal people's welfare; and
- The possibility of injury to the Milpuddie family cannot be excluded.

Its final conclusion was that indigenous people continued to inhabit the Prohibited Zone for six years after the tests.[39]

The Antler series in 1957 followed similar lines, except that the Minister of Supply, Howard Beale, weighed in with several bumbling comments. At one point the British seized on one of Beale's more bizarre statements about the treatment of Aborigines. The Commonwealth Relations Officer wrote to the UK High Commissioner in Australia saying that 'No natives had been driven out of Maralinga or Woomera' – yet this was exactly what had been attempted, admittedly without 100 per cent success. He then made a statement about disease and malnutrition among the Aborigines during the last centuries, implying that they had always been badly off. In fact, at the time of white settlement, the Aborigines of the area seemed to be in excellent health and were rarely ill.[40]

That year also saw a distinct change in attitude towards the tests, with the public now aware of increasing international concerns about atmospheric testing. Eminent scientists, including one Australian, Mark Oliphant, attending the first Pugwash Conference in Canada, published a statement about the increasing global dangers of atmospheric testing and called for a ban. Once the Labor opposition in the Federal parliament got wind of the Australian public's changing perceptions they began actively to harass the Menzies government.

In 1984 the Maralinga Tjarutja people obtained land rights over the Maralinga area from the State government and demanded compensation and a clean-up of the Maralinga site from the British and Australian governments. In October of 1991 three Aboriginal elders took contaminated soil to London to press their case; AU$13.5 million dollars were eventually paid in compensation.

IN CONCLUSION

There is no better way to conclude than in Walter MacDougall's words:

> Mr. MacDougall noted in one of his reports to Captain Newman [Superintendent of the Weapons Research Establishment at Woomera] that the result [the Australian and British attitude towards the indigenous people] was certain to be a degeneration from self-respecting tribal communities to 'pathetic and useless parasites ... we might as well declare war on them and make a job of it.'[41]

NOTES

1. T. Rowse, 'Terra nullius', in G. Davison, J. Hirst and S. Macintyre (eds.), The Oxford Companion to Australian History (Melbourne: Oxford University Press, 1998), p.638.
2. D. Watson, Caledonia Australis (Sydney: William Collins, Vintage Edn. 1997).
3. 'Referendum', in Davison et al., The Oxford Companion to Australian History, p.548.
4. R. Cross, Fallout: Hedley Marston and the British Bomb Tests in Australia (Adelaide: Wakefield Press, 2001).
5. J. McClelland, J. Fitch and W.J.A. Jones, Report of the Royal Commission into British Nuclear Tests in Australia (Canberra: Australian Government Printing Service, 1985), Vol.1, pp.234–5. Emphasis added.
6. McClelland et al., Report of the Royal Commission, p.118.
7. L. Beadell, Blast the Bush (Adelaide: Rigby, 1967).
8. McClelland et al., Report of the Royal Commission, p.168.
9. Beadell, Blast the Bomb, pp.1–4.
10. McClelland et al., Report of the Royal Commission, pp.151–2.
11. R. Milliken, No Conceivable Injury: The Story of Britain and Australia's Atomic Cover-up (Ringwood: Penguin, 1986), p.165.
12. McClelland et al., Report of the Royal Commission, pp.169–71.
13. 'New evidence on A-tests claimed', Advertiser (Adelaide), 7 July1980.
14. South Australian Health Commission, A Survey of Diseases that may be Related to Radiation among Pitjantjatjara on Remote Reserves (Adelaide: SAHC, 1981), p.2.
15. I have attempted to obtain the correspondence between Cutter and the relevant departments of the South Australian government through its Freedom of Information Act. Disclosure was refused on the grounds that it is covered by the secrecy provisions of the State Radiation and Protection and Control Act 1982.
16. 'Killer "Black Mist"', Advertiser (Adelaide), 23 May 1980.

17. Y. Lester, *Yami: The Autobiography of Yami Lester* (Alice Springs: IAD Press, 2000), p.187.
18. McClelland *et al.*, *Report of the Royal Commission*, pp.174–7.
19. 'Illness, Death after a "Black Mist"', *Advertiser* (Adelaide), 3 May 1980.
20. McClelland *et al.*, *Report of the Royal Commission*, pp.187–90.
21. Available at http://www.iratiwanti.org/iratiwanti.php3?page=atomic_tests.
22. Milliken, *No Conceivable Injury*, p.197.
23. McClelland *et al.*, *Report of the Royal Commission*, pp.259, 261.
24. Cross, *Fallout*, p.42.
25. H. Beale, *This Inch of Time* (Melbourne: Melbourne University Press, 1977).
26. McClelland *et al.*, *Report of the Royal Commission*, p.300.
27. 'Maralinga Move Devastated Culture', *Advertiser* (Adelaide), 1 Dec. 1984.
28. Lester, *Yami*, p.163.
29. McClelland *et al.*, *Report of the Royal Commission*, p.311.
30. Ibid., pp.309–11.
31. Ibid., p.373.
32. Cross, *Fallout*, p.32.
33. McClelland *et al.*, *Report of the Royal Commission*, pp.313–19.
34. 'Blacks barefoot on "hot" earth: witness', *Courier-Mail* (Brisbane), 6 Feb. 1985.
35. A. Tame and F.R.J. Robotham, *Maralinga: British A-Bomb Australian Legacy* (Melbourne: Fontana Collins, 1982).
36. McClelland *et al.*, *Report of the Royal Commission*, p.320.
37. 'Aboriginal family "near test site"', *Canberra Times*, 20 Oct. 1984; ibid., p.321.
38. McClelland *et al.*, *Report of the Royal Commission*, pp.319–21.
39. 'Maralinga discovery kept secret: embarrassment avoided', *Canberra Times*, 6 Nov. 1984.
40. McClelland *et al.*, *Report of the Royal Commission*, pp.323–4, 371, 381.
41. 'How a "handful of natives" disturbed the plans of the bomb tests', *Sydney Morning Herald*, 28 Oct. 1984.

Cleaning-Up Maralinga

ALAN PARKINSON

This chapter describes the process of cleaning-up one of the sites where British nuclear weapons were tested. Worse stories can doubtless be told of the test sites of other nuclear powers, particularly in the Soviet Union and the United States, but this account may also give some idea of the problems that could be created by the detonation of a crude nuclear device by terrorists (Chapter 11).

TESTS AND TRIALS

Between October 1952 and September 1958 Britain carried out 21 nuclear bomb tests in Australia and various Pacific islands (Appendix 2). Seven of these were at Maralinga, a tract of Aboriginal land in the state of South Australia (Map 1). The 3,200 square kilometre site was commandeered by the Australian government and handed over to Britain for atomic bomb development. There is ample evidence that the Australian government had its own plans for nuclear-weapons development;[1] indeed, it probably thought that co-operation with Britain would further its own aspirations.

The last nuclear bomb exploded at Maralinga was at Taranaki on 9 October 1957, the third of the Antler series. With the exception of the Tadje explosion, the first of the Antler series, none of these major trials were deemed to have caused any contamination necessitating removal. The Tadje bomb was a 'fizzer' – although the site became highly contaminated with plutonium and cobalt, it did not figure in the subsequent clean-up despite the fact that the ARL said the site would be a concern long into the future.[2] While there were no more nuclear explosions, there were many minor trials in the period 1959 to 1963 which caused considerable contamination. The Tims trials in 1960 and 1961 contaminated the TM site with plutonium; the Vixen A trials contaminated the Wewak site, also with plutonium. By far the worst contamination occurred at Taranaki through the Vixen B trials in 1960, 1961 and 1963.

These trials were said to be to confirm the safety of nuclear bombs in storage or in transit, but evidently there was also some measure of weapons development. In the trials, a nuclear bomb was placed on a large structure, known as a featherbed, built from heavy steel joists and plates with barytes and lead bricks all assembled on a concrete firing pad. Twelve of the trials used a core made from plutonium and uranium; the other three were calibration rounds in which the core was pure uranium. These were 'one point' trials, in which the explosive charges were not detonated simultaneously, so there was no nuclear explosion. The heat of the chemical explosion melted the core of the bomb and hurled the molten mix some 800 to 1,000 metres into the air, where it was caught by the wind and spread over many square kilometres in an arc, generally to the north of Taranaki (Plate 4).

Between ten and 20 per cent of the uranium and plutonium went downwards and contaminated the featherbeds and the surrounding soil. So apart from any damage done by the explosion, the featherbeds became contaminated and could not be used again. This raised the problem of disposal of the contaminated debris; the British solution was to dig pits, generally close to the firing pads, and bury the featherbeds and concrete pads.

The other trials involving plutonium at TM100, TM101 and Wewak were on a far smaller scale than anything at Taranaki, but they still contaminated wide areas of those two sites.

OPERATION 'BRUMBY'

In 1967 the British Army conducted a final clean-up of the Maralinga range under the code name Operation 'Brumby'. According to the final report:

> The operation was progressing well at the beginning of July, and every effort was made to complete the major tasks for inspection by the Atomic Weapons Tests Safety Committee (AWTSC), and assuming that they would be satisfied, to complete all the remaining tasks and withdraw from the Range, and Australia, by the end of the month.[3]

The Australian government had established the AWTSC supposedly to advise on the safety of the atomic trials in Australia. This paragraph of the report suggests that the AWTSC was not represented on site while the clean-up was in progress. It also hints at haste to complete the work before the committee arrived.

The main activities of Operation 'Brumby' were ploughing and mixing to dilute the contamination at Taranaki, the TM sites and Wewak in an attempt to reduce the radioactivity to what was considered an acceptable level. Some parts of central Taranaki failed to meet this (undefined) level, so 4,200 cubic metres of soil were spread over the offending areas.

Radioactive debris was disposed of in 32 pits around the sites, 21 of which were at Taranaki. Other debris was disposed of in some 60 other pits and in the crater left by the Marcoo bomb, which was filled and covered. Nineteen of the Taranaki pits were covered with 300-millimetre reinforced concrete caps, which were supposed to extend a metre beyond the pit boundary on all sides. The other two pits simply had a plug of concrete placed over them to finish at ground level (which was a rock surface).

Committee members arrived at the site on 8 July 1967 and left on 10 July 1967. In that period they visited Emu and inspected the Maralinga range. According to the report:

> The Committee was extremely satisfied with the operation and on Sunday [9 July], the Chairman, Professor Titterton, spoke to the Force and thanked them for the work they had done. A statement saying that they were satisfied was given by the Committee to the British Government, and a formal handover document is now in course of preparation.[4]

On the strength of that three-day visit by those members of the committee, the Australian government was persuaded that the site was in an acceptable condition for it to be abandoned and absolved Britain of any further responsibility.

THE ROYAL COMMISSION

In the mid-1980s scientists from the ARL visited the site and monitored the surface radioactivity. Their opinion was that the site was not in a proper and safe state. Additional fencing was erected, particularly around the northern part of Taranaki and around the TM sites.

In 1984 the Australian government established a Royal Commission to inquire into the status of both Emu and Maralinga. The President of the Commission was Robert McClelland, a former Labor government minister. McClelland found that previous clean-up attempts were inadequate, having been based on wrong assumptions and in some ways making any future clean-up more difficult. The Commission identified the plutonium contamination as the most significant hazard and noted that inhalation by children digging and playing in the contaminated soil, ingestion through eating bush food, or the contamination of an open wound by plutonium were unacceptable risks. Key recommendations were that the site should be cleaned-up to allow unrestricted access by the Aboriginal population and the cost of the clean-up should be borne by Britain.

PLANNING THE CLEAN-UP

In response, the Australian government set up TAG to investigate many aspects of the site and the lifestyle of Aborigines and to develop costed options for the clean-up. An aerial survey of the contaminated areas was conducted in 1987, backed-up by a ground survey by technicians from the ARL. The group reported to the Australian parliament in 1990 with some 30 options, ranging from simply erecting a fence around the whole contaminated area, to removing all the contaminated soil within a yet to be delineated boundary.[5] The government decided that Option 6(c) of that report was the most appropriate: it was a half-way scheme between simply fencing the contaminated area and scraping up all of the contaminated soil for burial. This option was agreed by the Commonwealth Government, the South Australian Government and the traditional owners, the Maralinga Tjarutja. In outline, the scheme was to:

- Remove the plutonium contaminated soil from the ploughed areas (2.1 square kilometres) and bury it in trenches at the three contaminated sites (Taranaki, Wewak and TM);
- Import clean soil to cover the scraped areas and re-vegetate those areas;
- Treat the 32 pits containing contaminated debris by a process of ISV;
- Sort through the 60 or so pits which contained non-radioactive debris and remove any contamination that might be found, disposing of it in the main burial trench; and
- Erect a fence around the contaminated area to the north of Taranaki to prevent access.

The Australian government then negotiated with the British government for some contribution to the cost of the clean-up. Britain contributed £20 million (about AU$44 million) towards the AU$104 million cost, to be paid in instalments.

Consideration of the potential dose to an Aborigine living a semi-traditional lifestyle on the range resulted in clean-up criteria for the three main sites and for location of the fence around Taranaki. The TAG proposed the risk of one in 10,000 of contracting a cancer by the age of 50 as a criterion to guide the clean-up. This led to an estimated dose of five millisieverts per annum (five times that allowed for a member of the public), which could be encountered by an Aborigine in areas contaminated at 3,000 becquerels (three kBq) of americium-241 per square metre. The proposition was accepted by the Maralinga Tjarutja and this level of contamination became the basic clean-up criterion.

Establishment of the clean-up criteria meant that the ARL could mark out which soil had to be removed for burial. This resulted in most of the ploughed area being included for removal, plus some that had not been ploughed. The soil removal boundary at Taranaki was set at about 40 kBq of americium-241/square metre, with further allowance made for the presence of contaminated fragments. The end-state criterion at Taranaki was three kBq of americium-241/square metre averaged over one hectare. The criteria varied slightly for other sites to take account of the differing ratios of plutonium to americium.

Since this criterion would have required the removal of 120 square kilometres of contaminated soil at Taranaki, a compromise was agreed. This was to remove the most contaminated soil from Taranaki for burial and to fence the remainder. Later, the notion of fencing was dropped in favour of a line of boundary markers which carry warning signs advising the Aborigines that the enclosed area is not suitable for permanent residence, but is safe enough to allow hunting and transit. All of the contaminated soil above the end-state criterion would be removed at the other two sites for burial.

The boundary markers were generally placed around the three kBq of americium-241/square metre contour but, for operational reasons and to prevent any future confusion, the markers were placed along existing (but sometimes barely discernable) tracks. As a consequence, although some 120 square kilometres remains contaminated above the criterion, the enclosed area to which occupancy is restricted is closer to 450 square kilometres.

PROGRESS ON THE PROJECT

Responsibility for the clean-up was vested in the Commonwealth DPIE. At that time, there was no nuclear regulatory organization in Australia. It was on 5 February 1999 that the ARPANSA came into being, absorbing all of the ARL. In 1993 DPIE established the MARTAC to advise them and the Minister on the progress of the project. In effect, this committee specified the scope of the project.

Work on the clean-up started in earnest in 1994. A contract was let to ARL to delineate the soil removal boundary at the three plutonium-contaminated sites and also to specify the health physics policy for the project. Another contract was awarded to the government-owned ACS to manage the early phases of the project and to provide health physics services. The scope of that contract was to erect a construction camp for the site workforce and upgrade the site infrastructure, this was followed by the excavation of three trenches 15 metres deep at the three main sites, collection of contaminated soil and burial of that soil in the trenches. Of lesser importance was the rehabilitation of 60 or so burial pits that contained general, uncontaminated, debris. While the end-state criteria were generally satisfied in the soil removal phase, the operation was not a total success since thousands of tonnes of contaminated soil blew away because the dust suppression techniques were inadequate.

The Commonwealth also let a contract to Geosafe Corporation of the United States to develop the ISV process to match the Taranaki geology. The purpose of ISV is to use electricity to convert the pit contents into a stable glass-like rock, which immobilizes the plutonium for hundreds of thousands of years. When the development showed that ISV was suitable for the treatment of the Taranaki pits, DPIE let a contract in mid-1996 to Geosafe Australia to design and build the ISV plant and then to use it to treat the Taranaki pits. In selecting ISV, DPIE stated: 'The ISV technology was selected over exhumation and reburial at the Taranaki site because of advantages of improved occupational, public and environmental safety, and superior containment of radioactive materials in the glassy product.'[6]

As work proceeded, further study resulted in modifications to the original scope of work. It was decided to restrict ISV to the 21 pits at Taranaki. The debris from the pits at Wewak and the TM site (including the Tietkens Plain Cemetery) was placed at the bottom of the burial trenches at those sites. Some radioactive debris was removed from the Airfield Cemetery and transported to Taranaki for burial. Also, the lumps of uranium on the surface at Kuli were collected and buried and the central area was scraped and the soil buried. The soil removal phase of the project was completed in early 1998.

In mid-1997, ACS was sold to the private firm GHD, a company that had not made the final six considered to manage the project. This was accepted since their part of the project was nearing completion, except for some on-going provision of health physics services.

As the soil was scraped from central Taranaki, it became apparent that the pits were very much larger than had been understood from the British reports. Consequently, ISV would cost more to complete than had been quoted and Geosafe was asked to provide a revised estimate of cost.

By the end of 1997, the equipment had been built and tested and was ready to be shipped to site when DPIE did a very strange thing. On the day after asking for the revised estimate, they told Geosafe that GHD would be taking over as manager of that phase of the project. This take-over had been discussed in three meetings held between DPIE and GHD without Geosafe's knowledge. The Commonwealth's Representative overseeing the whole project was also excluded. The future of the most expensive and complex part of the whole project was decided at three clandestine meetings attended by two people from DPIE who had little knowledge of the project and no experience in project management, whose only knowledge of ISV was a half-hour inspection of some of the equipment, and two from GHD who had never even seen the full-scale equipment, nor had they been involved in any way in the three-year development programme to match the ISV technology to the Taranaki geology. The ignorance of those from DPIE in radiation and other technical matters was amply demonstrated in hearings before a Senate Committee in May 2000.[7]

In the event, GHD was appointed both Project Manager and Project Authority and so Geosafe, the world's experts in ISV, found themselves reporting to a company that had absolutely no knowledge of the process or the equipment and to a client which was similarly ignorant. From then on, partly because of GHD's lack of knowledge and partly because of the way that the take-over was handled, the project had an uncertain future.

In addition to asking Geosafe for a revised estimate, DPIE started to seek ways to minimize the cost of this part of the project. This was towards the end of 1997, eight months before ISV operations started on-site. They considered various schemes to exhume some of the pits, sort the contents, bury some of the debris and vitrify the remainder. This was known as the hybrid option and was announced to the South Australian Government and the Maralinga Tjarutja in September 1998, an announcement which was not endorsed by the Tjarutja. Sorting was done on the basis of size, not level of radioactivity; the larger pieces were to be vitrified and the smaller items and soil buried, even though the latter could be far more radioactive. The government then started exhuming eight large pits around the periphery of central Taranaki, while 13 inner pits were being vitrified.

There were no criteria by which the effectiveness of ISV could be gauged. Although some criteria were in draft form, they had not been included in the contract. Ten melts had been completed before any criteria were agreed and even then some were rather impractical.

As treatment of the pits continued, the lack of knowledge of ISV on the part of DPIE and GHD became all too apparent. As a consequence, MARTAC became much more involved than would be expected of an advisory committee. By now the committee comprised scientists who had expectations that were neither constant nor contractual. Even though all members of the committee had supported the recommendation to adopt the ISV process, agreeing it was the best solution available, some started to express concerns about whether or not the non-contractual criteria were satisfied. They undertook a quality control function, which one would have expected to have been the responsibility of GHD or Geosafe, but instead of using a drill to take core samples, they started to break up the blocks searching for evidence or otherwise of compliance with the draft criteria. One factor in particular that received a lot of attention was unmelted steel in the block, in spite of the fact that there was never a requirement to melt the steel. Instead the criterion stated that 'There should be a high degree of confidence that the contaminated soils and debris within the pits are completely melted *or encased* in the vitrified product'.[8]

On 21 March 1999, as treatment of Pit 17 (the thirteenth melt) was almost complete, something in the pit exploded and molten glass was spewed some 50 metres from the pit, causing extensive damage to the hood in the process. Geosafe conducted an investigation into the possible cause of the explosion and GHD arranged for an audit of the Geosafe report. On 23 June 1999 DPIE announced that it was abandoning any form of vitrification, claiming that there was no conclusive evidence as to the cause of the explosion and stating that it was unsafe to continue. This decision was taken several months before the two reports were delivered in October and December 1999. Although the reports did not agree as to the most likely cause of the explosion, they did agree that it was caused by something in the pit and not by the ISV process. The Maralinga Tjarutja dissociated themselves from the decision simply to cancel the ISV project and to exhume and bury the debris.

AFTER VITRIFICATION

Having abandoned vitrification, DPIE was left with the 'exhume and bury' option. But instead of segregating the debris, they simply exhumed everything and dropped it all into a bare hole in the ground. They then broke up all of the ISV blocks and placed the pieces over the debris as a kind of barrier and covered the whole with about five metres of soil, which extends two to three metres above the surface – so the top of the debris is actually within three metres of ground level.

The government claimed that the decision to cancel ISV had nothing to do with cost, but there is clear evidence in discussion papers of the time that the cancellation had more to do with cost than any other factor.[9] The government also claimed that the decision was made partly because the amount of plutonium in the pits was less than had been expected when ISV was proposed,[10] but they had started work on the hybrid scheme long before there was any indication of the plutonium content of the pits. A report that was received in Australia in 1987 estimated the total amount of plutonium in the Taranaki pits as 2.2 kilograms,[11] this estimate was in turn based on earlier reports which quoted one to three kilograms. These early estimates were accepted seven months before the contract was signed with Geosafe, as shown in the minutes of the meeting of MARTAC in November 1995 which concluded that there would be between 2.2 and 4.4 kilograms. DPIE later acknowledged the amount of plutonium to be two kilograms,[12] so validating the initial estimates.

After abandoning what every member of MARTAC and all other parties agreed was a far superior waste form, one could have expected DPIE to take the next best option, to segregate the debris so that it would be readily retrievable should a future generation not accept the simple burial option. For example, the debris could have been placed in a concrete vault so that it was segregated and retrievable.

SATISFYING THE CODE OF PRACTICE?

The government claims that the burial option is consistent with the 1992 Code of Practice for disposal of radioactive waste.[13] Sometimes they say that what has been done satisfies the code and sometimes that they did not need to satisfy it. Whether they were required to satisfy the code is immaterial because not a single requirement has been met, indeed it cannot even be said to have been used as a guide. For example, there was no environmental impact statement, no surface water management system, no radiation management plan and no institutional control period established. Most importantly, since the government hopes to return the land to Aboriginal ownership, the code stipulates that 'the [disposal] site should not be located in an area where land ownership rights or control could compromise retention of long-term control over the facility' – the debris has been buried in a shallow grave at Taranaki because that was the most convenient disposal route.

Sometimes, DPIE and ARPANSA describe the work at Maralinga as an *intervention* that required them only to improve the situation. While accepting that explanation, should not they have improved the situation as much as possible within the constraints of the budget? Should they not have spent the money in such a way that the improvements were the best that could be achieved? If the intention was simply to improve the situation, then there are far cheaper ways to achieve that end and obtain a better result; they did not need to spend AU$40 million on an aborted scheme to do so.

In July 2001 the government published a discussion paper seeking public comment on the process to find a site suitable for a store for intermediate level waste.[14] Twice that paper states that long-lived radioactive waste, whether low- or intermediate level, is not suitable for near-surface disposal. But that is exactly what has been done at Maralinga.

NOTES

A list of further relevant resources is available from the author. Please email
alanpark@ozemail.com.au.

1. W. Reynolds, *Australia's Bid for the Atomic Bomb* (Melbourne: Melbourne
   University Press, 2000); A. Cawte, *Atomic Australia* (Sydney: University of New
   South Wales Press, 1992); *Fortress Australia*, screened on ABC TV, 22 Aug.
   2002.
2. Australian Radiation Laboratory, *Maralinga Rehabilitation Project*, Submission
   to Parliamentary Standing Committee on Public Works, Public Hearing held at
   Ceduna, 23 Feb. 1995.
3. W. Cook, *Operation Brumbie Final Report* (Aldermaston: AWRE, 1967), p.1.
4. Ibid., p.5.
5. Technical Assessment Group, *Rehabilitation of Former Nuclear Test Sites in
   Australia* (Canberra: DPIE, 1990).
6. R. Rawson, P. Davoren and C. Perkins, *Status of Rehabilitation of the Maralinga
   and Emu Sites* (Canberra: DPIE, 1997).
7. Hansard of the Senate Economics Legislation Committee Hearings, Canberra,
   3 May 2000.
8. Maralinga Rehabilitation Technical Advisory Committee, *Minutes of the Sixth
   Meeting*, Maralinga, 14–18 Aug. 1995.
9. GHD, *Cost Comparison for the Treatment of Outer Pits*, Canberra, 21 Aug.
   1998; D.R. Davy, *A Role for Excavation in the Rehabilitation of the Waste
   Disposal Pits at Taranaki, Maralinga*, Report to Consultative Group on
   Maralinga Clean-Up Project, Canberra, 17 July 1998.
10. Senator N. Minchin, *Minister Confirms Maralinga Clean-Up is Safe*, Media
    release, Canberra, 17 April 2000.
11. F.W. Cornish, *Review of Contamination and Possible Treatment Options at
    Maralinga*, AWRE Report O 23/86 (Aldermaston: AWRE, 1987).
12. Catherine Hockley, 'Spectre that Still Haunts', *Advertiser* (Adelaide), 20 April
    2000, p.19.
13. National Health and Medical Research Council, *Code of Practice for the Near-
    Surface Disposal of Radioactive Waste in Australia (1992)*, Radiation Health
    Series No.35 (Canberra: Australian Government Publishing Service, 1992).
14. Department of Industry, Science and Resources, *Safe Storage of Radioactive
    Waste*, The National Store Project: Methods for Choosing the Right Site, A
    Public Discussion Paper (Canberra: Department of Industry, Science and
    Resources, 2001).

Long-term Health Effects in UK Test Veterans

SUE RABBITT ROFF

The United Kingdom's atmospheric atomic- and nuclear-weapons testing programme lasted for more than a decade from the first detonation at Monte Bello in 1952 to the completion of the joint United States–UK series at Christmas Island and the subsequent clean-up through 1964. Together with the studies of the survivors of the two atomic detonations at Hiroshima and Nagasaki in 1945, we now have longitudinal data on the health of at least half of the nearly 40,000 servicemen and civilians (22,000 British, 16,000 Australians, 535 New Zealanders and approximately 300 Fijians) who 'participated' in the tests including the attempted clean-ups at Maralinga (Chapter 8) and Christmas Island. Since the majority of the men (only a handful of women were ever sent to a UK nuclear test site) were in their 20s at the time they participated 40 to 50 years ago, we are now looking at a cohort who are in their 60s and 70s at least. What do we know about the long-term effects on their health of their work in radioactive-weapons development?

HIROSHIMA AND NAGASAKI

Follow-up of the survivors of the detonations at Hiroshima and Nagasaki may be suggestive, despite two important differences. The Japanese survivors are generally presumed to have been exposed to a high dose of radiation over a very short period of time (acute exposure), whereas it is likely that the nuclear test veterans were exposed to relatively low doses over a longer period, often 12 months (chronic exposure). In Japan, the exposed population did not consist predominantly of healthy young adult males but of the full age range of both genders in the two cities. Although dose level was probably an essential difference between the two exposures, it is now accepted that there is no threshold below which radiation exposure is safe – that is, even the smallest speck of radioactive material can be injurious. It is therefore useful to review the latency periods in the manifestation of the cancers attributed to exposure to the atom bombs which have been reported for the Japanese survivors. Although the longitudinal studies on the survivors have extended now for more than 50 years, it is not considered that the data are complete, since many of the exposed were *in utero* or infants at the time of the detonations and are still alive.

The incidence of leukaemia among the Japanese survivors peaked within five years, but it has still not returned to normal more than 50 years later. The increase of thyroid cancer was not apparent until the 1950s (ten years after the detonations); increases of breast and lung cancers, not until the 1960s (20 years); gastric and colon cancer and multiple myeloma, not until the late 1970s (over 30 years); and meningioma, not until the late 1990s (over 50 years). In general, an excess of solid cancers began to appear after ten years and increased for the next 30, possibly beginning to plateau 40 years after exposure. This means that the incidence of radiogenic cancers induced by the exposures in 1945 is greater among those survivors who have in any case reached the age when actuarially they are most likely to suffer cancers.

In general, the data from the Radiation Effects Research Foundation's Life Span Study indicate that during follow-up, the earlier years were dominated by cancers appearing in those aged over 20 at exposure. However, 50 per cent of all total *excess* cancers were observed in the last seven years of follow-up in those under 20 at exposure, a cohort that has 85 per cent of its members still alive and now entering the period when they are prone to cancer.[1]

SELF-REPORTED HEALTH STATUS OF UK TEST VETERANS

How do the veterans of the UK nuclear-weapons test regard their own health? In 1997, on behalf of the BNTVA, I undertook a study of the self-reported health status of 1,041 members of the BNTVA, which then had a membership of about 2,000, ten per cent of the approximately 21,000 who attended the tests. The survey was designed to ask specific questions, not to provide final answers, which do not – and with the passage of time may never – exist. The findings have been published in full elsewhere;[2] only an outline can be given here.

The membership rolls of the BNTVA were also utilized by the MoD in the construction of a database of 21,358 UK nuclear veterans who were studied using a different methodology by researchers under the auspices of the NRPB. The sample of 1,041 BNTVA members is slightly younger than the NRPB cohort and had virtually half the death rate of the full cohort in the period to December 1990. Any bias, therefore, is more likely to be in the direction of 'healthy volunteer' than 'unhealthy volunteer' sub-sample for these 1,041 men.

Of the 1,041 men, 877 (84 per cent) reported health problems; 164 men (16 per cent) reported no health problems. The 877 men reported 3,427 conditions: 136 men (13 per cent) reported severe dental problems, many losing all their teeth within five years of returning from the tests; 113 men (11 per cent) reported heavy hair loss in their 20s after returning from the tests. Sixty-five men (six per cent) reported cataracts, often before the age of 40 years; 93 men (nine per cent) reported other eye problems, including dry eyes, loss of tears, iritis and uveitis, and 27 men (three per cent) reported glaucoma. These three categories of conditions – dental, hair-loss and early cataracts – are usually considered indicators of possible radiation exposure.

Musculoskeletal problems, including a variety of inflammatory and degenerative back and joint diseases, accounted for 702 items, or one-fifth of all the non-cancer conditions reported. Two hundred and sixteen men (21 per cent) reported various skin conditions. Although the veterans would have been heavily sunburnt, it is noted that similar conditions were seen in Fijian attendees at the UK tests and are being observed in Tahitians who worked on the French nuclear tests. Ninety-six men (nine per cent) also reported one or more of dermatitis, eczema and psoriasis; 51 (five per cent) reported problems with their nails in the years following the tests. Eight of the 24 cancers reported were melanoma or other skin cancers. These 371 skin conditions constituted 11 per cent of the total number of conditions reported. Gastrointestinal problems – including the inflammatory bowel conditions Crohn's disease, ulcerative colitis and diverticulitis – accounted for 486 of the conditions reported (14 per cent of all non-cancer conditions). Most men reported the onset of these problems in their late 20s and early 30s. The categories of skeletal, skin and intestinal conditions accounted for the 45 per cent of all non-cancer conditions reported by the 1,041 men.

Of the 363 cancers reported for 262 men, 56 (15 per cent) were skin cancers and 70 (19 per cent) were gastro-intestinal. Together these accounted for one-third of the cancers reported. There were also 52 (14 per cent) cancers of haematopoietic (blood-forming) tissues.

About 15 per cent of the respondents reported post-test infertility. The incidence of stillbirths and neural tube defects (particularly spina bifida and hydrocephalus, of which 26 cases were reported among fewer than 5,000 children and grandchildren of these men) together with the occurrence of skeletal and skin co-morbidity in both children and grandchildren, suggests that there is a biological mechanism of teratogenic injury consistent with very recent advances in understanding of genomic instability, which can be transmitted from parents to offspring (Chapter 10).

The results in this preliminary study of 1,041 UK veterans have been mirrored in a parallel study of 238 New Zealand and 30 Fijian veterans of the same tests. It is therefore tentatively proposed that the irradiation of young men – by low level chronic irradiation perhaps from re-suspended radionuclides in the coral island environment of Christmas Island, or the desert sand of the Australian test sites or by acute prompt radiation from the detonations themselves – may have triggered pre-cancerous conditions. These could progress to haematopoietic cancers, such as multiple myeloma. Many men were required to witness multiple tests from a position less than 20 miles from ground zero. Most were required to stand with their backs initially to the explosions, possibly exposing their spines to radiation.

While these findings and hypotheses are still only tentative, they are compatible with other research in the field. The long-term symptoms reported by these veterans of UK nuclear-weapons tests may be similar to the chronic radiation sickness, characterized by depression, fatigue and an altered blood picture, described in nuclear workers in Russia.[3] An increase of acute myeloid leukaemia and lung cancer (with the suggestion that the exposure to plutonium could interact with smoking in the latter) has also been reported in Russian radiation workers,[4] though not multiple myeloma.

The non-cancerous conditions reported here are common and their categorization into 'syndromes' ascribed to an environmental cause is far from universally agreed. On the other hand, particularly in the light of the Japanese experience cited above, it is accepted that radiation is a cause of some cancers, especially leukaemia and multiple myeloma. But attempts to identify the cause of a possible small increase of a relatively uncommon cancer are fraught with difficulty from sampling error and other statistical pitfalls. In the present case acceptance of radiation exposure as a cause could open the floodgates to large claims for compensation, which may have contributed to the reluctance of the MoD to accept even the possibility of a relationship. The remainder of this chapter considers this aspect of the controversy, beginning with an account of the current consensus on the issue in the United States.

THE UNITED STATES

Since 1988 the US has in principle provided for compensation for nearly 500,000 'radiation-exposed veterans' who participated in the occupation of Hiroshima and Nagasaki, were prisoners of war in those cities at the time of the atomic detonations, or were involved in 'onsite participation in a test involving the atmospheric detonation of a nuclear device'. According to the governing legislation (Title 38 United States Code

Annotated Section 1112) 15 malignant conditions, including leukaemia other than chronic lymphocytic leukaemia, cancer of the thyroid, cancer of the breast and multiple myeloma, were considered possibly radiogenic for such veterans. Cancer of the prostate was added to the list in 1998 and six other cancers in 2002.

It was stated at the time that the list was extended that the intended effect of this amendment to the legislation was to ensure that veterans who may have been exposed to radiation during military service do not have a higher burden of proof than civilians exposed to ionizing radiation who may be entitled to compensation for these cancers under comparable Federal statutes. Although the list of conditions is extensive, in fact only approximately 500 veterans have succeed in claims under these provisions because of the difficulties of establishing their eligibility. Nearly two-fifths of the successful claims have been made by veterans of the occupation of Hiroshima and Nagasaki.

The Department of Veterans' Affairs receives advice on the relationship of various diseases to ionizing radiation from the Veterans' Advisory Committee on Environment Hazards. It should be noted though that the decisions of the Advisory Committee apparently override the reservations of several epidemiological studies on the relevance and absence or otherwise of crucial data on matters such as the size of study groups and adequacy of sampling and information on radiation doses.[5]

As well as its compensation provisions, the US Department of Veterans Affairs runs an Ionizing Radiation Registry Examination Program, which offers a complete medical history, physical examination and standard diagnostic tests, plus additional specialized tests and consultations if necessary. More than 22,000 examinations have been performed under this programme. Eligible veterans also receive special, free treatment for radiogenic diseases.

THE UNITED KINGDOM

The United Kingdom Veterans Agency (formerly the WPA) states as its normal policy: 'In general an award of war pension will be considered where there is evidence of service exposure to ionising radiation *and* there is a recognised causal link between the claimed condition and such exposure.'[6] 'Service related ionising radiation exposure' is defined as 'exposure to a measurable level of ionising radiation due to service in the armed forces and as determined by radiological dosimetry specialist report'. This requirement replaced an earlier provision that to succeed in a pension application a nuclear test veteran needed to show that he had been exposed to 'excess' (that is, higher than background) levels of radiation during his service.

Although the UK policy statement recognizes more conditions as potentially radiogenic than the US statement – including polycythaemia rubra vera, non-melanoma skin cancer, cancer of uterus and vagina, testis and kidney – the award of pensions was very parsimonious until recent years. For instance, in 1997 the then Secretary of State for Defence stated in the House of Commons that:

> It is not possible to say precisely how many claims for compensation from the Ministry of Defence have been made by British nuclear test veterans. However, my Department's computer records show that since 29 June 1976 109 claims for compensation for radiation linked illnesses have been made by ex-service personnel who were involved in the British nuclear test programme. All of these cases have been repudiated because independent studies of the health of the test veterans showed that participation in the nuclear testing programme had no detectable effect on the veterans' life expectation, or on their risk of developing cancer. However, nuclear test veterans may receive a war pension...[7]

In a letter to a Member of Parliament,[8] the Chief Executive of the WPA stated in 1998 that 159 pension claims had been received, of which 30 were awarded – 12 being listed as 'radiation award'.

In the years since this statement, at least 26 pensions have been awarded by the WPA (which became the Veterans Agency under the aegis of the MoD in 2001). The marked increase in successful applications in the past five years is probably due to more effective advocacy before the Pensions Appeals Tribunals, largely based on archival material that has become available in recent years together with changes in medical knowledge. It may also reflect an increasing rate of applications as the veterans reach the 'cancer prone' age.

Initial applications are still routinely denied at the administrative level, even for conditions which have been recognized as potentially radiogenic in the Agency's own policy statement and for which other veterans or their widows have received pensions. This is because of the Agency's policy of considering each case on its merits without dependence on precedents. The Agency has routinely offered two reasons for rejection at this level. The first is the 'radiological dosimetry specialist report' commissioned by the War Pensions/Veterans Agency from the Atomic Weapons Authority, which usually asserts that the individual was not exposed to radiation during his service at the tests. In the case of Christmas Island, for instance, a MoD mimeo concluded that:

> The background dose received by civilians and members of HM Forces serving at or off Christmas Island in the years 1956 to 1964 was only about 35 per cent of that which they would have received on average had they remained, for that period of their lives, in the United Kingdom – that is, some 100 micro-sieverts per calendar month less at Christmas Island than in the United Kingdom.[9]

PLATE 1: A Vulcan bomber carries a Blue Steel missile over Niagara Falls
© Crown Copyright/MoD

PLATE 2: Test firing of a Polaris missile
© Crown Copyright/MoD

PLATE 3: 'Widening the Web', Greenham Common, 14 December 1985
© Rosemary Douglas

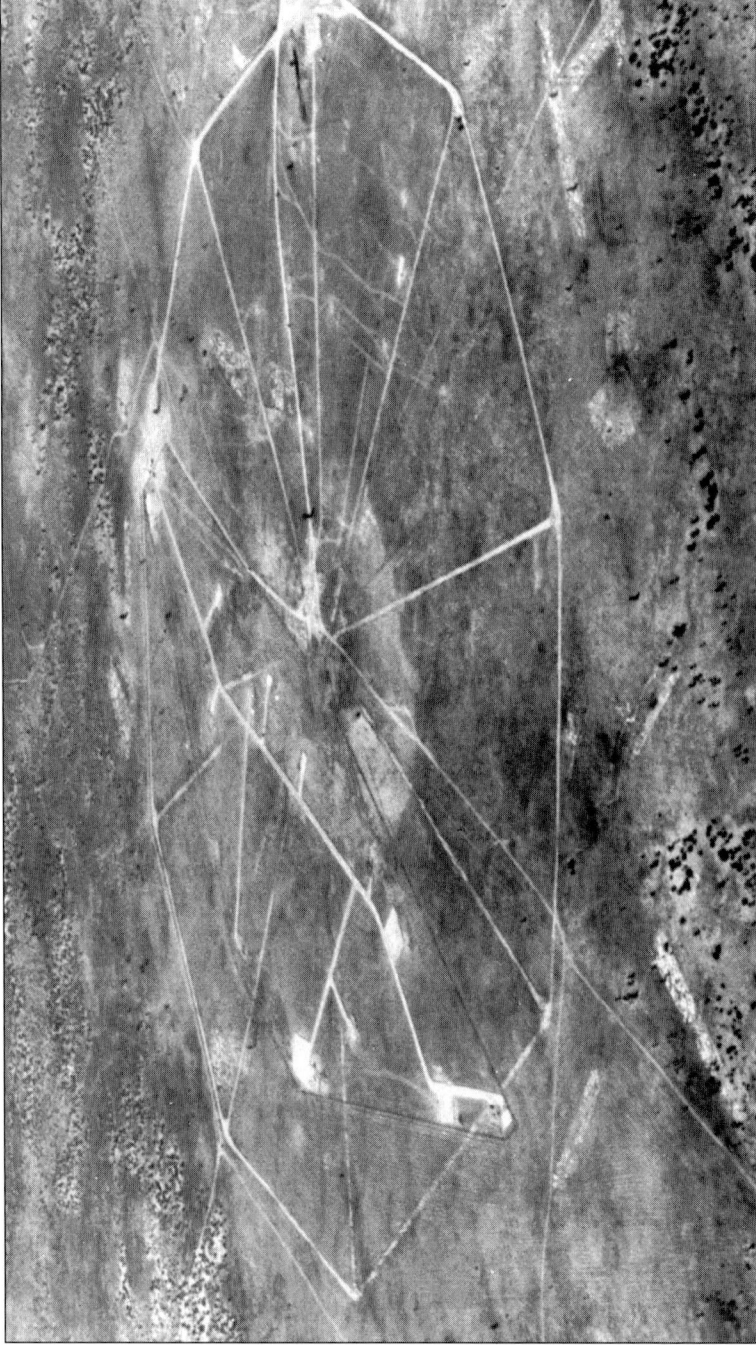

PLATE 4: The Taranaki test site, Maralinga, South Australia
© Alan Parkinson

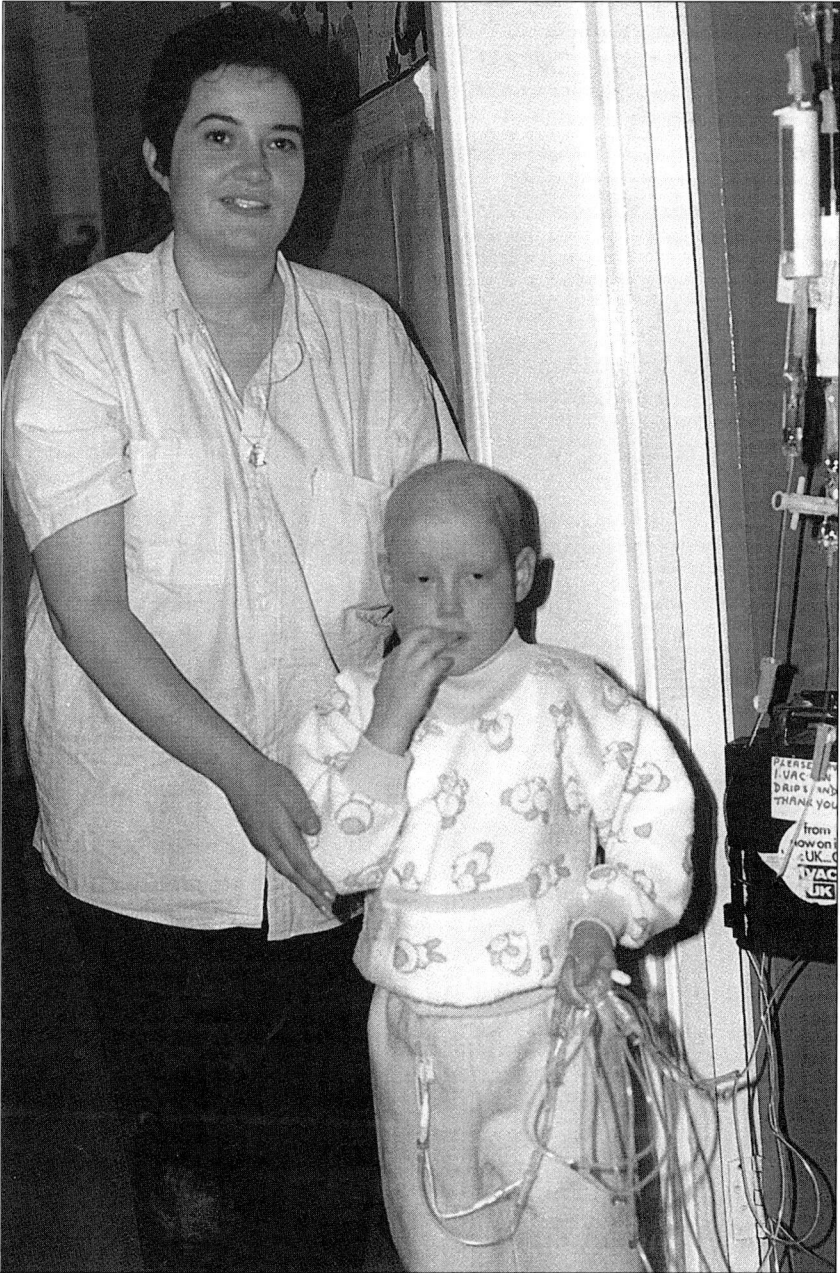

PLATE 5: Childhood leukaemia
Jemma D'arcy and her mother Sue. Jemma, who lived near the Sellafield nuclear
site and whose father worked there, died of leukaemia in 1990.
Photograph with kind permission of Susan D'arcy

PLATE 6: Effects of a ten-tonne terrorist explosion in Trafalgar Square, London
From artist's impression by Pat Fogarty, with thanks. Note that the effects of scattered radioactivity cannot be shown

MAP 1: Australia showing nuclear test sites
© Australian Nuclear Veterans Association

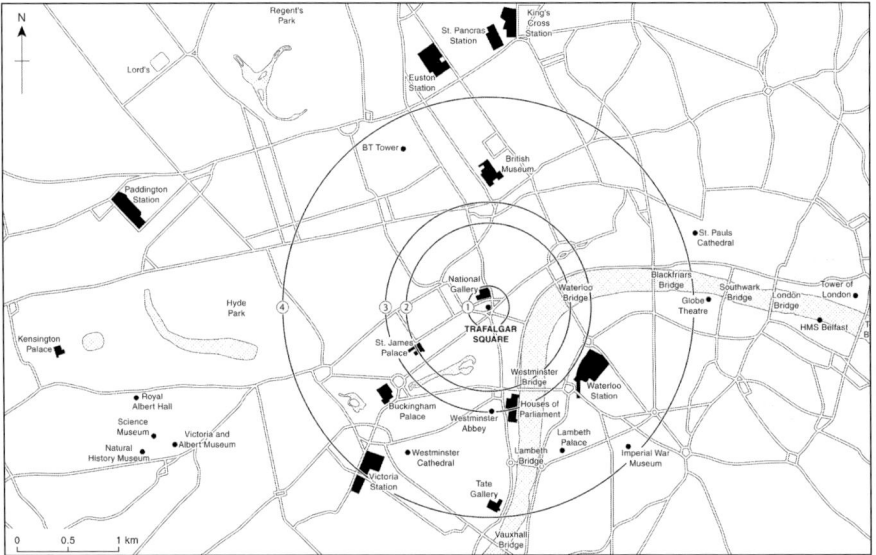

MAP 2: Effects of a one-kiloton nuclear explosion
centred on Trafalgar Square, London

Within Circle 1 (200 metres), almost 100 per cent fatality in those directly exposed
to thermal radiation; within Circle 2 (800 metres), almost 100 per cent fatality in
those directly exposed to blast; within Circle 3 (one kilometre), almost 100 per cent
fatality in those directly exposed to prompt nuclear radiation; within Circle 4
(two kilometres), almost all directly exposed suffer immediate injuries from burns
and blast.
Map by Antony Smith with additional graphics by Richard Prime

Although this period covered the 1957 Windscale/Sellafield accident in the UK (Introduction), Pensions Appeals Tribunals have found it hard to credit, especially considering that in the last Christmas Island series of joint UK–US tests, 25 nuclear weapons were detonated over the course of six months – or one a week – on a small Pacific island where several thousand servicemen were living, working and eating fish caught in the lagoons.

The second reason that was given for these routine rejections was that the two epidemiological studies commissioned by the MoD from the NRPB reported that there have been no detectable excess cancers among the 22,000 UK veterans, with the possible exceptions of leukaemia and multiple myeloma.[10]

However, these arguments have not survived the scrutiny of the PATs (consisting of a legally qualified member, a medically qualified member and a representative of the service branch of the applicant) now that there is clear evidence that detectable fallout radiation was measured at Christmas Island. Since Monte Bello and Maralinga are clearly contaminated (and Maralinga has been the recipient of a £20,000,000 decontamination attempt, paid for by the UK government – Chapter 8) this claim has never withstood scrutiny by the PATs for veterans of the Australian tests.

The PATs have also set aside the earlier NRPB studies, primarily on the grounds that epidemiological studies do not actually address, far less resolve, individual cases, as successive Ministers have acknowledged. For instance, a junior minister at the MoD wrote that:

> I accept that some ex-Servicemen who were present at the atmospheric nuclear texts [sic] are ill. Some of them have a war pension because their illness is accepted as in some way attributable to their time in service. There is, however, no evidence of excess illness or mortality amongst the veterans as a group, which could be linked to exposure to radiation as a result of their participation in the tests.[11]

His successor, a public health consultant before he became a Member of Parliament, wrote that: 'Ms Roff … questions the power of the [NRPB] study and points out that it tells us nothing about individuals. The second point is a statement of the obvious and does not need to be laboured over.'[12]

The irrelevance of the NRPB epidemiological studies in relation to individual pension applications can be seen in particular in relation to the six known awards for multiple myeloma since publication of the second NRPB report. The Agency's policy was to award pensions for those who had been present at the test sites who suffered leukaemia (other than chronic lymphatic leukaemia which has never been shown to be radiogenic), multiple myeloma and primary polycythaemia rubra vera when the leukaemia or polycythaemia manifested itself within 25 years of first presence at the sites. This was based on the findings of the first NRPB report, published in 1988. But the 1993 report stated that the excess of multiple myeloma was probably due to chance and the Agency ceased to award pensions for this condition on the basis of 'presence at the tests' only. However, at least six pensions for multiple myeloma have been awarded since this decision based on the evaluation of the probable aetiology at the individual, rather than the epidemiological level. Similarly, the '25-year latency' rule for leukaemia has been overtaken by greater medical knowledge, which indicates that it is unfortunately premature to assume that the hazard passes within that time. Another trend in recent PAT decisions has been a concern with consistency of decision-making which, it can be hoped, may one day translate into more equitable policies governing the power of precedents. At present each veteran or widow has to go through a process of appeal that commonly takes two years, sometimes five, and is rarely successful without professional legal advocacy.

The third NRPB study was commissioned by the MoD from the NRPB in February 1999 and reported in early 2003.[13] According to the MoD's announcement:

> The decision to conduct a new study is in response to recent analysis of the National Radiological Protection Board (NRPB) database, which noted a recent rise in the incidents [*sic*] of MM [multiple myeloma] in both test participants and the control group. (The recent analysis recorded 29 cases of MM in veterans and 24 in controls.) These new figures suggest no explicit evidence of a difference in the occurrence of MM between the two groups (participants and controls). But in order to make a valid comparison between the two groups, and between these groups and national rates, a detailed and scientifically based analysis is necessary.

The study would be carried out by the NRPB 'and will be subject to independent oversight by a committee including eminent academics and scientists'. The statement further noted that:

> The first NRPB study (in 1988) found that test participation may have caused a small risk of developing leukaemia and MM. The evidence was weak because of the exceptionally few cases found in the control population. A further study in 1993 did not support the earlier findings for MM in this period and concluded that the apparent increase in MM in participants seen in the previous study was a chance finding mainly due to the exceptionally low rate of diseases seen in the control group at that time.

The statement insisted that 'The MoD has every confidence in these studies and the conclusions drawn. However, MoD will respond positively and constructively to any concerns about illness brought about by new data.' In fact, this third study was a response to the longstanding concerns of the BNTVA about possible under-ascertainment of cases among participants in the first two studies. Their records, and the study of self-reported morbidity and death certificates that I conducted,[14] had led them to suspect that there were more cases of certain conditions than had been reported in the first two NRPB studies. The MoD argued that my sample was biased, on the assumption that individuals only joined the BNTVA once they fell ill and were therefore self-selected. It was therefore decided, on the suggestion of the late Alice Stewart, to check the possibility that my sample was reporting a higher incidence of some conditions than were reported for the estimated 85 per cent sample in the NRPB studies. The prime example of this possibility seemed to be multiple myeloma, a known radiogenic condition. The central issue was whether the detection and ascertainment methods used by the NRPB (based on the interrogation of service databases in relation to cancer registries) was adequate to detect all the known cases of a condition such as multiple myeloma. The BNTVA and I agreed to make available our data for an inter-comparison with that held by the NRPB after a double-blind study had been conducted.

The first meeting of the oversight Advisory Committee for the third NRPB study virtually coincided with the release of the US Five Series study on the Operation 'Crossroads' nuclear test veterans in October 1999. This had stressed the limitations of such studies, especially in relation to the question of attaining sufficient statistical power with a small sample for relatively uncommon conditions. The UK researchers and their Advisory Committee apparently did not place weight on the caveat issued by their corresponding member, John Kaldor of the University of New South Wales, who commented that:

> The authors [of the first two NRPB studies] were undoubtedly aware that their study would not have the statistical power to detect small increases in mortality or cancer incidence or increases in the occurrence of rate conditions that may have been associated with participation in the nuclear tests. For example, if the risk of multiple myeloma was truly increased as a result of participant exposure to radiation by a factor of 20 per cent, this increase is very unlikely to have been detected as statistically significant.[15]

Kaldor had acknowledged the force of the warning that:

> Epidemiological methods may be capable of detecting relative risks perhaps as low as 1.3 to 1.4. However, the relative risks of interest following low doses of radiation (1–10cGy) are of the order of 1.01 to 1.05. Thus not much should be anticipated from direct observations at 1cGy...[16]

The Advisory Committee and researchers for the third NRPB study also apparently did not consider another caveat, issued on publication of the US National Institute of Medicine report on the Five Series Study:

> Only a study cohort four times the size of the one available would have been likely to identify the observed leukemia risk as statistically significant. The sample size presently available does not provide sufficient power to achieve statistical significance for risks of the magnitude we observed.[17]

This was despite the fact that the Five Series cohort was three times as large as those in the NRPB studies and claimed that there had been a 99 per cent ascertainment of cases. This was achieved by a complex variety of detection strategies. For instance:

> The assembled information for this epidemiologic study comes from more than 100 distinct sources. Handwritten paper logs, microfilm or microfiche, computer files, medical records, work orders, transport orders, memoirs, interoffice memoranda, testimony, secondary compilations of primary sources, letters from spouses, death certificates, film badge records, computer programs, and benefits and compensation claims represent a diverse sample.[18]

As well as these labour-intensive methods, the Five Series study relied on the Nuclear Test Personnel Review database, which included a nation-wide toll-free call-in programme for veterans of the atmospheric nuclear tests to report details of their participation in a test. The National Association of Atomic Veterans Medical Survey of 1,784 veterans, advertised in a range of veterans' journals and held a public meeting for veterans. The Five Series researchers also searched the claims files of the Veterans Administration. Similar strategies have been used in other studies of veterans' epidemiology.[19]

Although the third UK study was provoked by concerns about ascertainment and despite the inherent lack of statistical power of the study, the Advisory Committee and the NRPB have repeated the methodology of the first two studies, which had relied solely on data linkage between service records and cancer registries. In fact, 'inclusion in the main cohort' of the study was dependent on having been ascertained by these methods. Any subject/case identified by any other means was classified as an 'independent responder' and excluded from the study because, it was argued, the same detection methods were not used to identify subjects/cases in the control group. This decision was taken even though it was acknowledged from the first report onwards that there was at least a 15 per cent under-ascertainment in the study.[20] In the first six months of the planning period of the third NRPB a comparison of national cancer registry and direct follow-up in the ascertainment of ovarian cancer was brought to the attention of the Advisory Committee and the researchers by the Director of

Cancer Registration in Scotland.[21] This study reported that in an analysis of a similar size cohort of 22,000 post-menopausal women who had participated in a study of screening for ovarian cancer, only 78 per cent of cases were detected from NHSCR files, while direct follow-up by postal questionnaire had ascertained 96 per cent of cases and concluded that a complementary method of follow-up is also required, not least considering the four-year time lag that often occurs in information reaching the NHSCR. A subsequent study of the completeness and accuracy of cancer registrations notified by the NHSCR for England and Wales, published two years later in the middle of the third NRPB study, concluded that it would be incautious to use NHSCR cancer registrations as the sole basis for an epidemiological study.[22]

When these issues were put to the NRPB researchers and the Advisory Committee they continued to insist that the third study must be conducted along exactly the same lines as the first two, in order to make their results comparable. It had, though, always been acknowledged that, 'For the study to be definitive, either all participants needed to be included or the authors needed to be able to show that those who were included were fully representative of all those who had participated'.[23] The Advisory Group also agreed upon the importance of treating data for the test participants and controls equally and relegating the cases identified by Dundee/BNTVA or any other means outside the NRPB strategies to the status of 'independent responders'.

THE THIRD NRPB SURVEY

In the event, the third NRPB study is of 21,357 test participants identified from the Service Office Records and stated to represent 85 per cent of the total of the approximately 25,000 participants.[24] It reports 35 cases of multiple myeloma among participants up to the end of 1998 and another 35 among 22,333 controls.

Of the 35 cases in participants, 23 were detected both by the NRPB and Dundee/BNTVA, 12 by the NRPB alone. At the time of the inter-comparison, the NRPB indicated that it was also aware of five 'independent responders', three of whom were also detected by the Dundee/BNTVA study, and it accepted six further 'independent responders' from Dundee. At least six of these ten independent responders had received war pensions for multiple myeloma and so could have been ascertained from the MoD's own claim files.

Three additional cases identified by Dundee/BNTVA and acknowledged by the NRPB are confirmed. Their data did not appear in the cancer registries in time for the study, although their diagnoses were made within its timeframe and all three men had been active applicants before the WPA throughout that time. Two other individuals received pensions for multiple myeloma during the timeframe of the study. These five cases could have all been detected by searching the WPA claims files, yet are not in either the main NRPB study or their list of independent responders. Together with the 11 accepted by the NRPB, they bring the number of known cases of multiple myeloma to 51. Two other additional known cases were excluded from the NRPB study because one man served in the Merchant Navy at the tests and one was a civilian meteorologist seconded to the RAF. Although the NRPB study included civilians with the AWE and AWRE, it did not extend to other civilians present at the tests and it did not include members of the Merchant Navy. The third NRPB study thus omits at least 30 per cent of the known cases of multiple myeloma among men who participated in the UK nuclear-weapons tests.

Part of the explanation for the discrepancy may be the fact that 11 of these 'independent responders' (including five of the six cases accepted by the NRPB from Dundee/BNTVA) served in the RAF at the tests in capacities ranging from ground crew servicing contaminated planes, to a base commander. The NRPB estimated that only 74 per cent of eligible RAF participants had been included in the main cohort of their second study.[25] Of the 21,538 test participants included in this study, 39.5 per cent were from the RAF,[26] yet their first study had estimated that the ascertainment rate for the RAF participants in Operation 'Grapple' was only 70 per cent.[27] Eight of the 11 'independent responders' acknowledged by the NRPB were from the RAF; this should have alerted them to the problem of under-ascertainment in their sample in relation to a service known to have participated in highly vulnerable activities with regard to radiation exposure.

It appears, then, that by relying solely on data linkage between the Service Records Office and cancer registries, the NRPB have identified barely 70 per cent of the verified cases of multiple myeloma among documented participants at the UK nuclear-weapons tests. The individuals whose cases were not identified may have been missed by the Service Records Office, the cancer registries, or both. As noted, the NRPB claims that their subjects represent 85 per cent of participants in the tests, but if, as it appears, the incidence of multiple myeloma is twice their reported level in the remaining 15 per cent, their sample is clearly not fully representative. As also noted, reliance on data linkage alone is inadequate for epidemiological studies; this is especially likely to be true when service records dating back 50 years form one arm of the linkage. Meanwhile, though the possibility that the incidence of multiple myeloma is indeed significantly increased in test participants, particularly those such as flight crews and ground workers exposed to higher doses of radiation, has not been ruled out.

It has recently been reported that in a study of 4,563 nuclear workers followed retrospectively from 1950 to 1994, all of the radiation doses contributing to mortality from cancers of the blood and lymph system were received before the age of 50. This led to the conclusion that 'effects of low-level radiation doses may depend on exposure age, and that patterns of effect modification by age may differ between types of cancer'.[28] Since most of the men who contracted multiple myeloma were in their 20s at the time they participated in the UK tests, their fate may be corroborating these findings. Certainly, after 50 years, full information on the UK nuclear test participants could still be compatible with the comment that 'chronic, low-level radiation exposure may have more generalised carcinogenic effects than have been observed in most previous investigations'.[29] Such effects may only become apparent with extended follow-up in depth and over time. While further cases of multiple myeloma could also have been overlooked in the NRPB's control sample, the comparison between the NRPB and our own ascertainment exercises suggest that such extended follow-up will have to use the full range of standard detection strategies rather than relying solely on database linkages. It is vital that this issue is clearly resolved, both to allow adequate compensation for those who may be suffering from the aftermath of participation in the UK nuclear tests and to avoid any possibility of similar risks to others in the future. Hago Zeeb of Bielefeld, who reviewed the NRPB paper, and Dudley Goodhead of the Medical Research Council, who resigned from the Advisory Committee due to pressure of work before these issues were raised, regard the criticism of the NRPB study as important and valid. They propose that the new evidence should be further considered, and perhaps another study carried out before the matter can be regarded as cleared up.[30] Keith Baverstock of WHO notes the disagreement on the ascertainment of myeloma, and says that the NRPB report seems unlikely to resolve the controversy or the very real concerns of the test veterans. He comments that in the Australian tests there could have been a higher risk of internal radiation from fallout, which would not have been recorded by film badges.[31]

NOTES

1. L.E. Peterson and S. Abrahamson, *Effects of Ionizing Radiation Atomic Bomb Survivors and their Children (1945–1995)* (Washington: Joseph Henry Press, 1998), p.x.
2. S.R. Roff, 'Mortality and Morbidity of Members of the British Nuclear Tests Veterans Association and the New Zealand Nuclear Tests Veterans Association and their Families', *Medicine, Conflict and Survival*, Vol.15 Suppl.I (1999).
3. N.S. Shilnikova *et al.*, 'Mortality Among Workers With Chronic Radiation Sickness', *Health Physics*, Vol.71, No.1 (1996), pp.86–9.
4. N.A. Koshurnikova *et al.*, 'Mortality Among Personnel Who Worked at the Mayak Complex in the First Years of its Operation', *Health Physics*, Vol.71, No.1 (1996), pp.90–93; N.D. Okladnikova *et al.*, 'Occupational Diseases from Radiation Exposure at the First Nuclear Plant in the USSR', *Science of the Total Environment*, Vol.142, Nos.1–2 (1994), pp.9–17.

5. S. Thaul (ed.), *The Five Series Study: Mortality of Military Participants in U.S. Nuclear Weapons Tests* (Washington: National Academy Press Institute of Medicine, 2000), p.75.
6. War Pensions Agency, *Policy Statement on Claims for Ionising Radiation Related Conditions* (London: WPA, 2001). Original emphasis.
7. *Hansard, House of Commons* (1 July 1997), Col.71.
8. G. Hextall, Letter to Michael Wills MP (15 June 1998).
9. Ministry of Defence, *Note on Exposure to Background Ionising Radiations at Christmas Island 1956–64* (London: Ministry of Defence, 1986).
10. S.C. Darby *et al.*, *Mortality and Cancer Incidence in UK Participants in UK Atmospheric Nuclear Weapons Tests and Experimental Programmes*, Document NRPB-R214 (Didcot: National Radiological Protection Board, 1988), p.37; idem, *Mortality and Cancer Incidence 1952–1990 in UK Participants in the UK Atmospheric Nuclear Weapons Tests and Experimental Programmes*, Document NRPB-R266 (Didcot: National Radiological Protection Board, 1993), p.16.
11. J. Spellar, Letter to Lord Ashley of Stoke (11 July 1997).
12. L. Moonie, Letter to Michael Ancram QC MP (24 Oct. 2001).
13. Press release (London: Ministry of Defence, 25 Feb. 1999).
14. Roff, 'Mortality and Morbidity of Members of the British Nuclear Tests Veterans Association'.
15. J. Kaldor, 'Report to the Minister Assisting the Minister for Defence on Recent Studies of Nuclear Test Veterans (Sydney: University of New South Wales, 1999).
16. J.D. Boice, 'Techniques for Detecting and Determining Risks from Low-level Radiation', *American Journal of Forensic Medicine and Pathology*, Vol.1, No.4 (1980), pp.318–23.
17. Thaul (ed.), *The Five Series Study*, p.75.
18. Ibid., p.19.
19. A list of sources is available from the author. Please email s.l.roff@dundee.ac.uk.
20. Darby *et al.*, *Mortality and Cancer Incidence in UK Participants*, p.37.
21. N. MacDonald *et al.*, 'A Comparison of National Cancer Registry and Direct Follow-up in the Ascertainment of Ovarian Cancer', *British Journal of Cancer*, Vol.80, No.11 (1999), pp.1826–7.
22. H.O. Dickinson *et al.*, 'How Complete and Accurate are Cancer Registrations Notified in the National Health Service Central Register for England and Wales?', *Journal of Epidemiology and Community Health*, Vol.55, No.6 (2001), pp.414–22.
23. Darby *et al.*, *Mortality and Cancer Incidence in UK Participants*, p.3.
24. C.R. Muirhead *et al.*, 'Follow Up of Mortality and Incidence of Cancer 1952–98 in Men from the UK Who Participated in the UK's Atmospheric Nuclear Weapon Tests and Experimental Programmes', *Occupational and Environmental Medicine*, Vol.60, No.3 (2003), pp.165–72.
25. Darby *et al.*, *Mortality and Cancer Incidence 1952–1990*, p.16.
26. Ibid., p.4.
27. Darby *et al.*, *Mortality and Cancer Incidence in UK Participants*, p.35.
28. B. Ritz, H. Morgenstern and J. Moncau, 'Age at Exposure Modifies the Effects of Low-Level Ionizing Radiation on Cancer Mortality in an Occupation Cohort', *Epidemiology*, Vol.10, No.2 (1999), pp.135–40.
29. B. Ritz, H. Morgenstern, J. Froines and B.B. Young, 'Effects of Exposure to External Ionizing Radiation on Cancer Mortality in Nuclear Workers Monitored for Radiation at Rocketdyne/Atomics International', *American Journal of Industrial Medicine*, Vol.35, No.1 (1999), pp.21–31.
30. Alan Rimmer, personal communication, 19 March 2003.
31. K. Baverstock, 'The 2003 NRPB Report on UK Nuclear-test Veterans', *Lancet*, Vol.361 (2003), pp.1759–60.

Health Effects at Home

DOUGLAS HOLDSTOCK

It has been claimed that not only did United States and United Kingdom nuclear weapons prevent a third World War, but that there were no NATO/Warsaw Pact combat-related deaths. Yet work on nuclear weapons involves handling radioactive materials and it was known from the lives of early radiologists and radiation workers (including Marie Curie) that radiation exposure can be lethal. Any survey of the history of nuclear weapons should therefore include a critical look at the health consequences of the nuclear-weapons programme itself.

The UK programme was far less extensive than those of the United States and the then Soviet Union. There is evidence of massive radioactive contamination around nuclear-weapons facilities in both countries,[1] which must have resulted in many cancers and perhaps birth defects. Earlier chapters discuss the health effects of the UK programme in Australia (Chapter 7) and on test veterans (Chapter 9), but there could also have been direct harm at home. This chapter examines possible health effects in two areas, around Sellafield (formerly Windscale) in Cumbria and around Aldermaston and Burghfield in West Berkshire (Introduction), with specific reference to the 1957 explosion at Windscale (as it was then known) and to the clusters of childhood leukaemia around Sellafield and in West Berkshire.

THE WINDSCALE FIRE AND ITS CONSEQUENCES

The two reactors (Piles 1 and 2) on the Windscale site, which began operating in 1950 and 1951 respectively, were designed to generate plutonium from uranium for the first UK test programme (Appendix 2).[2] The design installation and early operation of the plant took place far more rapidly, because of the urgency that the test programme was given, than would have been the case for a commercial project. Its operation was plagued with technical problems, particularly the accumulation of energy in the graphite moderator ('Wigner energy'),[3] which required periodic shutdown of the reactors. During one of these shutdowns, from 7 October 1957, fire broke out in Pile 1 and was not extinguished until 11 October. Estimates of the amount of radioactivity released to the environment have varied, ranging from 20,000–32,000 curies in the units of the time, 7.4 – 11.8 × 10^{14} becquerels in today's units, principally iodine-131 with a half-life of eight days. The escapes were almost all volatile; particulates such as uranium and plutonium were trapped by a filter at the top of the stack above the pile. Pile 1 remains sealed to this day; Pile 2 was shut down and never operated again.

HEALTH EFFECTS

The principal health risk was recognized to be from the radio-iodine release on the thyroid gland, particularly of young children, and the major health response was to prevent milk produced in the surrounding area from entering the food chain. Opinions differ as to whether this was carried out as expeditiously as possible or over a sufficient area, and therefore as to the possible health consequences. Early claims were that there would be no adverse effects outside the site, but subsequent estimates ranged up to 250 non-fatal cancer cases and a maximum of 100 cancer deaths, with up to ten hereditary deaths.[4] All these estimates emphasize that the likely numbers are lower, spread over many years and could be zero.

The high proportion of non-fatal cancers assumes that the majority would be thyroid cancer, which is usually curable, though later experiences after the Chernobyl accident shows that radiation-induced thyroid cancer in children occurs sooner after exposure and is more aggressive than previously realized. A relatively localized increase in thyroid cancer deaths might just have been detectable if today's standards of cancer registration were in place; the true effect, if any, will probably never be known.

LEUKAEMIA CLUSTERS

Reprocessing of spent nuclear fuel to extract plutonium at Sellafield, as it became known soon after the 1957 fire, was at first an integral part of its contribution to the UK nuclear-weapons programme, subsequently extended to cover spent fuel from the civil nuclear power programme. This contributed (and contributes) to a large extent to the emissions of radioactive material from Sellafield. The discharges have been the subject of continued controversy. They have been mostly within the legally permitted discharges for the time, though on several occasions accidental discharges (not accurately quantified) may have exceeded today's limits.

The most noteworthy of these was in November 1983, when up to 4,500 curies (1.6 × 10^{14} becquerels) of radioactive waste was discharged in error from a storage tank into the sea.[5] This led to the beach nearby being closed for six months.

There was therefore considerable concern when it was reported (not in the medical or scientific press, but by Yorkshire Television) that there was an increased rate of childhood leukaemia and the related disorder non-Hodgkin's lymphoma around Sellafield. The finding was, though, soon officially confirmed;[6] subsequently similar clusters have been identified in West Berkshire, in an area incorporating the Royal Ordnance Factory at Burghfield and the AWRE at Aldermaston, around the civil reprocessing plant and prototype fast reactor at Dounreay in Caithness, Scotland and around Cap de la Hague, the French equivalent of Sellafield. The controversy then and since has been over the role of radiation in causing these clusters.

RADIATION AND CANCER

After a few years, follow-up of the survivors of the Hiroshima and Nagasaki atom-bombings revealed a raised incidence of acute leukaemia and several other malignancies, including thyroid, breast and lung cancer. Thyroid cancer in children has increased significantly in the high fallout area from the Chernobyl explosion. Both of these followed relatively acute exposure to high doses of radiation, principally external gamma rays and neutrons in Japan and ingested radio-iodine in Belarus. Chronic exposure to low-dose radiation is also now accepted as carcinogenic; for example, radon is responsible for a proportion of domestic lung cancer in non-smokers.

Attempts have been made to quantify the cancer risk from radiation exposure. For obvious reasons, controlled studies on humans are not available and estimates have been based on extrapolations from observations of atom-bomb survivors. Over time there has been a steady reduction in the accepted exposures of survivors, based on estimates of the degree of shielding, quality of radiation and biological factors, such as age at time of exposure.[7] It is not known how far the effects of acute irradiation can be extrapolated to chronic exposure and little information is available on the specific effects of internal radio-isotopes, but it is now accepted that for regulatory purposes there is no threshold, that is, no absolutely safe dose of radiation.

LEUKAEMIA AND ITS CAUSES

Leukaemia is a cancer of the white-blood-cell producing cells of the bone marrow and lymph nodes, in which the excess white cells spill over into the bloodstream; the lymphomas are cancers of lymphoid tissue without excess of white cells in the peripheral blood. Leukaemias are classified into acute and chronic, depending on the rapidity of onset and severity and which cell series is affected. Childhood leukaemia is most often acute lymphoblastic – blasts are very immature cells. Untreated, it is rapidly fatal (Plate 5), but a significant proportion of cases can now be apparently cured by intensive, but highly unpleasant, chemotherapy.

All cancers are now thought to be clones of a single rogue mutation progenitor cell, which has escaped from normal control by somatic mutation, but do not become clinically evident until 1 billion or more cells have formed. This process usually takes years and several stages.[8] Childhood acute leukaemia is unusual in that as few as two stages may be needed. The first stage, which may occur during foetal life, is often a chromosomal translocation; the second is thought to be in some way related to exposure to infection (see below). Radiation and toxic chemicals (for example, benzene) are among the recognized causes of leukaemia, though in the majority of cases no cause can be identified. Leukaemia in animals is commonly due to specific viruses, but no virus has been identified as a cause of human leukaemia.[9] Genetic factors may predispose to leukaemia in several ways.

With respect to the leukaemia clusters, it is regarded as unlikely that radiation exposure is the sole direct cause. The amount, distribution and type of radioactive discharges from the various sites have been exhaustively studied and the radiation exposures are far too low on standard measures to cause the observed effects. A variant of the radiation hypothesis, which attracted considerable attention, is that of pre-conceptual parental irradiation. A careful study proposed that the fathers of affected children in the Sellafield cluster had received significantly higher exposures in the months before the later-affected child was conceived,[10] although this finding is currently regarded as due to chance.[11]

The alternative proposed is that the clusters are related in some way to infection, perhaps related to population mixing.[12] This could takes two forms, either exposure to an infection brought in from outside, or to an aberrant immunological response to infection. In either case, the infective agent could be an unrecognized pathogen, presumably a virus, or a common agent initiating an uncommon response; so far no agent has been identified. A statistical study of the Sellafield cluster suggests that up to half of the excess cases could be attributable to population mixing.[13]

NEW CONCEPTS IN RADIATION BIOLOGY

Recent work in radiation biology has re-opened the debate on the role of radiation. The 'classical' account of radiation-induced damage is that a particle passes close to a DNA strand and the ionization it induces causes a break, often double-stranded. This may then be corrected by the cellular mechanisms that also repair the frequent changes in DNA that may be spontaneous, for example, caused by oxidants in the cell. If not corrected, these mutants either result in the death of the cell or are transmitted clonally to its progeny, when they may cause mutations or cancer. Small 'targets' are hit apparently at random.

Recently discovered phenomena collectively known as radiation-induced genomic instability present a radically different picture.[14] Genomic instability is caused particularly, though not exclusively, by high linear energy transfer radiation, such as alpha particles. Damage to irradiated cells may not be manifest until several cell divisions after exposure, after which it is transmissible by further cell divisions. The damage can consist of breaks in DNA which can affect both strands, making repair much more difficult, and are more likely to give the resulting clone potentiality for malignant change. They can apparently occur not only in the direct track of the radiation but anywhere in the genome.[15] Radiation can also cause mutations in the so-called 'repeat' sequences of DNA (micro- and mini-satellites),[16] which are part of DNA not in specific genes, but perhaps having a controlling effect on nearby genes. The relationship of repeat sequences to human disease is uncertain, but some believe that such mutations could affect susceptibility to cancer.

Genomic instability can also occur in cells not directly traversed by radiation – the 'bystander' effect. Radiation-induced mutations in repeat sequences of germ lines (ova and sperm) can be transmitted to later generations; the offspring of mice treated with plutonium are at greater risk of leukaemia in response to chemicals or radiation.[17]

Collectively, these phenomena suggest that the radiation risk, from internal alpha particles in particular, could be significantly greater than previously recognized.[18] They also raise the possibility that the effect of pre-conceptual irradiation of parents, particularly fathers, should be reconsidered.

A UNIFYING HYPOTHESIS

The epidemiological evidence for an infective agent acting through population mixing of course remains strong, but the roles of radiation and infection are not mutually exclusive. In the two-stage development of childhood leukaemia, radiation could be the initiating effect, perhaps transmitted from an exposed father and with its effect enhanced by genomic instability, and the infective agent could be responsible for the second or promoting stage. In fact, both could be necessary; such interaction is now well recognized in clinical medicine. If two unrelated medications are given together in normal dosage, serious and unexpected, even fatal, side-effects may occur, which are not seen from either agent alone.

The Committee on Medical Aspects of Radiation in the Environment has been investigating the leukaemia clusters for several years. It accepts their reality, agrees that on conventional measures radiation dose is too small to cause them and accepts that there is circumstantial evidence for the role of population mixing. A new group, the Committee Examining Radiation Risks from Internal Emitters, based in the Department for Environment, Food and Rural Affairs, has now been set up and has been asked to consider the possibility that alpha-emissions from environmental polonium-210 or plutonium-239 (which after inhalation can migrate to bone or testis) could through genomic instability allow an infective agent that does not normally do so to initiate leukaemia.

IMPLICATIONS

Much more will be learned in the near future on genomic instability and its implications and work on the genome of leukaemia sufferers may identify an infective agent – though more than one could be responsible. Meanwhile, if the UK government decides not to replace Trident, production of military plutonium need not resume and the civil nuclear power programme (which could still continue after the recent governmental energy review) can manage on low-enriched uranium. Reprocessing to produce plutonium, which is responsible for a large proportion of the radioactive emissions from Sellafield, can cease. Indeed, it is hard to see how the UK's commitment under the Oslo–Paris agreement to reduce emissions from Sellafield to 'near zero' can be achieved in any other way.

Finally, a cynic might point out that the debate over the role of radiation *versus* infection need never have arisen. Whether either or both is the cause of the leukaemia clusters, these would not have occurred if AWE Aldermaston, the Royal Ordnance Factory at Burghfield and Sellafield had never existed – in other words, if the UK had had no nuclear-weapons programme.

NOTES

I am grateful to Keith Baverstock, Bryan Bridges and Dudley Goodhead for constructive comments on earlier drafts of some of the material in this chapter and to Rosemary Herring and her colleagues at the Education Centre Library, Ashford Hospital, Middlesex for help in obtaining source material.

1. M. Renner, 'Environmental and Health Effects of Weapons Production, Testing and Maintenance', in B.S. Levy and V.W. Sidel (eds.), *War and Public Health* (New York and Oxford: Oxford University Press, 1997), pp.126–33.
2. L. Arnold, *Windscale 1957: Anatomy of a Nuclear Accident* (Dublin: Macmillan Academic and Professional, 1992), pp.1–42.
3. Ibid., pp.31–4.
4. Ibid., pp.187–8.
5. H. Bolter, *Inside Sellafield* (London: Quartet Books, 1996), pp.97–106.
6. Independent Advisory Group, *Investigation of the Possible Increased Incidence of Cancer in West Cumbria*, The Black Report (London: HMSO, 1984).
7. Arnold, *Windscale 1957*, passim.
8. M. Greaves, *Cancer: The Evolutionary Legacy* (Oxford: Oxford University Press, 2000).
9. M. Greaves, 'Childhood Leukaemia', *British Medical Journal*, Vol.324 (2002), pp.283–7.
10. M.J. Gardner *et al.*, 'Results of Case-Control Study of Leukaemia and Lymphoma among Young People near Sellafield Nuclear Plant in West Cumbria', *British Medical Journal*, Vol.300 (1990), pp.423–9.
11. R. Doll *et al.*, 'Paternal Exposure Not to Blame', *Nature*, Vol.367 (1994), pp.678–80.
12. L.J. Kinlen, 'Epidemiological Evidence for an Infective Basis in Childhood Leukaemia', *British Journal of Cancer*, Vol.71 (1995), pp.1–5.
13. H.O. Dickinson and L. Parker, 'Quantitating the Effect of Population Mixing on Childhood Leukaemia', *British Journal of Cancer*, Vol.81 (1999), pp.144–51.
14. E.G. Wright, 'Inducible Genomic Instability: New Insights into the Biological Effects of Ionizing Radiation', *Medicine, Conflict and Survival*, Vol.16, No.1 (2000), pp.117–30.
15. K. Baverstock, 'Radiation-Induced Genomic Instability: A Paradigm-Breaking Phenomenon and its Relevance to Environmentally Induced Cancer', *Mutation Research*, Vol.454 (2000), pp.89–109.
16. B.A. Bridges, 'Radiation and Germline Mutation at Repeat Sequences: Are We in the Middle of a Paradigm Shift?', *Radiation Research*, Vol.156 (2001), pp.631–41.
17. B.I. Lord *et al.*, 'Induction of Lympho-Haemopoietic Malignancy: Impact of Preconception Paternal Irradiation', *International Journal of Radiation Biology*, Vol.74 (1998), pp.721–8.
18. H. Zhou *et al.*, 'Radiation Risk to Low Fluence of α Particles may be Greater than We Thought', *Proceedings of the National Academy of Sciences*, Vol.98 (2001), pp.14410–15.

Nuclear Terrorism: Today's Nuclear Threat

FRANK BARNABY

> Nothing could have anything like the impact of a nuclear explosion, which could be more physically damaging, psychologically shocking, and politically disruptive than any event since World War II. Although the casualties from a single act of nuclear terrorism might not match those of a nuclear war, they would still dwarf other forms of terrorism by many orders of magnitude and could easily exceed those of most conventional wars.[1]

The terrorist attacks on New York and Washington on 11 September 2001 brought home the willingness of a new breed of terrorists, now sometimes called 'new terrorists', to kill as many people as possible and cause the maximum amount of social and economic disruption. To discuss future terrorism it is useful and important to distinguish between the 'old' terrorists, who are likely to continue with 'business as usual', using conventional weapons to 'kill one and frighten thousands', and the 'new terrorists', who aim to 'kill thousands to frighten the hemisphere' with WMDs.

Different types of 'old' terrorism can be identified:

- Political terrorism, usually with separatist or nationalist aims;
- Terrorism by far right- and left-wing political groups;
- Terrorism by single-issue groups, such as right-to-lifers and radical environmentalists; and
- Terrorism by an individual.

Current trends suggest that political terrorism with separatist or nationalist aims is likely to decrease in the future and terrorism by single-issue groups is likely to remain roughly constant, but the other types of terrorism are likely to increase.

THE NEW TERRORISM AND
WEAPONS OF MASS DESTRUCTION

Terrorist actions by the 'new' terrorists – religious fundamentalists, particularly Islamic Fundamentalist groups and American Christian white supremacists – are likely to become increasingly frequent and violent. Whereas secular terrorists are likely to exercise constraint, and to avoid killing many when killing a few suits their purposes, religious fundamentalists are unlikely to feel any moral constraint about killing very large numbers of people.

In fact, mass killing by WMDs may fit well into the Armageddon and apocalyptic visions of some religious groups, some of which believe that they are under divine instruction to maximize killing and destruction. The likelihood that terrorist violence by fundamentalist groups will escalate to indiscriminate mass killing is the greatest future terrorist risk, the main consequence of increasing religious terror and decreasing radical political terror.

The best way the new terrorists can achieve their objective is to use a WMD. There is, therefore, clearly a danger, some would say an inevitability, that new terrorists will acquire, or develop and fabricate, and use WMDs – chemical, biological or nuclear.

Recent experience – for example, the use of nerve agents by the *Aum Shinrikyo* in Tokyo and of anthrax in the United States – shows that biological and chemical weapons are unpredictable and difficult to use effectively, that is, to cause a large number of casualties. Effective dispersal of both biological and chemical weapons is very difficult, so these weapons may not well serve the purposes of the new terrorists.

To fulfil their aims, therefore, I believe that future new terrorists are more likely to make nuclear attacks; these are not only more likely to succeed, but their Armageddon nature is likely to appeal to fundamentalists. Nuclear terrorism may be the most likely future use of nuclear explosives, replacing the spread of nuclear weapons to countries (nuclear-weapon proliferation) as perhaps the most serious threat to national security. The success of recent attacks against American targets indicates that nuclear weapons do not deter terrorism by protecting countries armed with nuclear weapons. Nuclear deterrence has no role in dealing with the new terrorism.

NUCLEAR TERRORISM

Nuclear terrorist groups may become involved in several activities:

- Stealing or otherwise acquiring fissile material and fabricating and detonating a primitive nuclear explosive;
- Making and detonating a radiological weapon to spread radioactive material;

- Attacking a nuclear-power reactor to disseminate radioactivity;
- Attacking the high-level radioactive waste tanks at reprocessing plants to spread the radioactivity contained within;
- Attacking a plutonium store to spread the plutonium contained within;
- Stealing or otherwise acquiring a nuclear weapon from the arsenal of a nuclear-weapon power and detonating it; and/or
- Attacking, sabotaging or hijacking a transporter of nuclear weapons or nuclear materials.

All these actions have the potential to cause large numbers of deaths.

Of these possibilities, terrorists will probably prefer to set off a nuclear explosive, perhaps using a stolen nuclear weapon or, more likely, a nuclear explosive fabricated by them from acquired fissile material. Terrorists would be satisfied with a nuclear explosive device that is far less sophisticated than the types of nuclear weapons demanded by the military. What is the risk that terrorists will fabricate and use a primitive nuclear explosive?

ACQUIRING FISSILE MATERIAL

As plutonium and highly-enriched uranium become more available world-wide, it is increasingly possible for a terrorist group to steal, or otherwise illegally acquire, civil or military fissile material that could be used to fabricate a nuclear explosive device. The group could then detonate, or threaten to detonate, its nuclear explosive. Large amounts of fissile material exist.

Terrorist groups may find it easiest to acquire plutonium produced in civil reprocessing plants. This can be used in nuclear weapons,[2] and has been tested by both the United States[3] and the United Kingdom.[4] About 300 tonnes of civil plutonium has been separated, about 80 tonnes in France, 56 tonnes in Japan, 40 tonnes each in Germany and Russia and smaller amounts in seven other countries.[5] The total could rise to about 550 tonnes by 2010.[6]

HEU, though easier for terrorists to use (see below), may be more difficult to acquire. There are about 1,900 tonnes of HEU in the world, about 1,000 tonnes in Russia and 700 tonnes in the US; the UK has about 15 tonnes. Almost all this is military; only about 19 per cent civil, used mainly as fuel for research reactors.[7] HEU can be more easily disposed of by mixing with natural or depleted uranium as low-enriched uranium, which can be used as reactor fuel but not as a nuclear explosive.

Of particular concern is the growing trade in civil MOX nuclear fuel. The plutonium oxide is produced in reprocessing plants by separating it from spent nuclear-power reactor fuel elements. If terrorists acquire MOX fuel, they could relatively easily remove the plutonium oxide from it chemically and use it to fabricate nuclear weapons. The global trade in MOX therefore increases the risk of nuclear terrorism.

Concern about the theft of fissile materials has been considerably enhanced by recent incidents of the smuggling of such materials from Russia. In December 1994 the Czech authorities seized three kilograms of HEU; security police were reported to have confiscated nearly 40 kilograms of weapons-grade uranium in December 1993 in Odessa in the Ukraine; more than 400 grammes of weapons-grade plutonium were seized in Germany in 1994. These and other smuggling incidents, which are almost certainly the tip of an iceberg, suggest that a significant black-market in fissile materials exists. If significant production of MOX fuel occurs at Sellafield, this would become a target for theft, particularly if it is traded abroad, as with Japan. Such possibilities have attracted attention with recent concern over whether Iraq could obtain nuclear-weapons capability.[8]

THE FISSION PROCESS

A nuclear explosion relies on producing a nuclear fission chain reaction to obtain nuclear energy. A fission chain reaction can be produced and sustained using one of two fissile isotopes, plutonium-239 and uranium-235. These nuclei undergo fission when they absorb (capture) a neutron. A nuclear explosive can only be fabricated from one of these isotopes.

When a uranium-235 nucleus captures a neutron, a nucleus of the isotope uranium-236 is formed. This is very unstable and rapidly splits (fissions) into nuclei of elements of medium atomic numbers, called fission products, generally radioactive. Similarly, if a plutonium-239 nucleus captures a neutron, plutonium-240 is formed which is very unstable and rapidly fissions.

In addition to the fission products, neutrons are emitted during the fission process – on average, between two and three neutrons are emitted – and energy is given off. The fission process can be represented by:

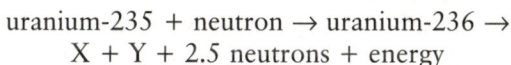

$$\text{uranium-235} + \text{neutron} \rightarrow \text{uranium-236} \rightarrow$$
$$X + Y + 2.5 \text{ neutrons} + \text{energy}$$

Or, where X and Y are fission products:

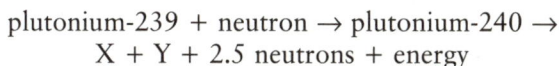

$$\text{plutonium-239} + \text{neutron} \rightarrow \text{plutonium-240} \rightarrow$$
$$X + Y + 2.5 \text{ neutrons} + \text{energy}$$

Energy is released during fission because the masses of the fission products (X and Y) and the fission neutrons is less than the mass of the uranium-236 nucleus. By Einstein's famous equation ($E = Mc^2$) the extra mass becomes energy; c, the velocity of light, is a huge number and, therefore, the amount of energy given off is very large.

THE CRITICAL MASS

If at least one of the neutrons produced when a nucleus undergoes fission produces the fission of another nucleus, a fission chain reaction is produced and maintained for a long enough time to produce an adequate explosion. The minimum mass of a fissile material that can sustain a nuclear fission chain reaction is called the critical mass.

If a mass of plutonium-239 or uranium-235 is increased above the critical level, the number of neutrons produced by fission builds up and considerably more fissions occur in each successive generation of fission. When the rate of production of fissile neutrons exceeds all neutron losses, a supercritical mass is created and a rapid and uncontrollable increase in the number of neutrons within the mass of fissile material occurs, producing enough energy to cause a nuclear explosion.

DESIGNING A PRIMITIVE NUCLEAR EXPLOSIVE

Terrorist groups are likely to be satisfied with a nuclear explosive device that is far less sophisticated than the types of nuclear weapons demanded by the military. The military demand that their nuclear weapons are highly reliable and explode with an explosive yield that can be accurately predicted; a terrorist group would be much less demanding and satisfied with a relatively unsophisticated device, much easier to design and fabricate.

Three designs of crude nuclear explosives would be adequate for most purposes of a terrorist group intent on nuclear terrorism. The first is a gun-type nuclear explosive device using HEU as the fissile material. This is the simplest crude device to design and construct and the one most likely to produce a powerful nuclear explosion.

The second is an implosion-type nuclear explosive device using a solid sphere of plutonium metal as the fissile material – a crude version of the atomic bomb that destroyed Nagasaki. This is the most difficult of the three to design and construct, but within the capabilities of a significantly large terrorist group.

The third, an implosion-type device using plutonium oxide as the fissile material, is perhaps the most likely nuclear device to be constructed by terrorists because of the increasing and widespread availability of plutonium oxide. It may be the most attractive of the three designs to terrorists because of the threat of the widespread dispersion of large amounts of plutonium even if the device produces no nuclear explosion.

126

Using Highly-Enriched Uranium

Luis Alvarez, a nuclear-weapon physicist, has emphasized the ease of constructing a nuclear explosive with HEU:

> With modern weapons-grade uranium, the background neutron rate is so low that terrorists, if they have such material, would have a good chance of setting off a high-yield explosion simply by dropping one half of the material onto the other half. Most people seem unaware that if separated highly-enriched uranium is at hand it's a trivial job to set off a nuclear explosion ... even a high school kid could make a bomb in short order.[9]

A primitive gun-type weapon could comprise a cylindrical 'barrel' 50 centimetres in length and eight centimetres in diameter, with a 40-kilogram mass of 90 per cent uranium-235 HEU at the bottom. This would be hollowed-out to the shape of a 15-kilogram mass of HEU at the top, with a high-explosive charge above it to be detonated electronically. The whole device could weigh about 300 kilograms, transportable by, and detonated in, an ordinary van.

Such a weapon could explode with the equivalent of several hundred, perhaps several thousand, tonnes of TNT. For comparison, the largest conventional bomb used in the Second World War, the 'earthquake bomb', contained about ten tonnes of TNT. The bomb used by Timothy McVeigh against the Federal Building in Oklahoma weighed about three tonnes.

Using Plutonium

The critical mass of crystalline plutonium oxide is about 35 kilograms, metallic reactor-grade plutonium is about 13 kilograms.[10] A sphere of the fissile material would be placed in the centre of a spherical shape of about 200 kilograms conventional high explosive, such as Semtex. If it were also surrounded by a tamper/reflector of beryllium or uranium the critical mass would be smaller but the explosive yield greater.

Such a device would have a radius of around 40 centimetres. It would be surrounded by a large number of detonators to be fired simultaneously by an electronic circuit triggered by a timer or a remote radio signal. It might explode with a power of a few tens to hundreds of tonnes of TNT, enough to devastate a city centre (see below). Plate 6 shows an artist's impression of what Trafalgar Square, London might look like after an explosion which only 'fizzled'. Even if there were no nuclear explosion and the plutonium was only scattered, it would be widely dispersed – as small particles if an incendiary material were mixed with the high explosive.

If inhaled, such material is very likely to cause lung cancer. The half-life of plutonium-239 is 24,000 years; Chapter 8 shows the difficulty of cleaning-up a remote area. A city centre so attacked could be uninhabitable for months or years and the initial explosion would cause mass panic over a much wider area.

EFFECTS OF A PRIMITIVE NUCLEAR EXPLOSION

100-Tonne Explosion

A 100-tonne nuclear explosion would produce a crater about 30 metres across. The lethal area for prompt radiation after such an explosion (1.2 square kilometres) is larger than that for blast (0.4 square kilometre) or heat (0.1 square kilometre). Anyone in the open within 600 metres would probably be killed by these direct effects.[11] For an explosion in Trafalgar Square, London the area would extend from Cambridge Circus to the Foreign and Commonwealth Office in Whitehall. Other deaths would be caused by buildings collapsing or debris falling and by fires from broken gas pipes or petrol in cars, the effects of fires could exceed those from the direct effects of heat. Many square kilometres (in this example, most of central London) would be contaminated by radioactive fallout.

Such an explosion would paralyze the emergency services. Many seriously injured would die from lack of care, from delays to ambulances and releasing those trapped in buildings. In the UK there are only a few hundred burns beds in the whole National Health Service. Panic could effect even trained emergency personnel, especially from awareness of radioactive fallout.

One-Kiloton Explosion

Thermal radiation from an explosion of this size would kill within one minute those outside or near windows up to 200 metres away. Blast would kill up to 800 metres away, prompt radiation up to one kilometre (in this example, all of Soho, the Royal National Theatre and Westminster Abbey). Heat injuries would extend to one kilometre and blast to two kilometres (including the Elephant and Castle, Euston and Victoria stations – Map 2).

The nuclear electronic pulse would damage communications equipment out to two kilometres and electronic equipment to ten kilometres (Stratford, Streatham and Willesden). This would have severe consequences for fire and police services and hospitals.

Assuming a 24-kilometres/hour wind, fallout would cause acute radiation sickness to those exposed in the open in a cigar-shaped area ten kilometres long and up to two kilometres wide. The risk of cancer long-term would extend about 80 kilometres downwind (with the prevailing south-westerly wind, almost to Colchester). Plutonium would be widely dispersed; depending on how uniformly it was distributed, an even larger area could, according to international regulations, need to be evacuated and decontaminated.

PREVENTION

In the short-term, vital measures against nuclear (and other) terrorism include efficient protection of key nuclear (and biological and chemical) materials and facilities, with effective intelligence on the activities of terrorist groups capable of such actions. So far as nuclear terrorism is concerned, special attention should be given to the control of plutonium. This protection must take into account the relatively small amounts of plutonium needed to make a nuclear explosive.

Society may decide that the terrorist risk of acquiring and using a nuclear explosive, and the awesome consequences of such use, are such that some nuclear activities should be given up. An obvious example is the reprocessing of spent nuclear-power reactor fuel to separate the plutonium from it and the use of this plutonium to produce MOX fuel for nuclear reactors. The steps of chemically separating the plutonium oxide from uranium oxide in MOX, converting the oxide into plutonium metal and assembling the metal or plutonium oxide together with conventional explosive to produce a nuclear explosion are not technologically demanding and do not require materials from specialist suppliers. The information required to carry out these operations is freely available in the open literature.

None of the concepts involved in understanding how to separate the plutonium are difficult; a second-year undergraduate would be able to devise a suitable procedure by reading standard reference works, consulting the open literature in scientific journals and searching the internet. A small number, three or so, of people with appropriate skills could separate the plutonium from MOX and design and fabricate a crude nuclear explosive. All the nuclear-physics data needed to design a crude nuclear explosive device are available in the open literature.

The storage and fabrication of MOX fuel assemblies, their transportation and storage at conventional nuclear-power stations on a scale currently envisaged by the nuclear industry will be extremely difficult to safeguard and protect. The risk of diversion or theft of MOX fuel by terrorist groups is an alarming possibility. The risk is thought by many to be great enough to justify the argument that the reprocessing of spent nuclear reactor fuel and the production and use of MOX fuel should be stopped.

But in the long run, the best, and perhaps the only, way to defeat nuclear – and other – terrorism is to remove people's justified grievances and to improve their social welfare.[12]

NOTES

1. J. Despres, 'Intelligence and the Prevention of Nuclear Terrorism', in P. Leventhal and Y. Alexander (eds.), *Preventing Nuclear Terrorism* (Boston, MA: Lexington Books, 1987), p.322.
2. R.W. Selden, *Reactor Plutonium and Nuclear Explosives* (Berkeley, CA: Lawrence Livermore Laboratory, 1976).
3. J.L. Bloom, *Plutonium Grade and the Risk of Nuclear Weapons Proliferation*, Congressional Research Service Report No.85-145S (Washington DC: Library of Congress, 1985).
4. L. Arnold, *A Very Special Relationship: British Atomic Weapon Tests in Australia* (London: HMSO, 1987), Chapter 4, pp.61–6.
5. P. Leventhal, 'Fissile Materials and Tritium: How to Verify a Comprehensive Production and Safeguard All Stocks', Presentation at International Network of Engineers and Scientists Against Proliferation Seminar, Geneva, 29–30 June 1995.
6. D. Albright, F. Berkhout and W. Walker, *Plutonium and Highly Enriched Uranium 1996: World Inventories, Capabilities and Policies* (Oxford: Oxford University Press for Stockholm International Peace Research Institute, 1997).
7. Ibid.
8. C.J. Mark, *Some Remarks on Iraq's Possible Nuclear Weapon Capability in Light of Some of the Known Facts Concerning Nuclear Weapons* (Washington DC: Nuclear Control Institute, 1991).
9. W. Alvarez, 'The Nuclear Threat', at http://www.nci.org/new/about-nci.htm.
10. A.B. Lovins, 'Nuclear Weapons and Power-reactor Plutonium', *Nature*, No.283 (1990), pp.817–23 (typographical correction, No.284 [1990], p.190).
11. J. Rotblat, *Nuclear Radiation in Warfare* (London: Taylor and Francis, 1981).
12. F. Barnaby, *The New Terrorism: A 21st Century Biological, Chemical and Nuclear Threat* (Oxford: Oxford Research Group, 2001), pp.66–70, 75.

An End to British Nuclear Weapons?

R.S. PEASE

Fifty years ago the first British nuclear weapon, a plutonium bomb with an estimated yield of 25 kilotons of TNT equivalent, was tested on the Monte Bello islands off the north-west coast of Australia (Map 1). The test was the culmination of extraordinary efforts by the British government to acquire what it perceived to be both a decisive military weapon and an assertion of national independence.

In the 1980s the number of United Kingdom nuclear weapons grew to about 350 warheads deployed on aircraft, missiles and ships; it is now reduced to somewhat less than 200 warheads, all deployed on submarine-borne Trident missiles (Appendix 1).

In 1995 a British Pugwash Group report concluded that even at the height of the cold war, Britain's nuclear weapons had no detectable influence on the course of events: no allied country depended on them, not even the Commonwealth countries that assisted their development; no enemy appears to have been deterred by them; none of the UK wars was lost or won by them; and their actual use by the UK would invite nuclear counter-attack terminally disastrous to the UK.[1]

The conclusion that Britain could dispense forthwith with its nuclear weapons was (and is) based on the uselessness of the weapons during the entire 50 years since the Monte Bello test. However, the 1995 recommendation for a UK initiative to secure multilateral nuclear disarmament has not been realized and indeed looks to be improbable in the current international climate.

This chapter addresses the question of eliminating British nuclear weapons in the twenty-first century. It does so against a background where all the main political parties and a large fraction of public opinion in Britain still support the retention of Trident nuclear weapons, at least as long as there are other nuclear-armed nations. Consequently, the principal policy options considered are within this constraint. One of these – for the UK to announce now that it will not build a nuclear successor to the Trident system – is examined in more detail.

BRITAIN'S NUCLEAR WEAPONS

Four UK-built submarines each carry up to 16 Trident D-5 missiles, purchased from America. Each missile is armed with up to eight independently-targeted warheads. These UK-designed and built warheads have a yield believed to be about 100 kilotons. The number of warheads mounted on each missile varies and can be as few as one. Each submarine will deploy 48 warheads, a voluntary restraint, and the stockpile is fewer than 200 operationally available warheads. At least one submarine is always on patrol, but in a reduced state of alert at a notice to fire measured in days and the missiles are not targeted routinely.[2]

The principal military function of these weapons is to threaten unacceptable damage to the cities and military-industrial complexes of an enemy. The ceiling on deployed warhead numbers was announced without explanation in 1998; it corresponds to the criterion used during the cold war of penetrating the ABM defence system around Moscow. These Trident deterrent weapons could inflict barbaric large-scale damage, but the number is fewer than that needed on its own to secure military defeat of a large country such as Russia.

There are lower yield warheads,[3] probably in the one- to ten-kiloton range, available, or potentially so, by detonating just the primary of the multistage warhead, for 'sub-strategic' use. The sub-strategic function is envisaged for use in circumstances where a demonstration of nuclear capability and determination to use it may avert a full-scale war. Presumably, it could also be used in military applications where the smaller warheads are effective. The aiming accuracy (circular error probable, the radius about the aiming point within which 50 per cent of the warheads fall), is asserted to be 120 metres, but we do not have hard evidence that UK test firings have achieved this. The figure is reminiscent of claims for numerous Second World War bombing devices prior to their actual combat use. The number of warheads deployed on each of the 58 missiles will almost certainly be less than the up-to-eight used in the strategic role. The area devastated by a one-kiloton warhead is estimated to be two square kilometres; for a 100-kiloton warhead, 15 to 30 square kilometres.[4]

INFRASTRUCTURE

The warheads are designed, manufactured and maintained by the AWE, which is run for the MoD by a consortium of companies. No new warhead systems are currently being designed or developed, but AWE is charged with maintaining the capability to do so.

For maintenance of the Trident warheads there is a programme of regular surveillance. In addition, a small number of weapons withdrawn annually from the total deployed, are disassembled and re-manufactured with renewed materials and components. The underlying stewardship programme comprises hydrodynamics, high-powered laser-light studies, materials and especially the ageing-of-material properties. New facilities are to be constructed on the Aldermaston site to replace those at outstations due for closure.[5] The UK maintains strong links with the weapons development and stewardship programmes of the United States, including a now much reduced contribution to the National Ignition Facility under construction at the Lawrence Livermore Laboratory in California.

The UK has declared stocks of military plutonium and HEU of several tonnes each and has large-scale facilities for reprocessing spent fuel from nuclear reactor. Military fissile material is no longer produced; the production reactor at Calder Hall has just closed; that at Chapelcross is now scheduled to close in 2005. The infrastructure and stocks of material can maintain both the Trident warheads and a nuclear warhead capability for the foreseeable future.

The Trident D-5 missiles produced in the US are used extensively by the US Submarine-Launched Ballistic Missile programme. No end to their production has been declared. The current UK nuclear-weapon system is dependent on the US in this long-term sense. In the short term, we know of no restrictive supply clause that prevents the UK firing the Trident missiles once they have been acquired.

The Vanguard submarines, which carry the missiles, are built in the UK and have a 30-year life expectancy. None of the previous generation of missile-carrying submarines remained this long in service. But the US is now planning an extended life of 44 years for its Trident-carrying submarines and the D-5 missiles.

PUBLIC OPINION AND GOVERNMENT POLICY

British public opinion polls taken during the 1990s show a sharply decreased interest in nuclear weapons. Only about one per cent included 'nuclear-weapons disarmament' in their response to the question 'What would you see as the important issues facing Britain today?' On the retention of UK nuclear weapons the answers are sensitive to the wording of the question. For example, in answer to the question 'Should Britain keep its nuclear weapons?' 35 per cent said they should be kept in all circumstances and 35 per cent in some circumstances (30 per cent either said no or had no opinion). On the other hand only about 40 per cent agreed with the statement 'I feel that Britain needs nuclear weapons to increase my sense of security'. We do not yet have results of recent polls that might be influenced by the recent Bush–Putin agreement on nuclear weaponry in Russia and America, or by events in the Indian sub-continent and Iraq.

The most authoritative government statement of policy was given in the 1998 Strategic Defence Review:

> The UK Government wishes to see a safer world in which there is no place for nuclear weapons.[6] ... When satisfied with international progress towards the goal of a nuclear-weapon-free world, the Government will ensure that British nuclear weapons are included in the negotiations.[7]

At the NPT Review Conference of May 2000 the UK, together with the other nuclear-weapon states, gave an unequivocal commitment to accomplish nuclear disarmament, but without any timetable to give impetus and meaning to the agreement. The MoD was quick to point out that this agreement would have little practical impact on UK nuclear-weapon activities, whilst a Foreign Office minister spoke of the agreement as a major statement of intent. The twin commitment, to keep Trident and to work towards *global* nuclear disarmament, is reiterated in the Labour Party's 2001 election manifesto.[8]

THE POLICY OPTIONS

The case for the UK's *independent* nuclear disarmament was deployed in an earlier report.[9] I see no reason to alter my view that this straightforward abandonment of nuclear weapons would discharge the UK's commitment under the NPT and would be the best policy for Britain. For Britain to take a significant role in international negotiations for nuclear disarmament would be, if successful, a greater achievement, since it would lead to the abolition of all nuclear weapons. However, the experience of recent years suggests that Britain's influence in these matters is very limited. It is sometimes argued that possessing nuclear weapons gives Britain more influence in such international negotiations than it would have without them, a proposition difficult to substantiate or contradict, let alone quantify. The scope for the UK to have international co-operation in defence matters goes well beyond nuclear weapons: the contribution to NATO by way of bases, intelligence and readiness to contribute conventional military assistance far outweighs the relatively very small nuclear-weapon contribution from the UK.

The scope for reducing the number of warheads deployed appears, according to some officials to be limited if the potential to deter is to be maintained as a plausible military option against large nations. However, the UK government has offered only assertion in support of its present deployment of up to 48 warheads per submarine. Most governments of most countries would fear being the target of half this number and of their civil populations' reactions to such a catastrophe. For example, the UK could probably halve the number of deployed warheads. The UK government should at least venture a reasoned estimate of why such barbaric deployment is necessary for a credible deterrent.

The next option abandons altogether the 100-kiloton warheads and deterrence by mass destruction and retains only the lower-yield warheads to discharge the sub-strategic role only. It is not clear if all 200 such warheads would be retained because there seems to have been little detailed elaboration of this role and how it would be affected by the absence of 100-kiloton deterrent warheads. For example, we are told that no (serious) military attention has been devoted since 1949 to countering a military invasion of Britain [sic]. Military planning has assumed that the critical action will all be on the continent of Europe. If the conventional armies fail (as they did last time round), so that a large well-armed and hostile army appears in the Pas-de-Calais, the American nuclear weapons will be called into action and we will all go together in the subsequent Armageddon.

Thus it is argued that there is no plausible role for UK sub-strategic weapons and it would be bizarre to plan to defend Britain against invasion by these or any other means. However, we must both pray and expect that no American government would unleash strategic nuclear weapons merely to prevent an invasion of Britain. Such prevention is a matter primarily for the UK and its MoD.

RENOUNCING A NUCLEAR SUCCESSOR FOR TRIDENT

As discussed earlier, the operational life of the Trident nuclear-weapon system is likely to be limited to about 30 years by the lifetime of the submarines. The question of developing the successor system will occur much earlier because of the long lead time needed to develop a major new weapons system. Trident entered service in 1995, so the question of replacement would arise between 2010 and 2015. Developing a successor would be tantamount to committing the UK to being a nuclear-weapon state until well past the middle of the century, a discouraging prospect for the UK's commitment to Article VI of the NPT. Indeed, it was stated in 1998 that while it would be premature to abandon the capability to build a successor to Trident, 'the Government's aim is to take forward the process of nuclear disarmament to ensure that our security can in future be secured without nuclear weapons'.[10]

There are several advantages to renouncing a successor to Trident now: it is highly desirable to have some sort of timetable for implementing Article VI of the NPT, otherwise the whole treaty will fall into disrepair. The UK can give a clear lead in a matter within its own competence, which will enhance the pressure on other nations to follow the example of responding to the NPT. The UK can start developing its non-nuclear security so that the nightmare of the present arrangement can be dispelled; new roles must be found for the naval base at Faslane and for AWE, or their closure be anticipated. While the immediate consequences of this policy are few, in particular, the expense and danger of deploying Trident continues for several decades, a step towards nuclear disarmament, however small, is a step in the right direction, making the UK both safer and more civilized.

For the policy to be credible, it should be accompanied by the destruction of stored weapons components – for example, disassembly of decommissioned Chevaline warheads (the predecessor to Trident) was completed in February 2002.[11] The large stocks of military fissile material might be put to civilian use, by conversion to MOX fuel or otherwise. Production of military tritium should cease. All nuclear facilities and materials except those supporting the continuing Trident programme, and HEU for submarine propulsion, need to be put under Euratom and/or IAEA safeguards supervision.

Lastly, adopting this policy would be comparable to the decision in 1956 that the UK would no longer research and develop offensive chemical weapons, that the chemical weaponeers and their facilities should concentrate on defence against such weapons, especially means of enforcing the relevant arms limitation treaties. A similar step by the UK in the nuclear-weapons field could lead to reducing the major threat of nuclear warfare.

NOTES

This chapter is based on T. Milne, H. Beach, J. Finney, R.S. Pease and J. Rotblat, *An End to UK Nuclear Weapons* (London: British Pugwash Group, 2002), however this text is one for which I must take full responsibility. I am grateful for the comments and criticisms of my colleagues in the British Pugwash Group research project, especially for the help given by Tom Milne and Hugh Beach.

1. C.R. Hill, R.S. Pease, R.E. Peierls and J. Rotblat, *Does Britain Need Nuclear Weapons?* (London: British Pugwash Group, 1995).
2. *The Strategic Defence Review*, Cm.3999 (London: HMSO, 1998).
3. AWE, *A New Beginning*, Annual Report (Aldermaston: AWE, 2000).
4. F. von Hippel and D. Schroer, *Physics, Technology and the Nuclear Arms Race* (New York: American Institute of Physics, 1983), pp.5–10.
5. L. Moonie, Letter, *Observer*, 30 June 2002.
6. *The Strategic Defence Review*, para.60.
7. Ibid., Supporting Essay 5, paras.1–5.
8. *The Choices for Britain* (London: Labour Party, 2001), p.39.
9. Hill *et al.*, *Does Britain Need Nuclear Weapons?*, *passim*.
10. *The Strategic Defence Review*, Supporting Essay 5, para.4.
11. AWE, *AWE Today*, 11 April 2002.

Afterword

RONALD McCOY

This book, which is a collection of writings by scientists, doctors, soldiers, researchers, peace activists and others, assesses the military relevance, political impact, legal status and health and environmental effects of the British nuclear-weapons programme from the time it began in 1952. Although scientists in Britain had first recognized the possibility of producing a bomb from nuclear fission in 1940, the project was subsequently subsumed by the fateful Manhattan Project of the United States, which produced the atomic bombs responsible for the destruction of Hiroshima and Nagasaki in 1945.

The book gives an absorbing account of the development of Britain's nuclear arsenal, the environmentally disastrous atmospheric tests in Australia and the South Pacific, the health effects on Australian indigenous people and test participants, an imaginary nuclear battlefield and British civil society's resistance to its government's nuclear-weapons programme and its efforts to achieve nuclear disarmament. It shows that Britain's addiction to nuclear weapons remains as strong as ever, as it continues to base its security on the flawed and discredited doctrine of nuclear deterrence.

That war is demonstrably cruel and destructive has apparently not been sufficient reason for eschewing preparations for war or eliminating war from the conduct of international affairs. Although war can be avoided or its effects mitigated by diplomacy, the eternal problem has been to conceive of a stable, functional international system in which national security would not ultimately have to rely, in some way, on the use of force.

A government has an obligation to ensure the safety of its people and the survival of its institutions. This involves preventing conflict within its borders and meeting aggression from without. In doing so, a prudent and responsible government would proceed from a set of principles and assumptions upon which it can fashion rational policies, designed to ensure human security within a stable international order, based on international law. But what if the assumptions are wrong and the policies are not rational? What if international order is unstable and conflict pervasive?

NUCLEAR DISARMAMENT

Nuclear disarmament has been a matter of human survival ever since the world witnessed the complete destruction of Hiroshima and Nagasaki in a matter of seconds by two nuclear bombs. It has now taken on even greater urgency in a turbulent world threatened by rampant terrorism, militarism and increasingly perilous nuclear policies.

The Baruch Plan to control and regulate all nuclear research and development was the first nuclear disarmament proposal to the newly formed United Nations in 1946. It failed to receive the support of the Soviet Union. The United Nations was eventually subverted by the cold war and disempowered from taking effective action against the ensuing nuclear arms race or preventing proxy wars. The argument that the elimination of nuclear weapons is a realistic proposition gained some ground for the first time, when the joint communiqué of the first meeting between Mikhail Gorbachev and Ronald Reagan in 1985 declared that 'A nuclear war cannot be won and must never be fought'. In the early 1990s, Robert McNamara, the former US Secretary of Defense who was closely involved in the Cuban missile crisis of 1962, admitted that the US and the Soviet Union came within a whisker of nuclear war because of flawed information and misperceptions on both sides. He concluded that: 'The indefinite combination of nuclear-weapons and human fallibility will lead to a nuclear exchange.'[1]

By the mid-1990s several statements and reports, including the report of the 1996 Canberra Commission on the Elimination of Nuclear Weapons,[2] demolished the doctrine of nuclear deterrence and argued that the nuclear-weapon states should make an unequivocal commitment to the elimination of nuclear weapons. The logical arguments advanced were not new, having been kept alive by peace and disarmament groups worldwide, but they carried the force and credibility of military and political leaders, nuclear-weapons experts and analysts, who were prominently involved in cold war nuclear policies and strategies.

In 1996 the Advisory Opinion of the ICJ on the legal status of nuclear weapons unanimously declared that there existed 'an obligation to pursue in good faith and bring to a conclusion negotiations leading to nuclear disarmament in all its aspects under strict and effective international control'. The ICJ ruled that any threat or use of nuclear weapons would be illegal, but could not conclude definitively whether this ruling was applicable in 'extreme circumstances of self-defence, in which the very survival of a State would be at stake' (Chapter 2).[3] The ICJ ruling implies that the use or threat of use of nuclear weapons against non-nuclear-weapon states is illegal and that, if the sole function of nuclear weapons is to deter their use by another nuclear power, this function would lapse if there were no nuclear-weapon states.

There are few signs that the nuclear-weapon states have been convinced of the need to disarm completely. Their objections are reasoned and based on fears that the verification of nuclear disarmament is unreliable and that the clandestine production of nuclear weapons cannot be prevented or detected in good time because knowledge of nuclear-weapons technology cannot be erased. But these objections are outweighed by the greater risk of nuclear war by accident or miscalculation, as in the Cuban missile crisis.

History shows that the world is often confronted by a problem whose solution lies outside the political acceptability or wisdom of the international community at the time. The unopposed rise of Hitler in the 1930s, which led to the Second World War, and the feared communist threat to Southeast Asia in the 1960s, which led to the Vietnam War, are examples.

The nuclear predicament in the post-cold war world, now further complicated by the events of 11 September 2001, continues to defy resolution as the mindsets of political realists continue to argue that nuclear abolition is utopian and delusional. Yet what could be more delusional than the argument that nuclear weapons provide a rational and realistic military option for security? The inescapable reality is that nuclear war annihilates both sides. Risking mutual suicide is not realistic or rational, but 'political reality' and 'circumstantial reality' still clash, while the world becomes a more dangerous place.

The ideological struggle of the cold war is over, but cold-war thinking and the doctrine of nuclear deterrence are very much alive, still masquerading as the ultimate guarantee of security. That is, until 11 September 2001, when the United States discovered its own vulnerability and inability to deter terrorists with its nuclear arsenal. The continued possession of nuclear weapons makes the diversion of nuclear materials or nuclear weapons into the hands of terrorists more likely. Terrorists cannot be deterred by the threat of nuclear retaliation, as a nation would. The only policy that can reduce the danger of nuclear terrorism is abolition, because abolition alone can impose a comprehensive prohibition on nuclear-weapons technology.

In the long term, the real alternatives are either the proliferation of nuclear weapons and 'nuclear anarchy' or the abolition of nuclear weapons by international agreement. The current American policy of pre-emptive military counter-proliferation and counter-terrorism, while simultaneously retaining its own nuclear weapons indefinitely, is a recipe for catastrophic, endless war.

THE NON-PROLIFERATION TREATY

The proliferation of nuclear weapons and other WMDs has been a major concern to all states. In their legitimate concern about proliferation, the nuclear-weapon states all too easily forget that nuclear and other dangers flow from their own arsenals and that their double standards are a stimulus to other states to exercise their nuclear, biological and chemical options.

Although discriminatory in nature, the 1970 NPT (Appendix 3) has largely succeeded in preventing the horizontal proliferation of nuclear weapons, apart from the clandestine efforts of a few states and the nuclear conversion of India and Pakistan in 1998, both non-signatories of the NPT. The recent withdrawal of the Democratic People's Republic of Korea from the NPT is another blow to the non-proliferation regime and a warning that the NPT must achieve its main goal of eliminating nuclear weapons, before it begins to unravel.

The nature of diplomacy and the ambiguity of the language of the NPT have allowed states parties, particularly the nuclear-weapon states, to procrastinate and avoid their treaty obligations through innovative interpretations of phraseology, including the linking of nuclear disarmament with 'general and complete disarmament'.

When the NPT was extended indefinitely in 1995, a set of 'Principles and Objectives for Nuclear Non-Proliferation and Disarmament' was adopted as an explicit commitment to the 'determined pursuit by the nuclear weapon states of systematic and progressive efforts to reduce nuclear weapons globally, with the ultimate goal of eliminating those weapons'.

When the Final Document of the 2000 NPT Review Conference was adopted, it advocated 13 practical steps for systematic and progressive nuclear disarmament, including 'an unequivocal undertaking by the nuclear-weapon states to accomplish the total elimination of their nuclear arsenals'. In addition, it called for states to ratify the CTBT, ban the production of fissile materials, diminish the role of nuclear weapons in security policies and engage in a process leading to the total elimination of nuclear weapons. Since then, the 2002 meeting of the NPT Preparatory Committee has concluded without substantive agreement on vital issues – a mere papering over the cracks, until the next meeting.

Although no single state can be held solely responsible, the United States, Russia and China could be apportioned some blame for indicating that the world would remain nuclearized indefinitely after the cold war. The United States, however, can be singled out as the essential circuit-breaker. Without American leadership and commitment, any effort in nuclear disarmament will fail.

It is no surprise that the arms control regime has been brought to a standstill by the Bush administration's undivided attention to the 'war on terrorism', which is reshaping international security. The 2001 US Nuclear Posture Review and the recent National Security Strategy indicate that the United States has raised the stakes further, by lowering the threshold and reserving the 'right' to use nuclear weapons in any war it fights and to launch pre-emptive military strikes against any state or non-state actor judged to be a security threat. The resurgence in terrorism by militant religious extremists is a timely reminder to the nuclear-weapon states and the international community that nuclear disarmament is a matter of urgency, as existing stockpiles of nuclear weapons and fissile materials are potential sources of weapons for nuclear terrorism.

BRITAIN'S ROLE

Within this bleak geopolitical landscape, it could be said that the British government is well positioned to provide visionary, moral leadership, if it would only seize the moral high ground and renounce nuclear weapons. As a permanent member of the UN Security Council and one of the five declared nuclear-weapons states, Britain appears to have accepted its responsibility to comply with the NPT only in principle, without making an unequivocal commitment or taking the lead in nuclear disarmament. It has shown little interest in nuclear disarmament issues since the 1995 NPT Review and Extension Conference or in implementing the 13 practical steps in the 'Plan of Action' agreed to at the 2000 NPT Review Conference. On the contrary, the Secretary of State for Defence told the House of Commons on 5 June 2000 that 'the non-proliferation treaty agreement is an aspiration; it is not likely to produce results in the short term'.[4]

When the ICJ delivered its advisory opinion on the legal status of nuclear weapons in 1996, the British government rejected it on the grounds that Britain did have a legal justification for the continued possession of nuclear weapons. Similarly, the report of the Canberra Commission was considered and then dismissed. The recent disarmament efforts by a group of seven middle-power states – known as the New Agenda Coalition – to move the nuclear disarmament agenda forwards in the UN General Assembly was criticized as being incompatible with Britain's 'credible minimum deterrent'.

Although the British government has signed and ratified the CTBT, its strong support of US security policies and the frequent visits of government personnel to the US Nevada test site in 2001 have given rise to fears that Britain may abandon its commitments to the CTBT and resume testing with the United States. Britain has refused to consider stopping the production of tritium or making a commitment not to withdraw fissile materials from military stockpiles for use in nuclear-weapons production.

Within the UN Conference on Disarmament in Geneva, Britain has not renewed efforts to break the impasse on the fissile materials cut-off treaty negotiations or reach agreement on the establishment of subsidiary bodies to advance the stalled process of nuclear disarmament.

Britain's nuclear capability is now concentrated within one system under the command of one force and at one location: four Royal Navy Trident submarines based at Faslane on the River Clyde in Scotland. Although the conversion from Polaris to Trident has reduced the number of operational nuclear warheads, each Trident warhead has greater accuracy, is potentially more destructive and can now be targeted individually. More importantly, there is no firm commitment that the present Trident nuclear-weapons system will not be replaced or extended when its current service life runs out. Such a commitment would represent the one step that would ensure the total elimination of Britain's nuclear arsenal (Chapter 12).

The British government has declared support for the proposed US National Missile Defense system, indicating that it will grant permission to the United States to use its two North Yorkshire bases, Fylingdales radar station and Menwith Hill listening post.

Britain's nuclear policy has changed over the years and now includes the 'first use' of nuclear weapons. The Secretary of State for Defence, in answering questions in Parliament over Iraq, stated that in conditions of extreme self-defence Britain would retain the right to use nuclear weapons pre-emptively against a non-nuclear-weapon state, such as Iraq, in the event of an imminent threat from biological or chemical weapons.

The 1998 Strategic Defence Review confirmed the retention of a sub-strategic role for Trident as a minimum nuclear deterrent, with one submarine constantly on patrol, carrying a reduced load of 48 warheads, each with an explosive yield of 100 kilotons, which is about five times the destructive power of the Nagasaki bomb. Although the Strategic Defence Review declares that 'The submarine's missiles will not be targeted and will normally be at several days "notice to fire"',[5] the reality is that modern communications enable the submarine to 'go nuclear' very rapidly if ordered to do so. The obvious way to immediately lower the nuclear threshold would be to take Trident off its 24-hour patrol, remove the warheads from the missiles and store them ashore.

Britain's continuing commitment to nuclear deterrence and its non-compliance with its NPT obligations are also mirrored in its increasing collaboration with the United States on nuclear-weapons research at Los Alamos and Lawrence Livermore laboratories, including advanced computer simulation technology that enables scientists to design, develop and test new weapons without the need for underground testing. Funds are also being allocated towards new facilities at the AWE in Aldermaston for the production of Trident warheads, as well as to the laser fusion programme of the US National Ignition Facility.

THE UNITED NATIONS AND THE RULE OF LAW

The end of the cold war brought false hopes of a 'peace dividend' and a new world order, based on the UN Charter and international law. The UN Charter, as a multilateral agreement articulating principles and rules for the conduct of states, is itself an instrument and contributor to the development of international law.

The Charter affirms the legally binding quality of rules for international state conduct, including the principles of non-intervention, peaceful settlement of disputes, de-colonization, respect for human rights, the sovereign equality of states and the duty of co-operation. But the Charter goes beyond that and actually authorizes the creation of organs and agencies, committees and commissions and an interacting network of specialized agencies, regional organizations and NGOs world-wide.

The ICJ is the principal juridical arm of the UN and, by ratifying its Statute, governments are obliged to accept it as an independent organ of the UN that reaches decisions, that are final and binding, on the basis of international law, not international political considerations.

Although the UN may not have succeeded in eradicating the scourge of war, it has reduced it to a level below that of world war and defined more clearly the permissible legal parameters for using force in international disputes. Under the UN system, responsibility for maintaining peace and security and settling disputes peacefully is invested in the Security Council, which is empowered to adopt resolutions and make decisions, such as sanctions, which carry the force of law and are binding on all member states. Although at times governments have resisted compliance for various reasons, the fact remains that the Security Council possesses the authority to create international law and impose binding obligations.

The UN has influenced the establishment of international legal order over the past five decades with varying success, although the future course of UN-derived prescriptive law to regulate the conduct of member states promises to be more problematic, including imposing measures against governments, major and minor, that violate the NPT and other treaties. The UN Charter has provided a set of values for the international system: democracy, human rights, equality, social progress, freedom and justice. The fundamental purposes and principles in the Charter express international concern over the need to suppress aggression and support principles of international law, non-violent resolution of conflict and international co-operation. In other words, the Charter codifies normative values into hard legal principles for regulating international behaviour.

Critical problems arise when states lack political will to comply with and enforce those legal principles. When states fail or refuse to comply in matters affecting peace and security, how should the UN react? The key lies in the composition and political will of the Security Council and its

ability to enforce resolutions. Experience has shown that political considerations and the veto power of its permanent members hold sway.

The UN is an important seedbed for germinating new rules and norms
of international law. It provides a global forum for negotiating and formu-
lating international agreements, for furnishing opportunities for dialogue
and the exchange of ideas on almost any issue affecting international
relations and for offering legal channels for governments to seek peaceful
redress for any grievance.

Ultimately, UN contributions to a just and peaceful international order
depend upon the political will of its member states to establish and adhere
to the rule of law. The UN is a political organization that acts along political lines, often for political gains. The UN can only be as strong or effective as its member states are willing to make it, particularly the permanent
members of the Security Council.

International law is manifestly intended to function for the benefit of
all member states, but it can only do so with the genuine co-operation and
goodwill of the governments of those same states. That fundamental truth
will remain the overriding challenge in determining the effectiveness of
the UN in eliminating WMDs and maintaining peace in the years to come.

NOTES

1. F. Blackaby, 'Introduction and Summary', in J. Rotblat (ed.), *Nuclear Weapons: The Road to Zero* (Oxford: Westview Press, 1998), pp.1–2.
2. *Report of the Canberra Commission on the Elimination of Nuclear Weapons* (Canberra: Commonwealth of Australia, 1996), pp.18–47.
3. ICJ, *Legality of the Threat or Use of Nuclear Weapons*, Doc A/51/218 (New York: United Nations, 1996), para.105 E, F.
4. G. Hoon, quoted in Campaign for Nuclear Disarmament, *The United Kingdom's Record on Nuclear Disarmament* (London: CND, 6th Edn. 2002), p.5.
5. The Strategic Defence Review, Cm.3999 (London: HMSO, 1998), para.68.

Appendix 1
British Nuclear Weapons

A variety of nuclear weapons and missiles and delivery systems have been developed in the 50 years of the British nuclear-weapons programme. Aircraft-delivered bombs were carried on Buccaneer, Canberra, Jaguar, Scimitar, Sea Harrier, Sea Vixen, Shackleton, Tornado, Valiant, Victor and Vulcan aircraft. Of the missiles, Blue Steel was an air-to-surface strategic missile carried on Vulcan and Victor bombers. Polaris/Chevaline were carried on Polaris submarine-launched ballistic missiles.

The United Kingdom's sole nuclear warheads at the end of 2002 are the approximately 200 (including spares) available for deployment on Trident nuclear submarines, four of which are operational. Each submarine can carry 16 Trident II D-5 SLBMs (bought from the United States). The warheads on each SLBM are Multiple Independently-targeted Re-entry Vehicles (designed and built at the AWE facilities at Aldermaston and Burghfield, Berkshire). The Trident SLBMs have ranges of about 12,000 kilometres.

The UK government has announced that it will not deploy more than 48 Trident II D-5 SLBM warheads on each Trident submarine. The 1998 Strategic Defence Review states that 'We will have only one submarine on patrol at any one time, carrying a reduced load of 48 warheads'.[1] This implies that each of the 16 missiles will carry three strategic Multiple Independently-targeted Re-entry Vehicles.

The SDR states that Trident 'covers both strategic and sub-strategic requirements'. Trident strategic warheads are generally assumed to have an explosive yield equivalent to that of 100,000 tonnes of TNT (100 kilotons). The MoD keeps the yield secret, but independent experts assume that the strategic warhead is similar to the American W76 warhead carried on the American Trident I C-4 SLBM, which has an explosive power of 100 kilotons.

Presumably a single 'sub-strategic' warhead will be carried on a Trident SLBM. The yield of the 'sub-strategic' warhead to be carried on British Trident SLBMs has not been announced. It may well be about one kiloton. This could be achieved by removing the tritium bottle from the boosted fission trigger in the warhead, a simple operation.

The yield of the trigger without boosting is probably about one kiloton, with boosting it is probably ten kilotons. The thermonuclear stage will then give a thermonuclear yield of 100 kilotons. The warhead could then have variable yields of about one kiloton (achieved by removing the tritium bottle), ten kilotons (by 'switching out' the thermonuclear stage) and 100 kilotons (using the total fission plus fusion yield).

TABLE 1
TYPES OF BRITISH NUCLEAR WEAPONS

Name	Type	Weight	Deployed	Yield
Aircraft Bombs				
Blue Danube	fission	5 tonnes	1953–62	up to 40 kilotons
Red Beard	fission	1 tonnes	1961–71	up to 20 kilotons
Violet Club	fission	4 tonnes	1958–60	500 kilotons
Yellow Sun	thermonuclear	3 tonnes	1961–72	1 megaton
WE177-A	thermonuclear	272 kilograms	1966-84	200 kilotons
WE177-B	thermonuclear	431 kilograms	1966–96	400 kilotons
WE177-C	fission	classified	1971–92	10 kilotons
Missiles				
Blue Steel	thermonuclear	6,800 kilograms	1963–70	1 megaton
Polaris A3TK	thermonuclear	16,200 kilograms	1967–92	225 kilotons
Trident D-5	thermonuclear	57,700 kilograms	1992–	100 kilotons

NOTE

1. *The Strategic Defence Review*, Cm.3999 (London: HMSO, 1998).

Appendix 2
British Nuclear Weapon Tests

Between 1952 and 1991 (inclusive) the UK is known to have carried out 45 nuclear tests. Of these, 21 were in the atmosphere, 18 in 1956–58. Up to the end of 1957, tests were performed in Australia; and in 1957 and 1958 off Malden and Christmas Islands in the Pacific. Details of these tests are given in Table 2. From 1962, 24 underground tests, from one to three yearly were conducted jointly with the United States at its Nevada test site, though the UK observed a unilateral moratorium on testing from 1965 to 1974.

The UK is one of seven nuclear-weapon powers (China, France, India, Pakistan, Russia/the Soviet Union, the United Kingdom and the United States) that have tested nuclear weapons. These countries are known to have conducted a total of at least 2,052 nuclear tests. Israel, the eighth known nuclear-weapon power has not, so far as is publicly known, tested a nuclear weapon.

The total explosive yield of all the nuclear tests conducted so far is equivalent to that of roughly 510 million tonnes (megatonnes) of TNT. Of this total, the British tests accounted for about nine megatonnes.

The 12 nuclear tests in Australia were basically to develop knowledge about fission weapons and the effects of nuclear explosions and to conduct initial research into thermonuclear explosions. Some of these were carried out at Maralinga in South Australia, as were a series of trials of the 'safety' of nuclear weapons that dispersed radioactive material but did not result in a full-scale nuclear explosion (Chapter 8). The nine nuclear tests at Christmas and Malden Islands were to develop thermo-nuclear warheads, including operational ones.

The tests in the Pacific were more important than those in Australia for the development of British nuclear weapons but, in the end, none of the British nuclear tests were crucial for this purpose. The development and deployment of effective operational British nuclear weapons depended mostly on collaboration between British and American nuclear-weapon designers.

The British Nuclear Weapons Programme

TABLE 2
ATMOSPHERIC BRITISH TESTS

Operation	Location	Date	Yield	Launch
Hurricane	Monte Bello	03.10.52	25 kilotons	ocean surface
Totem 1	Emu	14.10.53	10 kilotons	tower
Totem 2	Emu	26.10.53	8 kilotons	tower
Mosaic 1	Monte Bello	16.05.53	15 kilotons	tower
Mosaic 2	Monte Bello	19.06.53	60 kilotons	tower
Buffalo	Maralinga	27.09.56	15 kilotons	tower
Buffalo	Maralinga	04.10.56	1.5 kilotons	tower
Buffalo	Maralinga	11.10.56	3 kilotons	aircraft
Buffalo	Maralinga	21.10.56	10 kilotons	tower
Grapple	off Malden Island	15.05.57	0.3 megaton	aircraft
Grapple	off Malden Island	31.05.57	0.72 megaton	aircraft
Grapple	off Malden Island	19.06.57	0.2 megaton	aircraft
Antler	Maralinga	15.09.57	1 kiloton	tower
Antler	Maralinga	25.09.57	6 kilotons	tower
Antler	Maralinga	09.10.57	25 kilotons	balloon
Grapple	Christmas Island	08.11.57	1.8 megatons	aircraft
Grapple	Christmas Island	28.04.58	3.0 megatons	aircraft
Grapple	Christmas Island	22.08.58	24 kilotons	balloon
Grapple	Christmas Island	02.09.58	1.0 megaton	aircraft
Grapple	Christmas Island	11.09.58	0.8 megaton	aircraft
Grapple	Christmas Island	23.09.58	25 kilotons	balloon

Appendix 3
Treaty on the Non-Proliferation of Nuclear Weapons

The *States concluding this Treaty*, hereinafter referred to as the 'Parties to the Treaty',

Considering the devastation that would be visited upon all mankind by a nuclear war and the consequent need to make every effort to avert the danger of such a war and to take measures to safeguard the security of peoples,

Believing that the proliferation of nuclear weapons would seriously enhance the danger of nuclear war,

In conformity with resolutions of the United Nations General Assembly calling for the conclusion of an agreement on the prevention of wider dissemination of nuclear-weapons,

Undertaking to co-operate in facilitating the application of International Atomic Energy Agency safeguards on peaceful nuclear activities,

Expressing their support for research, development and other efforts to further the application, within the framework of the International Atomic Energy Agency safeguards system, of the principle of safeguarding effectively the flow of source and special fissionable materials by use of instruments and other techniques at certain strategic points,

Affirming the principle that the benefits of peaceful applications of nuclear technology, including any technological by-products which may be derived by nuclear-weapon States from the development of nuclear explosive devices, should be available for peaceful purposes to all Parties to the Treaty, whether nuclear-weapon or non-nuclear-weapon States,

Convinced that, in the furtherance of this principle, all Parties to the Treaty are entitled to participate in the fullest possible exchange of scientific information for, and to contribute alone or in co-operation with other States to, the further development of the applications of atomic energy for peaceful purposes,

Declaring their intention to achieve at the earliest possible date the cessation of the nuclear arms race and to undertake effective measures in the direction of nuclear disarmament,

Urging the co-operation of all States in the attainment of this objective,

Recalling the determination expressed by the Parties to the 1963 Treaty banning nuclear weapon tests in the atmosphere, in outer space and under water in its preamble to seek to achieve the discontinuance of all test explosions of nuclear weapons for all time and to continue negotiations to this end,

Desiring to further the easing of international tension and the strengthening of trust between States in order to facilitate the cessation of the manufacture of nuclear weapons, the liquidation of all their existing stockpiles, weapons and the means of their delivery pursuant to a Treaty on general and complete disarmament under strict and effective international control,

Recalling that, in accordance with the Charter of the United Nations, States must refrain in their international relations from the threat or use of force against the territorial integrity or political independence of any State, or in any other manner inconsistent with the purposes of the United Nations, and that the establishment and maintenance of international peace and security are to be promoted with the least diversion of armaments of the world's human and economic resources,

Have agreed as follows:

ARTICLE I

Each nuclear-weapon State Party to the Treaty undertakes not to transfer to any recipient whatsoever nuclear weapons or other nuclear explosive devices or control over such weapons or explosive devices directly, or indirectly; and not in any way to assist, encourage, or induce any non-nuclear-weapon State to manufacture or otherwise acquire nuclear weapons or other nuclear explosive devices, or control over such weapons or explosive devices.

ARTICLE II

Each non-nuclear-weapon State Party to the treaty undertakes not to receive the transfer from any transferor whatsoever of nuclear weapons or other nuclear explosive devices or of control over such weapons or explosive devices directly, or indirectly; not to manufacture or otherwise acquire nuclear weapons or other nuclear explosive devices; and not to seek or receive any assistance in the manufacture of nuclear weapons or other nuclear explosive devices.

ARTICLE III

1. Each non-nuclear-weapons State Party to the Treaty undertakes to accept safeguards, as set forth in an agreement to be negotiated and concluded with the International Atomic Energy Agency in accordance with the Statute of the International Atomic Energy Agency and the Agency's safeguards system, for the exclusive purpose of verification of the fulfilment of its obligations assumed under this Treaty with a view to preventing diversion of nuclear energy from peaceful uses to nuclear weapons or other nuclear explosive devices. Procedures for the safeguards required by this Article shall be followed with respect to source or special fissionable material whether it is being produced, processed or used in any principal nuclear facility or is outside any such facility. The safeguards required by this Article shall be applied on all source or special fissionable material in all peaceful nuclear activities within the territory of such State, under its jurisdiction, or carried out under its control anywhere.

2. Each State Party to the Treaty undertakes not to provide: (a) source or special fissionable material, or (b) equipment or material especially designed or prepared for the processing, use or production of special fissionable material, to any non-nuclear-weapon State for peaceful purposes, unless the source or special fissionable material shall be subject to the safeguards required by this Article.

3. The safeguards required by this Article shall be implemented in a manner designed to comply with Article IV of this Treaty, and to avoid hampering the economic or technological development of the parties or international co-operation in the field of peaceful nuclear activities, including the international exchange of nuclear material and equipment for the processing, use or production of nuclear material for peaceful purposes in accordance with the provisions of this Article and the principle of safeguarding set forth in the preamble.

4. Non-nuclear-weapon States Party to the Treaty shall conclude agreements with the International Atomic Energy Agency to meet the requirements of this Article either individually or together with other States in accordance with the Statute of the International Atomic Energy Agency. Negotiation of such agreements shall commence within 180 days from the original entry into force of this Treaty. For States depositing their instruments of ratification or accession after the 180-day period, negotiation of such agreements shall commence not later than the date of such deposit. Such agreements shall enter into force not later than eighteen months after the date of initiation of negotiations.

ARTICLE IV

1. Nothing in this Treaty shall be interpreted as affecting the inalienable right of all the Parties to the Treaty to develop research, production and use of nuclear energy for peaceful purposes without discrimination and in conformity with Articles I and II of this Treaty.
2. All the Parties to the Treaty undertake to facilitate, and have the right to participate in, the fullest possible exchange of equipment, materials and scientific and technological information for the peaceful uses of nuclear energy. Parties to the Treaty in a position to do so shall also co-operate in contributing alone or together with other States or international organizations to the further development of the applications of nuclear energy for peaceful purposes, especially in the territories of non-nuclear-weapons States Party to the Treaty, with due consideration for the needs of the developing areas of the world.

ARTICLE V

Each Party to this Treaty undertakes to take appropriate measures to ensure that, in accordance with this Treaty, under appropriate international observation and through appropriate international procedures, potential benefits from any peaceful applications of nuclear explosions will be made available to non-nuclear-weapon States Party to this Treaty on a non-discriminatory basis and that the charge to such Parties for the explosive devices used will be as low as possible and exclude any charge for research and development. Non-nuclear-weapon States Party to the Treaty shall be able to obtain such benefits, pursuant to a special international agreement or agreements, through an appropriate international body with adequate representation of non-nuclear-weapon States. Negotiations on this subject shall commence as soon as possible after the Treaty enters into force. Non-nuclear-weapon States Party to the Treaty so desiring may also obtain such benefits pursuant to bilateral agreements.

ARTICLE VI

Each of the Parties to the Treaty undertakes to pursue negotiations in good faith on effective measures relating to cessation of the nuclear arms race at an early date and to nuclear disarmament, and on a Treaty on general and complete disarmament under strict and effective international control.

ARTICLE VII

Nothing in this Treaty affects the right of any group of States to conclude regional treaties in order to assure the total absence of nuclear weapons in their respective territories.

ARTICLE VIII

1. Any Party to the Treaty may propose amendments to this Treaty. The text of any proposed amendment shall be submitted to the Depositary Governments which shall circulate it to all Parties to the Treaty. Thereupon, if requested to do so by one third or more of the Parties to the Treaty, the Depositary Governments shall convene a conference, to which they shall invite all the Parties to the Treaty to consider such an amendment.

2. Any amendment to this Treaty must be approved by a majority of the votes of all the Parties to the Treaty, including the votes of all nuclear-weapon States Party to the Treaty and all other Parties which, on the date the amendment is circulated, are members of the Board of Governors of the International Atomic Energy Agency. The amendment shall enter into force for each Party that deposits its instrument of ratification of the amendment upon the deposit of such instruments of ratification by a majority of all the Parties, including the instruments of ratification of all nuclear-weapon States Party to the Treaty and all other Parties which, on the date the amendment is circulated, are members of the Board of Governors of the International Atomic Energy Agency. Thereafter, it shall enter into force for any other Party upon the deposit of its instrument of ratification of the amendment.

3. Five years after the entry into force of this Treaty, a conference of Parties to the Treaty shall be held in Geneva, Switzerland, in order to review the operation of this Treaty with a view to assuring that the purposes of the Preamble and the provisions of the Treaty are being realized. At intervals of five years thereafter, a majority of the Parties to the Treaty may obtain, by submitting a proposal to this effect to the Depositary Governments, the convening of further conferences with the same objective of reviewing the operation of the Treaty.

ARTICLE IX

1. This Treaty shall be open to all States for signature. Any State which does not sign the Treaty before its entry into force in accordance with paragraph 3 of this Article may accede to it at any time.

2. This Treaty shall be subject to ratification by signatory States. Instruments of ratification and instruments of accession shall be deposited with the Governments of the Union of Soviet Socialist Republics, the United Kingdom of Great Britain and Northern Ireland and the United States of America, which are hereby designated the Depositary Governments.

3. This Treaty shall enter into force after its ratification by the States, the Governments of which are designated Depositaries of the Treaty, and forty other States signatory to this Treaty and the deposit of their instruments of ratification. For the purposes of this Treaty, a nuclear-weapon State is one which has manufactured and exploded a nuclear weapon or other nuclear explosion device prior to 1 January of 1967.

4. For States whose instruments of ratification or accession are deposited subsequent to the entry into force of this Treaty, it shall enter into force on the date of the deposit of their instruments of ratification or accession.

5. The Depositary Governments shall promptly inform all signatory and acceding States of the date of each signature, the date of deposit of each instrument of ratification or of accession, the date of the entry into force of this Treaty, and the date of receipt of any requests for convening a conference or other notices.

6. This Treaty shall be registered by the Depositary Governments pursuant to Article 102 of the Charter of the United Nations.

ARTICLE X

1. Each Party shall in exercising its national sovereignty have the right to withdraw from the Treaty if it decides that extraordinary events, related to the subject-matter of this Treaty, have jeopardized the supreme interests of its country. It shall give notice of such withdrawal to all other Parties to the Treaty and to the United Nations Security Council three months in advance. Such notice shall include a statement of the extraordinary events it regards as having jeopardized its supreme interests.

2. Twenty-five years after the entry into force of the Treaty, a Conference shall be convened to decide whether the Treaty shall continue in force indefinitely, or shall be extended for an additional fixed period or periods. This decision shall be taken by a majority of the Parties to the Treaty.

ARTICLE XI

This Treaty, the English, Russian, French, Spanish and Chinese texts of which are equally authentic, shall be deposited in the archives of the Depositary Governments. Duly certified copies of this Treaty shall be transmitted by the Depositary Governments to the Governments of the signatory and acceding States.

In witness whereof the undersigned, duly authorized, have signed this Treaty.

Done in .... at .... this .... day of ....

NOTES

The text is as taken from the UN Open Access Document published by United Nations Office of Public Information (DPI/324-80-40758-June 1980-3.5M). We are grateful for permission to reprint it here. The resolution was adopted by a roll-call vote of 95 in favour to four against, with 21 abstentions. At the end of 2002 there were 188 states parties. The United States, Russia, United Kingdom, France and China are parties as nuclear-weapon states. The only non-signatories among UN member states are India, Israel and Pakistan, but as this book goes to press the Democratic Republic of North Korea has given notice under Article X of its intention to withdraw from the Treaty.

Appendix 4
Some Useful Websites

Abolition 2000	http://www.abolition2000.org
Abolition 2000 UK	http://abolition2000uk.gn.apc.org
Aldermaston Campaign	http://www.aldermastonwpc.gn.apc.org
Atomic Mirror	http://www.earthways.org/atomicmirror
BASIC	http://www.basicint.org
CND	http://www.cnduk.org
IPPNW	http://www.ippnw.org
MEDACT	http://www.medact.org
Movement for the Abolition of War	http://www.abolishwar.freeuk.com
Oxford Research Group	http://www.oxfordresearchgroup.org.uk
Pugwash Conferences on Science and World Affairs	http://www.pugwash.org
Quaker Peace and Social Witness	http://www.quaker.org.uk
Scientists for Global Responsibility	http://www.sgr.org.uk
Trident Ploughshares 2000	http://www.tridentploughshares.org
VERTIC	http://www.vertic.org
World Court Project UK	http://www.wcp.gn.apc.org

Index

Index

Cook, James (Australia 1770) 76
Cook, Robin 60
'Corporal' missile 36, 41
'Corps counter stroke' 42
Corps Tactical Battle in Nuclear War, The see
  Purple Pamphlet, The
'counterforce' 39
Cox, John (Chair of CND 1977) 61
critical mass 126
Cross, Roger 8
Cruise missiles 2–3
  'answered' SS20s 67
  CND and 62
  CND and withdrawal 69
  Conservative government and 64
'crust' of enemy forces, between front lines
  42–3
CTBT (1996) 24, 71
  ban production of fissile materials 140
  ban on underground testing and 30
  failure to ratify by US and China 25
  signed and ratified by Britain 25, 141
Cuba, 2002 UN General Assembly and 24
Cuban missile crisis (1962) 2, 59, 138–9
Curie, Marie, radiation and 115
customary international law, UK domestic
  law and 28

Daily Worker/Morning Star 59
Dale, Geoffrey 86–7
Dale, Rowland 61
'Davy Crockett' 36–7
Declarations of Public Conscience to The
  Hague 74
decontamination centre, Maralinga village
  47–9
decontamination of motor vehicles 48
Democratic People's Republic of Korea *see*
  North Korea
de-targeting concept, fine distinctions 29
deterrence, overwhelming retaliation 13–15
Devonport dockyard, cost of work to refit
  nuclear submarines 9
direct defence, definition 39
Director of Cancer Registration (Scotland),
  ovarian cancer and 110–11
disarmament, linked with human rights 65
DNA, leukaemia and 119
Dounreay (Caithness) 117
DPIE 95–8
  established MARTAC (1993) 95
'dual key' control of weapons 37
Duff, Peggy 59
'Dulles doctrine' 37
Dundee/BNTVA, 'independent responders'
  and 111–12
Durance, Colonel 87–8

'earthquake bomb' 127
Eastern Europe, peaceful protests 3

Eggleston, Barbara 61
Eisenhower era 14
  nuclear war and 37
El Alamein 45
Emergency Committee for Direct Action
  Against Nuclear War (Direct Action
  Committee) 57
Emu Field 76–7, 84, 86
  Totem Tests 79–83
  visit by AWTSC committee 93
environment, radioactive containment of the
  4–5
EU, Britain and 20
Euratom and/or IAEA safeguards supervision
  136
Europe, Pershing and Cruise missiles
  stationed (1980s) 45
European Nuclear Disarmament Appeal
  (1980) 65
exercise 'Battle Royal', British corps attacked
  Belgian corps (1954) 44
'exhume and bury' option 98

Falkland Islands War 17–18, 53
Farebrother, George 74
Faslane 72, 136, 142
Federal Minister for Science and the
  Environment (18 September 1980) 81
Fijian test veterans 104
'first strike' guidelines (1972) 39
first test,
  day after 48–9
  description 48
  later 49–50
  today 50
First World War, conscientious objectors and
  law-breaking 67
fissile material,
  acquiring 124–5
  theft of 125
fission process 125–6
fission of uranium, observed 1938 and
  understood 1939
'flexible response' 15, 39, 41
Foot, Michael 57
Foy, Yet 50
France,
  NATO and 38
  NPT and 2
  nuclear programme 15, 20
  nuclear tests 4
  plutonium 124
  resumed nuclear testing after NPT review
    conference 73
  withdrawal from military structure (1966)
    40
free-fall bombs 35
Frisch, Otto 1, 12
Fundamentalist groups 123
Fylingdales radar station 142

161

Index